KEYSTONE WESTERN AMERICANA SERIES

Archibald Hanna and William H. Goetzmann,
General Editors

THE LEWIS AND CLARK EXPEDITION

THE LEWIS AND CLARK EXPEDITION

BY

MERIWETHER LEWIS

The 1814 Edition, Unabridged

IN THREE VOLUMES

Introduction by Archibald Hanna

Volume III

J. B. LIPPINCOTT COMPANY

PHILADELPHIA AND NEW YORK

FIRST EDITION

PRINTED IN THE UNITED STATES OF AMERICA

LIBRARY OF CONGRESS CATALOG CARD NUMBER: 61-14989

THE LEWIS AND CLARK EXPEDITION

A *map of the Lewis and Clark Expedition follows the listing of chapters in each volume.*

CONTENTS

VOL. III.

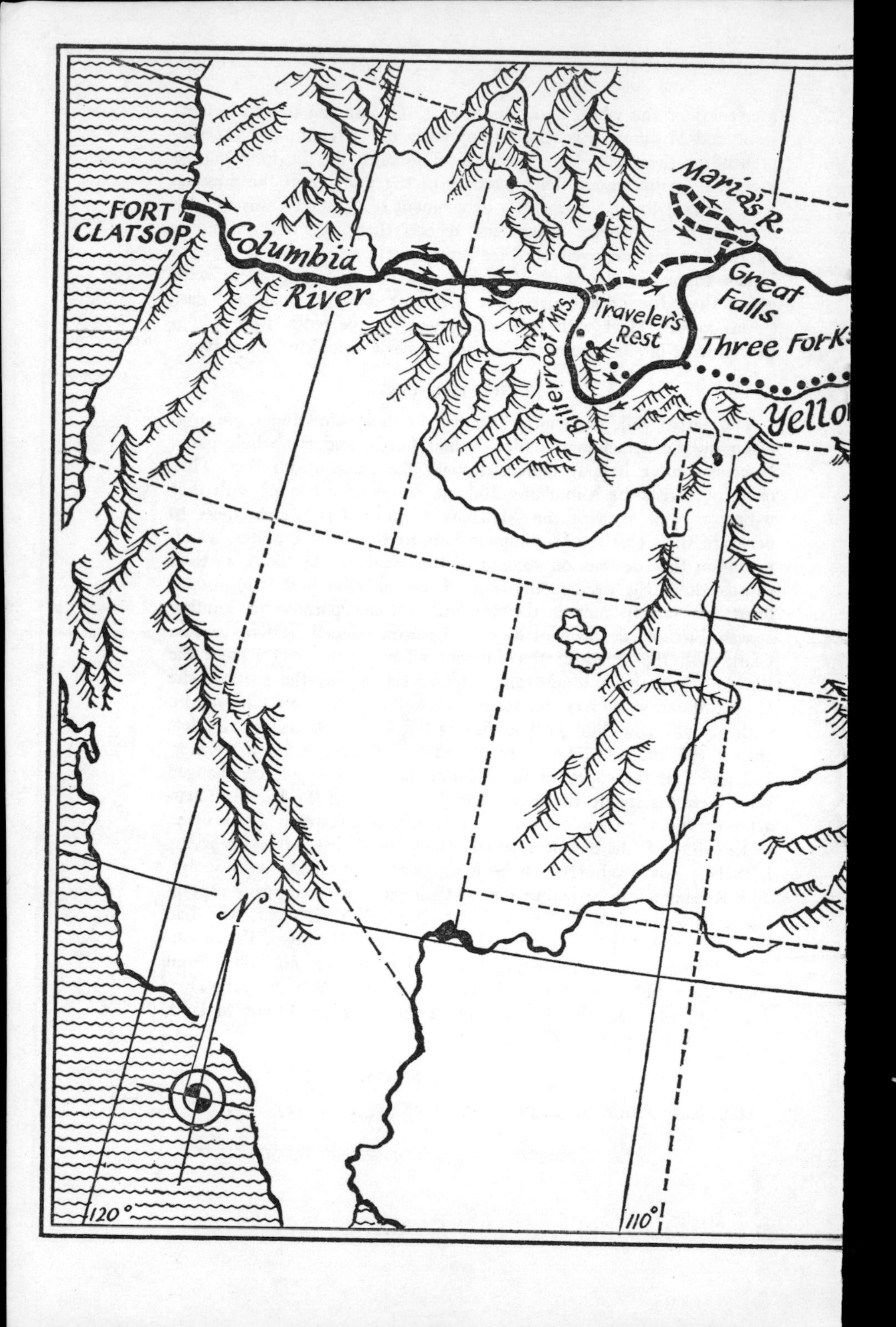
FORT CLATSOP
Columbia
River
Maria's R.
Great
Falls
Traveler's
Rest
Bitterroot Mts.
Three Forks
Yellow
N
120°
110°

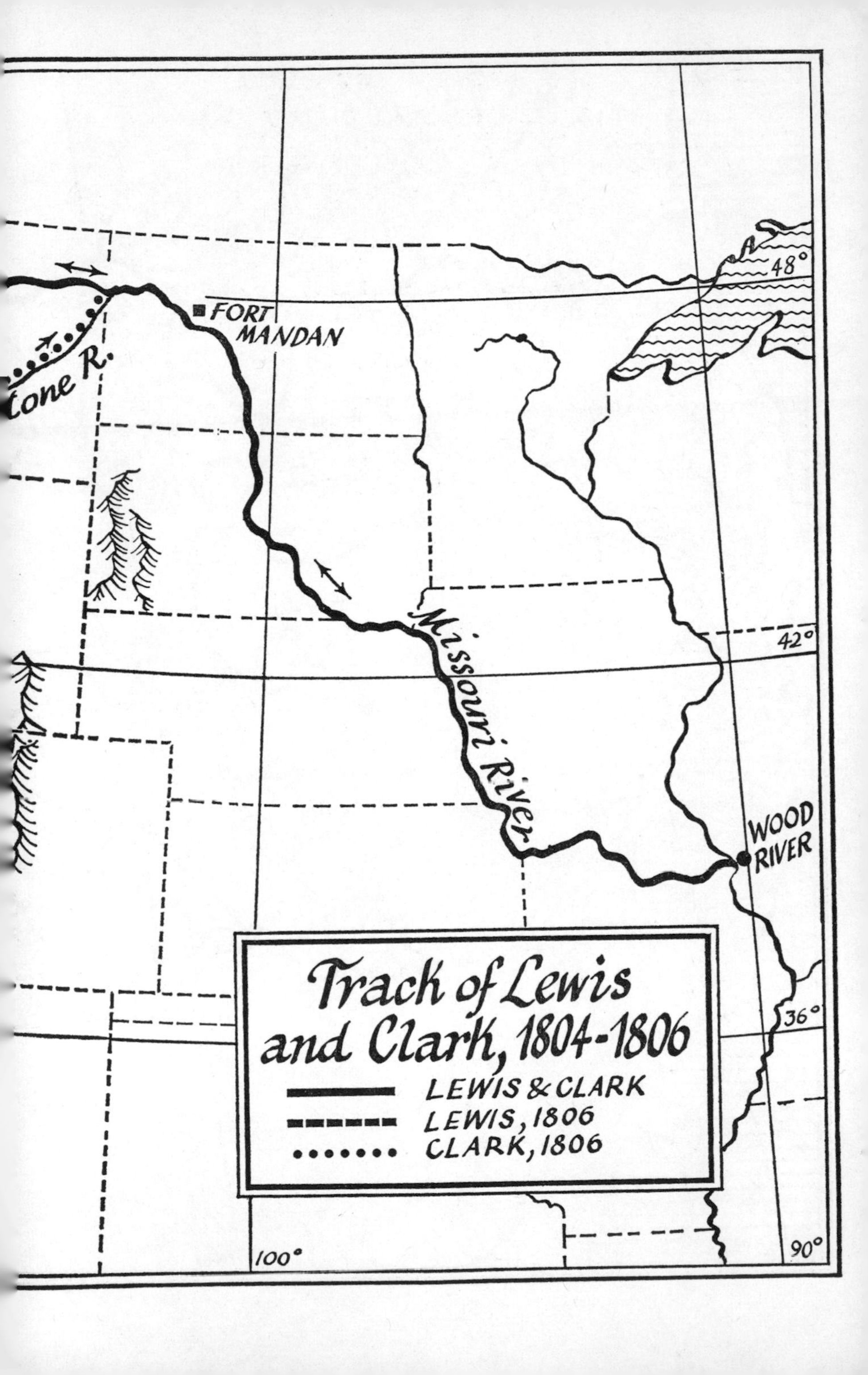

tone R.
FORT MANDAN
48°
Missouri River
42°
WOOD RIVER
36°
100°
90°
Track of Lewis and Clark, 1804-1806
LEWIS & CLARK
LEWIS, 1806
CLARK, 1806

LEWIS AND CLARKE'S EXPEDITION

UP THE MISSOURI.

CHAPTER XXV.

Difficulty of procuring means of subsistence for the party—they determine to resume their journey to the mountains—they leave in the hands of the Indians a written memorandum, importing their having penetrated to the Pacific, through the route of the Missouri and Columbia, and through the Rocky mountains—the party commence their return route—dexterity of the Cathlamah Indians in carving—description of the Coweliskee river—they experience much hospitality from the natives—an instance of the extreme voracity of the vulture—the party are visited by many strange Indians, all of whom are kind and hospitable—scarcity of game, and embarrassments of the party on that account—captain Clarke discovers a tribe not seen in the descent down the Columbia—singular adventure to obtain provisions from them—particular description of the Multomah village and river—description of mount Jefferson—some account by captain Clarke of the Neerchokio tribe, and of their architecture—their sufferings by the small-pox.

MANY reasons had determined us to remain at fort Clatsop till the first of April. Besides the want of fuel in the Columbian plains, and the impracticability of passing the mountains before the beginning of June, we were anxious to see some of the foreign traders, from whom, by means of our ample letters of credit, we might have recruited our exhausted stores of merchandise. About the middle of March however, we become seriously alarmed for the want of food: the elk, our chief dependence, had at length deserted their usual haunts in our neighbourhood, and retreated to the mountains. We were too poor to purchase other food from the Indians, so that we were sometimes reduced, notwithstanding all the exertions of our hunters, to a single day's provision in advance. The men too, whom the constant rains and confinement had rendered unhealthy, might we hoped be benefitted by leaving the coast, and resuming the exercise of travelling. We therefore determined to leave fort Clatsop, ascend the river slowly, consume the month of March in the woody country, where we hope to find subsistence, and in this way reach the plains about the first of April, before which time it will be impossible to attempt crossing them: for this purpose we began our preparations. During the winter we had been very industrious in dressing skins, so that we now had a sufficient quantity of clothing, besides between three and four hundred pair of moccasins. But the whole stock of goods on which we are to depend, either for the purchase of horses or of food, during the long tour of nearly four thousand miles, is so much diminished, that it might all be tied in two handkerchiefs. We have in fact nothing but six blue robes, one of scarlet, a coat and hat of the United States artillery uniform, five robes made of our large flag, and a few old clothes trimmed with riband. We therefore feel that our chief dependence must be on our guns, which fortunately for us are all in good order, as we had taken the precaution of bringing a number of extra locks, and one of our men proved to be an excellent artist in that way. The powder had been secured in leaden canisters, and though on many occasions they had been under water, it remained perfectly dry, and we now found ourselves in possession of one hundred and forty pounds of powder, and twice that quantity of lead, a stock quite sufficient for the route homewards.

After much trafficking, we at last succeeded in purchasing a canoe for a uniform coat and half a carrot of tobacco, and took a canoe from the Clatsops, as a reprisal for some elk which some of them had stolen from us in the winter. We were now ready to leave fort Clatsop, but the rain prevented us for several days from caulking the canoes, and we were forced to wait for calm weather, before we could attempt to pass point William. In the meantime we were visited by many of our neighbours, for the purpose of taking leave of us. The Clatsop Commowool has been the most kind and hospitable of all the Indians in this quarter: we therefore gave him a certificate of the kindness and attention which we had received from him, and added a more substantial proof of our gratitude, the gift of all our houses and furniture. To the Chinnook chief Delashelwilt, we gave a certificate of the same kind: we also circulated among the natives several papers, one of which we also posted up in the fort, to the following effect:

"The object of this last, is, that through the medium of some civilized person, who may see the same, it may be made known to the world, that the party consisting of the persons whose names are hereunto annexed, and who were sent out by the government of the United States to explore the interior of the continent of North America, did penetrate the same by the way of the Missouri and Columbia rivers, to the discharge of the latter into the Pacific ocean, where they arrived on the 14th day of November 1805, and departed the 23d day of March, 1806, on their return to the United States, by the same route by which they had come out." * On the

* By a singular casualty, this note fell into the possession of captain Hill, who, while on the coast of the Pacific, procured it from the natives. This note accompanied him on his voyage to Canton, from whence it arrived in the United States. The following is an extract of a letter, from a gentleman at Canton to his friend in Philadelphia:

Extract of a letter from ——— to ——— in Philadelphia.

CANTON, January, 1807.

I wrote you last by the Governor Strong, Cleveland, for Boston; the present is by the brig Lydia, Hill, of the same place.

Captain Hill, while on the coast, met some Indian natives near the mouth of the Columbia river, who delivered to him *a paper*, of which I enclose you a copy. It had been committed to their charge by captains Clarke and Lewis, who had penetrated to the Pacific ocean. The original is a rough draft with a pen of their outward route, and that which they intended returning by. Just below the junction of Madison's river, they found an immense fall of *three hundred and sixty-two* feet perpendicular. This, I believe, exceeds in magnitude any other known. From the natives captain Hill learned that they were all in good health and spirits; had met many difficulties on their progress, from various tribes of Indians, but had found them about the sources of the Missouri very friendly, as were those on Columbia river and the coast.

back of some of these papers, we sketched the connexion of the upper branches of the Missouri and Columbia rivers, with our route, and the track which we intended to follow on our return. This memorandum was all that we deemed it necessary to make; for there seemed but little chance that any detailed report to our government, which we might leave in the hands of the savages, to be delivered to foreign traders, would ever reach the United States. To leave any of our men here, in hopes of their procuring a passage home in some transient vessel, would too much weaken our party, which we must necessarily divide during our route; besides that, we will most probably be there ourselves sooner than any trader, who, after spending the next summer here, might go on some circuitous voyage.

The rains and wind still confined us to the fort; but at last our provisions dwindled down to a single day's stock, and it became absolutely necessary to remove: we therefore sent a few hunters ahead, and stopped the boats as well as we could with mud. The next morning,

Sunday, March 23, 1806, the canoes were loaded, and at one o'clock in the afternoon we took a final leave of fort Clatsop. The wind was still high, but the alternative of remaining without provisions was so unpleasant, that we hoped to be able to double point William. We had scarcely left the fort when we met Delashelwilt, and a party of twenty Chinnooks, who understanding that we had been trying to procure a canoe, had brought one for sale. Being, however, already supplied, we left them, and after getting out of Meriwether's bay, began to coast along the south side of the river: we doubled point William without any injury, and at six o'clock reached, at the distance of sixteen miles from fort Clatsop, the mouth of a small creek, where we found our hunters. They had been fortunate enough to kill two elk, but at such a distance that we could not send for them before the next morning,

Monday, March 24, when they were brought in for breakfast. We then proceeded. The country is covered with a thick growth of timber: the water however is shallow to the distance of four miles from shore; and although there is a channel deep enough for canoes on the south side, yet as the tide was low, we found some difficulty in passing along. At one o'clock we reached the Cathlamah village, where we halted for about two hours, and purchased some wappatoo and a dog for the invalids. This village we have already described, as situated opposite to the seal islands: on one of these the Indians have placed their dead in canoes, raised on scaffolds, above the reach of the tide. These people seem to be more fond of carving in wood than their neighbours, and have various specimens of their taste about the houses. The broad pieces supporting the roof and the board through which doors are cut, are the objects on which they chiefly display their ingenuity, and are ornamented with curious figures, sometimes representing persons in a sitting posture supporting a burden. On resuming our route among the seal islands, we mistook our way, which an Indian observing, he pursued us and put us into the right channel. He soon, however, embarrassed us, by claiming the canoe we had taken from the Clatsops, and which he declared was his property: we had found it among the Clatsops, and seized it as a reprisal for a theft committed by that nation; but being unwilling to do an act of injustice to this Indian, and having no time to discuss the question of right, we compromised with him for an elk skin, with which he returned perfectly satisfied. We continued our route along the shore, and after making fifteen miles encamped at an old village of nine houses, opposite to the lower village of the Wahkiacums. Here we were overtaken by two Chinnooks, who came to us after dark, and spent the night at our camp. We found plenty of wood for fires, which were quite necessary, as the weather had become cold. This morning,

Tuesday 25, proved so disagreeably cold that we did not set out before seven o'clock, when having breakfasted, we continued along the southern side of the river. The wind, however, as well as a strong current was against us, so that we proceeded slowly. On landing for dinner at noon, we were joined by some Clatsops, who had been on a trading voyage to the Skilloots, and were now on their return loaded with dried anchovies, wappatoo, and sturgeon. After dinner we crossed the river to a large island, along the side of which we continued about a mile till we reached a single house, occupied by three men, two women, and the same number of boys, all of the Cathlamah nation. They were engaged in fishing or trolling for sturgeon, of which they had caught about a dozen, but they asked so much for them that we were afraid to purchase. One of the men purchased the skin of a sea-otter, in exchange for a dressed elk skin and a handkerchief. Near adjoining this house was another party of Cathlamahs, who had been up the river on a fishing excursion, and been successful in procuring a large supply, which they were not disposed to sell. We proceeded on to the head of the island, and then crossed to the north side of the river. Here the coast formed a continued swamp for several miles back, so that it was late in the evening before we were able to reach a spot fit for our camp. At length we discovered the entrance of a small creek, opposite to the place where we were encamped on the sixth of November, and though the ground was low and moist, yet as the spot was sheltered from the wind, we resolved to pass the night there: we had now made fifteen miles. Here we found another party of ten Cathlamahs, who had established a temporary residence here for the purpose of fishing sturgeon and taking seal, in both of which they had been successful. They gave us some of the flesh of the seal, which was a valuable addition to the lean elk. The low grounds which we passed are supplied with cottonwood, and the tree resembling the ash, except in its leaf, with red willow, broad-leafed willow, seven bark, gooseberry, green briar, and the large-leafed thorn. The wind was very high towards evening, and continued to blow so violent in the morning,

March 26, that we could not set out before eight o'clock. In the meantime finding that one of our neighbours, the Cathlamahs, by name Wallale, was a person of distinction, we gave him a medal of a small size, with which he was invested with the usual ceremonies. He appeared highly gratified, and requited us with a large sturgeon. The wind having abated, we proceeded to an old village, where we halted for dinner, having met on the way Sahawacap the principal chief of all the Cathlamahs, who was on his return from a trading voyage up the river, with wappatoo and fish, some of which he gave us, and we purchased a little more. At dinner we were overtaken by two Wahkiacums, who have been following us for twenty-four hours, with two dogs, for which they are importuning us to give them some tobacco; but as we have very little of that article left, they were obliged to go off disappointed. We received at the same time an agreeable supply of three eagles and a large goose, brought in by the hunters. After dinner we passed along the north shore opposite to a high fine bottom and dry prairie, at the upper end of which, near a grove of white-oak trees, is an island which we called Fanny's island. There were some deer and elk at a distance in the prairie, but as we could not stay to hunt, we continued till late in the evening, when we encamped on the next island above Fanny's. According to the estimate we made in descending the river, which we begin, however, to think was short, our journey of to-day was eighteen miles. Some Indians came to us, but we were occupied in procuring wood, which we found it difficult to obtain in sufficient quantity for our purposes, and they therefore did not remain long.

Thursday, 27. We set out early, and were soon joined by some Skilloots, with fish and roots for sale. At ten o'clock we stopped to breakfast at two houses of the same nation, where we found our hunters, who had not returned to camp last night, but had killed nothing. The inhabitants seemed very kind and hospitable. They gave almost the whole party as much as they could eat of dried anchovies, wappatoo, sturgeon, quamash, and a small white tuberous root, two inches long, and as thick as a man's finger, which, when eaten raw, is crisp, milky, and of an agreeable flavour. The Indians also urged us to remain with them all day, and hunt elk and deer, which they said were abundant in the neighbourhood; but as the weather would not permit us to dry and pitch our canoes, we declined their offer and proceeded. At the distance of two miles we passed the entrance of Coweliskee river. This stream discharges itself on the north side of the Columbia, about three miles above a remarkably high rocky knoll, the south side of which it washes in passing, and which is separated from the northern hills by a wide bottom of several miles in extent. The Coweliskee is one hundred and fifty yards wide, deep and navigable, as the Indians assert, for a considerable distance, and most probably waters the country west and north of the range of mountains which cross the Columbia between the great falls and rapids. On the lower side of this river, a few miles from its entrance into the Columbia, is the principal village of the Skilloots, a numerous people, differing, however, neither in language, dress, nor manners, from the Clatsops, Chinnooks, and other nations at the mouth of the Columbia. With the Chinnooks they have lately been at war, and though hostilities have ceased, yet they have not resumed their usual intercourse, so that the Skilloots do not go as far as the sea, nor do the Chinnooks come higher up than the Seal islands, the trade between them being carried on by the Clatsops, Cathlamahs, and Wahkiacums, their mutual friends. On this same river, above the Skilloots, resides the nation called Hullooetell, of whom we learnt nothing, except that the nation was numerous. Late in the evening we halted at the beginning of the bottom land, below Deer island, after having made twenty miles. Along the low grounds on the river were the cottonwood, sweet-willow, the oak, ash, the broad-leafed ash, and the growth resembling the beech; while the hills are occupied almost exclusively by different species of fir, and the black alder is common to the hills as well as the low grounds. During the day we passed a number of fishing camps, on both sides of the river, and were constantly attended by small parties of the Skilloots, who behaved in the most orderly manner, and from whom we purchased as much fish and roots as we wanted on very moderate terms. The night continued as the day had been, cold, wet, and disagreeable.

Friday, 28. We left our camp at an early hour, and by nine o'clock reached an old Indian village on the left side of Deer island. Here we found a party of our men whom we had sent on yesterday to hunt, and who now returned after killing seven deer, in the course of the morning, out of upwards of a hundred which they had seen. They were the common fallow deer with long tails, and though very poor are better than the black-tailed fallow deer of the coast, from which they differ materially. Soon after our arrival the weather became fair, and we therefore immediately hauled the boats on shore, and having dried them by means of large fires, put on the pitch. We also took this opportunity of drying our baggage; and as some of the hunters had not yet returned, it was deemed advisable to pass the night at our present camp. This island, which has received from the Indians the appropriate name of Elalah, or Deer island, is surrounded on the water side by an abundant growth of cotton-wood, ash, and willow, while the interior consists chiefly of prairies interspersed with ponds. These afford refuge to great numbers of geese, ducks, large swan, sandhill cranes, a few canvass-backed ducks, and particularly the duckinmallard, the most abundant of all. There are also great numbers of snakes resembling our gartersnakes in appearance, and like them not poisonous. Our hunters brought in three deer, a goose, some ducks, an eagle, and a tyger-cat, but such is the extreme voracity of the vultures, that they had devoured in the space of a few hours, four of the deer killed this morning; and one of our men declared, that they had besides dragged a large buck about thirty yards, skinned it, and broke the back-bone. We were visited during the day by a large canoe with ten Indians of the Quathlapotle nation, who reside about seventeen miles above us. We had advanced only five miles to-day.

Saturday, 29. At an early hour we proceeded along the side of Deer island, and halted for breakfast at the upper end of it, which is properly the commencement of the great Columbian valley. We were here joined by three men of the Towahnahiook nation, with whom we proceeded, till at the distance of fourteen miles from our camp of last evening we reached a large inlet or arm of the river, about three hundred yards wide, up which they went to their villages. A short distance above this inlet a considerable river empties itself from the north side of the Columbia. Its name is Chawahnahiooks. It is about one hundred and fifty yards wide, and at present discharges a large body of water, though the Indians assure us that at a short distance above its mouth, the navigation is obstructed by falls and rapids. Three miles beyond the inlet is an island near the north shore of the river, behind the lower end of which is a village of Quathlapotles, where we landed, about three o'clock. The village consists of fourteen large wooden houses. The people themselves received us very kindly, and voluntarily spread before us wappatoo and anchovies, but as soon as we had finished enjoying this hospitality, if it deserves that name, they began to ask us for presents. They were, however, perfectly satisfied with the small articles which we distributed according to custom, and equally pleased with our purchasing some wappatoo, twelve dogs and two sea-otter skins. We also gave to the chief a small medal, which he, however, soon transferred to his wife. After remaining some time we embarked, and coasting along this island, which after the nation we called Quathlapotle island, encamped for this night in a small prairie on the north side of the Columbia, having made by estimate nineteen miles. The river is rising fast. In the course of the day we saw great numbers of geese, ducks, and large and small swans, which last are very abundant in the ponds where the wappatoo grows, as they feed much on that root. We also observed the crested king-fisher, and the large and small blackbird: and this evening heard, without seeing, the large hooting owl. The frogs, which we have not found in the wet marshes near the entrance of the Columbia, are now croaking in the swamps and marshes with precisely the same note common in the United States. The garter-snakes appear in vast quantities, and are scattered through the prairies in large bundles of forty or fifty entwined round each other: among the moss on the rocks we observed a species of small wild onions growing so closely together as to form a perfect turf, and equal in flavour to the shives of our gardens, which they resemble in appearance also.

Sunday, 30. Soon after our departure we were met by three Clanaminamums, one of whom we recognised as our companion yesterday. He pressed us very much to visit his countrymen on the inlet, but we had no time to make the circuit, and parted. We proceeded far before a party of Claxtars, and Cathlacumups, passed us in two canoes, on their way down the river; and soon after we were met by several other canoes, filled with persons of different tribes on each side of the river. We passed, also, several fishing camps, on Wappatoo island, and then halted for breakfast on the north side of the river, near our camp of the 4th of November. Here we were visited by several canoes from two villages on Wappatoo island; the first, about two miles above us, is called Clahnaquah, the other a mile above them, has the name of Multnomah. After higgling much in the manner of those on the seacoast, these Indians gave us a sturgeon with some wappatoo and pashequaw in exchange for small fishhooks. As we proceeded we were joined by other Indians, and on coming opposite to the Clahnaquah village, we were shown another village about two miles from the river on the northeast side, and behind a pond running parallel with it. Here they said the tribe called Shotos resided. About four o'clock the Indians all left us. Their chief object in accompanying us appeared to be to gratify curiosity; but though they behaved in the most friendly manner, most of them were prepared with their instruments of war. About sunset we reached a beautiful prairie, opposite the middle of what we had called Image-canoe island, and having made twenty-three miles, encamped for the night. In the prairie is a large pond or lake, and an open grove of oak borders the back part. There are many deer and elk in the neighbourhood, but they are very shy, and the annual fern which is now abundant and dry, make such a rustling as the hunters pass through it, that they could not come within reach of the game, and we obtained nothing but a single duck.

Monday 31. We set out very early, and at eight o'clock landed on the north side of the river and breakfasted. Directly opposite is a large wooden house, belonging to the Shahala nation, the inhabitants of which came over to see us. We had observed in descending the river last year, that there were at the same place, twenty-four other houses built of wood and covered with straw, all of which are now destroyed: on inquiry the Indians informed us, that their relations whom we saw last fall, usually visit them at that season for the purpose of hunting deer and elk, and collecting wappatoo, but that they had lately returned to their permanent residence at the Rapids, we presume in order to prepare for the salmon season, as that fish will soon begin to run. At ten o'clock we resumed our route along the north side of the river, and having passed Diamond island, and Whitebrant island, halted for the night at the lower point of a handsome prairie. Our camp which is twenty-five miles from that of last night, is situated opposite to the upper entrance of Quicksand river: a little below a stream from the north empties itself into the Columbia, near the head of Whitebrant island. It is about eighty yards wide, and at present discharges a large body of very clear water, which near the Columbia overflows its low banks, and forms several large ponds. The natives inform us that this river is of no great extent, and rises in the mountains near us, and that at a mile from its mouth it is divided into two nearly equal branches, both of which are incapable of being navigated, on account of their numerous falls and rapids. Not being able to learn any Indian name, we called it Seal river, from the abundance of those animals near its mouth. At the same place we saw a summer duck, or a wood duck, as it is sometimes called; it is the same with those of the United States, and the first we had seen since entering the Rocky mountains last summer.

The hunters who had been obliged to halt below Seal river on account of the waves being too high for their small canoe, returned after dark with the unwelcome news that game was scarce in that quarter.

Tuesday, April 1. Three Indians had followed us yesterday, and encamped near us last night. On putting to them a variety of questions relative to their country, they assured us that Quicksand river, which we had hitherto deemed so considerable, extends no further than the southwest side of mount Hood, which is south 85° east, forty miles distant from this place; that it is moreover navigable for a very short distance only, in consequence of falls and rapids, and that no nation inhabits its borders. Several other persons affirmed that it rose near mount Hood, and sergeant Pryor, who was sent for the purpose of examining it, convinced us of the truth of their statement. He had found the river three hundred yards wide, though the channel was not more than fifty yards, and about six feet deep. The current was rapid, the water turbid, the bed of the river is formed entirely of quicksand, and the banks low and at present overflowed. He passed several islands, and at three and a half miles distance a creek from the south, fifty yards wide; his farthest course was six miles from the mouth of the river, but there it seemed to bend to the east, and he heard the noise of waterfalls. If Quicksand river then does not go beyond mount Hood, it must leave the valley a few miles from its entrance, and run nearly parallel with the Columbia. There must therefore be some other large river, which we have not yet seen, to water the extensive country between the mountains of the coast and Quicksand river: but the Indians could give us no satisfactory information of any such stream.

Whilst we were making these inquiries, a number of canoes came to us, and among the rest a number of families were descending the river. They told us that they lived at the Great rapids, but that a great scarcity of provisions there, had induced them to come down in hopes of finding subsistence in this fertile valley. All those who lived at the rapids, as well as the nations above them, were in much distress for want of food, having consumed their winter store of dried fish, and not expecting the return of the salmon before the next full moon, which will happen on the second of May: this intelligence was disagreeable and embarrassing. From the falls to the Chopunnish nation, the plains afford no deer, elk, or antelope, on which we can rely for subsistence. The horses are very poor at this season, and the dogs must be in the same condition if their food the fish have failed, so that we had calculated entirely on purchasing fish. On the other hand it is obviously inexpedient to wait for the return of the salmon, since in that case we might not reach the Missouri before the ice would prevent our navigating it. We might besides hazard the loss of our horses, for the Chopunnish, with whom we left them, intend crossing the mountains as early as possible, which is about the beginning of May, and they would take our horses with them, or suffer them to disperse, in either of which cases the passage of the mountains will be almost impracticable. We therefore, after much deliberation, decided to remain here till we collect meat enough to last us till we reach the Chopunnish nation, to obtain canoes from the natives as we ascend, either in exchange for our periougues, or by purchasing them with skins and merchandise. These canoes may in turn be exchanged for horses with the natives of the plains, till we obtain enough to travel altogether by land. On reaching the southeast branch of the Columbia, four or five men shall be sent on to the Chopunnish to have our horses in readiness, and thus we shall have a stock of horses sufficient to transport our baggage and to supply us with provisions, for we now perceive that they will form our only certain resource for food.

The hunters returned from the opposite side of the river with some deer and elk, which were abundant there, as were also the tracks of the black bear; while on the north side we could kill nothing.

In the course of our dealings to-day we purchased a canoe from an Indian, for which we gave six fathom of wampum beads. He seemed perfectly satisfied and went away, but returned soon after, cancelled the bargain, and giving back the wampum requested that we would restore him the canoe. To this we consented, as we knew this method of trading to be very common and deemed perfectly fair.

Wednesday, 2. Being now determined to collect as much meat as possible, two parties, consisting of nine men, were sent over the river to hunt, three were ordered to range the country on this side, while all the rest were employed in cutting and scaffolding the meat which we had already. About eight o'clock several canoes arrived to visit us, and among the rest were two young men, who were pointed out as Cashooks. On inquiry, they said that their nation resided at the falls of a large river, which empties itself into the south side of the Columbia, a few miles below us, and they drew a map of the country, with a coal on a mat. In order to verify this information, captain Clarke persuaded one of the young men, by a present of a burning-glass, to accompany him to the river, in search of which he immediately set out with a canoe and seven of our men. After his departure other canoes arrived from above, bringing families of women and children, who confirmed the accounts of a scarcity of provisions. One of these families, consisting of ten or twelve persons, encamped near us, and behaved perfectly well. The hunters on this side of the river, returned with the skins of only two deer, the animals being too poor for use.

Thursday, 3. A considerable number of Indians crowded us to-day, many of whom came from the upper part of the river. These poor wretches confirm the reports of scarcity among the nations above; which, indeed, their appearance sufficiently prove, for they seem almost starved, and greedily pick the bones and refuse meat thrown away by us.

In the evening captain Clarke returned from his excursion. On setting out yesterday at half past eleven o'clock, he directed his course along the south side of the river, where, at the distance of eight miles, he passed a village of the Nechacohee tribe, belonging to the Eloot nation. The village itself is small, and being situated behind Diamond island, was concealed from our view as we passed both times along the northern shore. He continued till three o'clock, when he landed at the single house already mentioned, as the only remains of a village of twenty-four straw huts. Along the shore were great numbers of small canoes for gathering wappatoo, which were left by the Shahalas, who visit the place annually. The present inhabitants of the house are part of the Neerchokioo tribe of the same nation. On entering one of the apartments of the house, captain Clarke offered several articles to the Indians, in exchange for wappatoo, but they appeared sullen and ill-humoured, and refused to give him any. He therefore sat down by the fire, opposite to the men, and taking a port-fire match from his pocket, threw a small piece of it into the flame, at the same time took his pocket compass, and by means of a magnet, which happened to be in his inkhorn, made the needle turn round very briskly. The match now took fire, and burned violently, on which, the Indians terrified at this strange exhibition, immediately brought a quantity of wappatoo, and laid it at his feet, begging him to put out the bad fire: while an old woman continued to speak with great vehemence, as if praying and imploring protection. Having received the roots, captain Clarke put up the compas, and as the match went out of itself, tranquillity was restored, though the women and children still took refuge in their beds, and behind the men. He now paid them for what he had used, and after lighting his pipe, and smoking with them, he continued down the river. He now found what we had called Image-canoe island, to consist of three islands, the one in the middle concealing the opening between the other two in such a way, as to present to us on the opposite side of the river, the appearance of a single island. At the lower point of the third, and thirteen miles below the last village, he entered the mouth of a large river, which was concealed by three small islands in its mouth, from those who descend or go up the Columbia. This river, which the Indians call Multnomah, from a nation of the same name, residing near it on Wappatoo island, enters the Columbia, one hundred and forty miles from the mouth of the latter river, of which it may justly be considered as forming one fourth, though it had now fallen eighteen inches below its greatest annual height. From its entrance mount Regnier bears nearly north, mount St. Helen's north, with a very high humped mountain a little to the east of it, which seems to lie in the same chain with the conic-pointed mountains before mentioned. Mount Hood bore due east, and captain Clarke now discovered to the southeast, a mountain which we had not yet seen, and to which he gave the name of mount Jefferson. Like mount St. Helen's its figure is a regular cone covered with snow, and is probably of equal height with that mountain, though being more distant, so large a portion of it does not appear above the range of mountains which lie between these and this point. Soon after entering the Multnomah he was met by an old Indian descending the river alone in a canoe. After some conversation with him, the pilot informed captain Clarke, that this old man belonged to the Clackamos nation, who reside on a river forty miles up the Multnomah. The current of this latter river, is as gentle as that of the Columbia, its surface is smooth and even, and it appears to possess water enough for the largest ship, since, on sounding with a line of five fathoms, he could find no bottom for at least one third of the width of the stream. At the distance of seven miles, he passed a sluice or opening, on the right, eighty yards wide, and which separates Wappatoo island from the continent, by emptying itself into the inlet below. Three miles further up, he reached a large wooden house, on the east side, where he intended to sleep, but on entering the rooms he found such swarms of fleas that he preferred lying on the ground in the neighbourhood. The guide informed him that this house is the temporary residence of the Nemalquinner tribe of the Cushook nation, who reside just below the falls of the Multnomah, but come down here occasionally to collect wappatoo: it was thirty feet long, and forty deep; built of broad boards, covered with the bark of white cedar; the floor on a level with the surface of the earth, and the arrangement of the interior like those near the seacoast. The inhabitants had left their canoes, matts, bladders, train-oil, baskets, bowls, and trenchers, lying about the house at the mercy of every visiter; a proof, indeed, of the mutual respect for the property of each other, though we have had very conclusive evidence that the property of white men is not deemed equally sacred. The guide informed him further, that a small distance above were two bayous, on which were a number of small houses belonging to the Cushooks, but that the inhabitants had all gone up to the falls of the Multnomah, for the purpose of fishing. Early the next morning captain Clarke proceeded up the river, which, during the night, had fallen about five inches. At the distance of two miles he came to the centre of a bend under the highlands on the right side, from which its course, as could be discerned, was to the east of southeast. At this place the Multnomah is five hundred yards wide, and for half that distance across, the cord of five fathoms would not reach the bottom. It appears to be washing away its banks, and has more sandbars and willow points than the Columbia. Its regular gentle current, the depth and smoothness, and uniformity with which it rolls its vast body of water, prove that its supplies are at once distant and regular; nor, judging from its appearance and courses, is it rash to believe that the Multnomah and its tributary streams water the vast extent of country between the western mountains and those of the seacoast, as far perhaps as the waters of the gulf of California. About eleven o'clock he reached the house of the Neerchokioo, which he now found to contain eight families; but they were all so much alarmed at his presence, notwithstanding his visit yesterday, that he remained a very few minutes only. Soon after setting out, he met five canoes filled with the same number of families, belonging to the Shahala nation. They were descending the river in search of subsistence, and seemed very desirous of coming alongside of the boat; but as there were twenty-one men on board, and the guide said that all these Shahalas, as well as their relations at the house which we had just left, were mischievous bad men, they were not suffered to approach. At three o'clock he halted for an hour at the Nechecolee house, where his guide resided. This large building is two hundred and twenty-six feet in front, entirely above ground, and may be considered as a single house, because the whole is under one roof; otherwise it would seem more like a range of buildings, as it is divided into seven distinct apartments, each thirty feet square, by means of broad boards set on end from the floor to the roof. The apartments are separated from each other by a passage or alley four feet wide, extending through the whole depth of the house, and the only entrance is from this alley, through a small hole about twenty-two inches wide, and not more than three feet high. The roof is formed of rafters and round poles laid on them longitudinally. The whole is covered with a double row of the bark of the white cedar, extending from the top eighteen inches over the eaves, and secured as well as smoothed by splinters of dried fir, inserted through it at regular distances. In this manner the roof is made light, strong, and durable. Near this house are the remains of several other large buildings, sunk in the ground and constructed like those we had seen at the great narrows of the Columbia, belonging to the Eloots, with whom these people claim an affinity. In manners and dress these Nechecolees differ but little from the Quathlapotles and others of this neighbourhood; but their language is the same used by the Eloots, and though it has some words in common with the dialects spoken here, yet the whole air of the language is obviously different. The men too are larger, and both sexes better formed than among the nations below; and the females are distinguished by wearing larger and longer robes, which are generally of deer skin dressed in the hair, than the neighbouring women. In the house were several old people of both sexes, who were treated with much respect, and still seemed healthy, though most of them were perfectly blind. On inquiring the cause of the decline of their village, an old man, the father of the guide, and a person of some distinction, brought forward a woman very much marked with the small-pox, and said, that when a girl she was very near dying with the disorder which had left those marks, and that all the inhabitants of the houses now in ruins had fallen victims to the same disease. From the apparent age of the woman, connected with her size at the time of her illness, captain Clarke judged that the sickness must have been about thirty years ago, the period about which we have supposed that the small-pox prevailed on the seacoast.

He then entered into a long conversation with regard to all the adjacent country and its inhabitants, which the old man explained with great intelligence, and then drew with his finger in the dust a sketch of the Multnomah, and Wappatoo island. This captain Clarke copied and preserved. He now purchased five dogs, and taking leave of the Nechecolee village, returned to camp.

CHAPTER XXVI.

Description of Wappatoo island, and the mode in which the nations gather wappatoo—the character of the soil and its productions—the numerous tribes residing in its vicinity—the probability that they were all of the tribe of the Multnomahs originally, inferred from similarity of dress, manners, language, &c. —description of their dress, weapons of war, their mode of burying the dead—description of another village, called the Wahclellah village—their mode of architecture—extraordinary height of Beacon rock—Unfriendly character of the Indians at that place—The party, alarmed for their safety, resolve to inflict summary vengeance, in case the Wahclellah tribe persist in their outrages and insults—interview with the chief of that tribe, and confidence restored—difficulty of drawing the canoes over the rapids—visited by a party of the Yehugh tribe—short notice of the Weocksockwillackum tribe—curious phenomenon observed in the Columbia, from the Rapids to the Chilluckittequaws.

FRIDAY, April 4, 1804. The hunters were still out in every direction. Those from the opposite side of the river returned with the flesh of a bear and some venison, but the flesh of six deer and an elk which they had killed was so meagre and unfit for use, that they had left it in the woods. Two other deer were brought in, but as the game seemed poor, we despatched a large party to some low grounds on the south, six miles above us, to hunt there until our arrival. As usual many of the Indians came to our camp, some descending the rivers with their families, and others from below with no object except to gratify their curiosity.

The visit of captain Clarke to the Multnomahs, now enabled us to combine all that we had seen or learnt of the neighbouring countries and nations. Of these the most important spot is Wappatoo island, a large extent of country lying between the Multnomah, and an arm of the Columbia, which we have called Wappatoo inlet, and separated from the main land by a sluice eighty yards wide, which at the distance of seven miles up the Multnomah connects that river with the inlet. The island thus formed is about twenty miles long, and varies in breadth from five to ten miles: the land is high and extremely fertile, and on most parts is supplied with a heavy growth of cottonwood, ash, the large-leafed ash, and sweet willow, the black alder, common to the coast, having now disappeared. But the chief wealth of this island consists of the numerous ponds in the interior, abounding with the common arrowhead (sagittaria sagittifolia) to the root of which is attached a bulb growing beneath it in the mud. This bulb, to which the Indians give the name of wappatoo, is the great article of food, and almost the staple article of commerce on the Columbia. It is never out of season; so that at all times of the year, the valley is frequented by the neighbouring Indians who come to gather it. It is collected chiefly by the women, who employ for the purpose canoes from ten to fourteen feet in length, about two feet wide, and nine inches deep, and tapering from the middle, where they are about twenty inches wide. They are sufficient to contain a single person and several bushels of roots, yet so very light that a woman can carry them with ease; she takes one of these canoes into a pond where the water is as high as the breast, and by means of her toes, separates from the root this bulb, which on being freed from the mud rises immediately to the surface of the water, and is thrown into the canoe. In this manner these patient females remain in the water for several hours even in the depth of winter. This plant is found through the whole extent of the valley in which we now are, but does not grow on the Columbia farther eastward. This valley is bounded westward by the mountainous country bordering the coast, from which it extends eastward thirty miles in a direct line, till it is closed by the range of mountains crossing the Columbia above the great falls. Its length from north to south we are unable to determine, but we believe that the valley must extend to a great distance: it is in fact the only desirable situation for a settlement on the western side of the Rocky mountains, and being naturally fertile, would, if properly cultivated, afford subsistence for forty or fifty thousand souls. The highlands are generally of a dark rich loam, not much injured by stones, and though waving, by no means too steep for cultivation, and a few miles from the river they widen at least on the north side, into rich extensive prairies. The timber on them is abundant, and consists almost exclusively of the several species of fir already described, and some of which grow to a great height. We measured a fallen tree of that species, and found that including the stump of about six feet, it was three hundred and eighteen feet in length, though its diameter was only three feet. The dogwood is also abundant on the uplands: it differs from that of the United States in having a much smoother bark, and in being much larger, the trunk attaining a diameter of nearly two feet. There is some white cedar of a large size, but no pine of any kind. In the bottom lands are the cottonwood ash, large leafed ash, and sweet willow. Interspersed with these are the pashequaw, shanataque, and compound fern, of which the natives use the roots, the red flowering current abounds on the upland, while along the river bottoms grow luxuriantly the watercress, strawberry, cinquefoil, narrowdock, sandrush, and the flowering pea, which is not yet in bloom. There is also a species of the bear's-claw now blooming, but the large leafed thorn has disappeared, nor do we see any longer the huckleberry, the shallun, nor any of the other evergreen shrubs which bear berries, except the species, the leaf of which has a prickly margin.

Among the animals, we observe the martin, small geese, the small speckled woodpecker, with a white back, the blue-crested corvus, ravens, crows, eagles, vultures, and hawks. The mellow bug, long-legged spider, as well as the butterfly and blowingfly, and tick, have already made their appearance, but none of all these are distinguished from animals of the same sort in the United States. The musquetoes too have resumed their visits, but are not yet troublesome.

The nations who inhabit this fertile neighbourhood are very numerous. The Wappatoo inlet extends three hundred yards wide, for ten or twelve miles to the south, as far as the hills near which it receives the waters of a small creek whose sources are not far from those of the Killamuck river. On that creek resides the Clackstar nation, a numerous people of twelve hundred souls, who subsist on fish and wappatoo, and who trade by means of the Killamuck river, with the nation of that name on the seacoast. Lower down the inlet, towards the Columbia, is the tribe called Cathlacumup. On the sluice which connects the inlet with the Multnomah, are the tribes, Cathlanahquiah, and Cathlacomatup: and on Wappatoo island, the tribes of Clannahminamun, and Clahnaquah. Immediately opposite, near the Towahnahiooks, are the Quathlapotles, and higher up on the side of the Columbia, the Shotos. All these tribes, as well as the Cathlahaws, who live somewhat lower on the river, and have an old village on Deer island, may be considered as parts of the great Multnomah nation, which has its principal residence on Wappatoo island, near the mouth of the large river to which they give their name. Forty miles above its junction with the Columbia, it receives the waters of the Clackamos, a river which may be traced through a woody and fertile country to its sources in mount Jefferson, almost to the foot of which it is navigable for canoes. A nation of the same name resides in eleven villages along its borders: they live chiefly on fish and roots, which abound in the Clackamos and manners, or language from the tribes of Multnomahs. Two days' journey from the Columbia, or about twenty miles beyond the entrance of the Clackamos, are the falls of the Multnomah. At this place are the permanent residences of the Cushooks and Chahcowahs, two tribes who are attracted to that place by the fish, and by the convenience of trading across the mountains and down Killamuck river, with the nation of Killamucks, from whom they procure train oil. These falls were occasioned by the passage of a high range of mountains; beyond which the country stretches into a vast level plain, wholly destitute of timber. As far as the Indians, with whom we conversed, had ever penetrated that country, it was inhabited by a nation called Calahpoewah, a very numerous people whose villages, nearly forty in number, are scattered along each side of the Multnomah, which furnish them with their chief subsistence, fish, and the roots along its banks.

All the tribes in the neighbourhood of Wappatoo island, we have considered as Multnomahs; not because they are in any degree subordinate to that nation; but they all seem to regard the Multnomahs as the most powerful. There is no distinguished chief, except the one at the head of the Multnomahs; and they are moreover linked by a similarity of dress and manners, and houses and language, which much more than the feeble restraints of Indian government contribute to make one people. These circumstances also separate them from nations lower down the river. The Clatsops, Chinnooks, Wahkiacums and Cathlamahs understand each other perfectly; their language varies, however, in some respects from that of the Skilloots; but on reaching the Multnomah Indians, we found, that although many words were the same, and a great number differed only in the mode of accenting them, from those employed by the Indians near the mouth of the Columbia, yet there was a very sensible variation of language. The natives of the valley are larger and rather better shaped than those of the seacoast: their appearance too is generally healthy, but they are afflicted with the common disease of the Columbia, soreness of the eyes. To whatever this disorder may be imputed it is a great national calamity: at all ages their eyes are sore and weak, and the loss of one eye is by no means uncommon, while in grown persons total blindness is frequent, and almost universal in old age. The dress of the men has nothing different from that used below, but are chiefly remarked by a passion for large brass buttons, which they fix on a sailor's jacket, when they are so fortunate as to obtain one, without regard to any arrangement. The women also wear the short robe already described; but their hair is most commonly braided into two tresses falling over each ear in front of the body, and instead of the tissue of bark, they employ a piece of leather in the shape of a pocket handkerchief tied round the loins. This last is the only and ineffectual defence when the warmth of the weather induces them to throw aside the robe. The houses are in general on a level with the ground, though some are sunk to the depth of two or three feet into the ground, and like those near the coast adorned or disfigured by carvings or paintings on the posts, doors and beds: they do not possess any peculiar weapon except a kind of broad sword made of iron, from three to four feet long, the blade about four inches wide, very thin and sharp at all its edges, as well as at the point. They have also bludgeons of wood in the same form; and both kinds generally hang at the head of their beds. These are formidable weapons. Like the natives of the seacoast, they are also very fond of cold, hot, and vapour baths, which are used at all seasons, and for the purpose of health as well as pleasure. They, however, add a species of bath peculiar to themselves, by washing the whole body with urine every morning.

The mode of burying the dead in canoes, is no longer practised by the natives here. The place of deposit is a vault formed of boards, slanting like the roof of a house from a pole supported by two forks. Under this vault the dead are placed horizontally on boards, on the surface of the earth, and carefully covered with mats. Many bodies are here laid on each other, to the height of three or four corpses, and different articles, which were most esteemed by the dead, are placed by their side; their canoes themselves being sometimes broken to strengthen the vault.

The trade of all these inhabitants is in anchovies, sturgeon, but chiefly in wappatoo, to obtain which, the inhabitants both above and below them on the river, come at all seasons, and supply in turn, beads, cloth, and various other articles procured from the Europeans.

Saturday, April 5. We dried our meat as well as the cloudy weather would permit. In the course of his chase yesterday, one of our men who killed the bear, found a nest of another with three cubs in it. He returned to-day in hopes of finding her, but he brought only the cubs, without being able to see the dam, and on this occasion, Drewyer, our most experienced huntsman, assured us that he had never known a single instance where a female bear, who had once been disturbed by a hunter and obliged to leave her young, returned to them again. The young bears were sold for wappatoo to some of the many Indians who visited us in parties during the day, and behaved very well. Having made our preparations of dried meat, we set out next morning,

Sunday 6, by nine o'clock, and continued along the north side of the river for a few miles, and then crossed to the river to look for the hunters, who had been sent forward the day before yesterday. We found them at the upper end of the bottom with some Indians, for we are never freed from the visits of the natives. They had killed three elk, and wounded two others so badly, that it was still possible to get them. We therefore landed, and having prepared scaffolds and secured the five elk, we encamped for the night, and the following evening,

Monday 7, the weather having been fair and pleasant, had dried a sufficient quantity of meat to serve us as far as the Chopunnish, with occasional supplies, if we can procure them, of dogs, roots, and horses. In the course of the day several parties of Shahalas, from a village eight miles above us, came to visit us, and behaved themselves very properly, except that we were obliged to turn one of them from the camp for stealing a piece of lead. Every thing was now ready for our departure, but in the morning,

Tuesday 8, the wind blew with great violence, and we were obliged to unload our boats, which were soon after filled with water. The same cause prevented our setting out to-day; we therefore despatched several hunters round the neighbourhood, but in the evening they came back with nothing but a duck. They had, however, seen some of the black-tailed, jumping, or fallow deer, like those about fort Clatsop, which are scarce near this place, where the common long-tailed fallow deer are most abundant. They had also observed two black bears, the only kind that we have discovered in this quarter. A party of six Indians encamped at some distance, and late at night the sentinel stopped one of the men, an old man who was creeping into camp in order to pilfer: he contented himself with frightening the Indian, and then giving him a few stripes with a switch, turned the fellow out, and he soon afterwards left the place with all his party.

Wednesday, 9. The wind having moderated, we reloaded the canoes, and set out by seven o'clock. We stopped to take up two hunters who had left us yesterday, but were unsuccessful in the chase, and then proceeded to the Wahclellah village, situated on the north side of the river, about a mile below Beacon rock. During the whole of the route from our camp, we passed along under high, steep, and rocky sides of the mountains, which now close on each side of the river, forming stupendous precipices, covered with the fir and white cedar. Down these heights frequently descend the most beautiful cascades, one of which, a large creek, throws itself over a perpendicular rock three hundred feet above the water, while other smaller streams precipitate themselves from a still greater elevation, and evaporating in a mist, again collect and form a second cascade before they reach the bottom of the rocks. We stopped to breakfast at this village. We here found the tomahawk which had been stolen from us on the fourth of last November: they assured us they had bought it of the Indians below; but as the latter had already informed us that the Wahclellahs had such an article, which they had stolen, we made no difficulty about retaking our property. This village appears to be the wintering station of the Wahclellahs and Clahclellahs, two tribes of the Shahala nation. The greater part of the first tribe have lately removed to the falls of the Multnomah, and the second have established themselves a few miles higher up the Columbia, opposite the lower point of Brant island, where they take salmon, that being the commencement of the rapids. They are now in the act of removing, and carrying off with them, not only the furniture and effects, but the bark and most of the boards of their houses. In this way nine have been lately removed. There are still fourteen standing, and in the rear of the village are the traces of ten or twelve others of more ancient date. These houses are either sunk in the ground or on a level with the surface, and are generally built of boards and covered with cedar bark. In the single houses there is generally a division near the door, which is in the end; or in case the house be double, opens on the narrow passage between the two. Like those we had seen below at the Neerchokioo tribe, the women wear longer and larger robes than their neighbours the Multnomahs, and suspend various ornaments from the cartilage of the nose: the hair is, however, worn in the same sort of braid, falling over each ear, and the truss is universal from the Wappatoo island to Lewis's river. The men also form their hair into two queues by means of otter skin thongs, which fall over the ears so as to give that extraordinary width to the face which is here considered so ornamental. These people seemed very unfriendly, and our numbers alone seemed to secure us from ill treatment. While we were at breakfast the grand chief of the Chilluckittequaws arrived, with two inferior chiefs, and several men and women of his nation. They were returning home, after trading in the Columbian valley, and were loaded with wappatoo and dried anchovies, which, with some beads, they had obtained in exchange for chappelell, bear-grass and other small articles. As these people had been very kind to us as we descended the river, we endeavoured to repay them by every attention in our power. After purchasing, with much difficulty, a few dogs and some wappatoo from the Wahclellahs, we left them at two o'clock, and passing under the Beacon rock, reached in two hours the Clahclellah village. This Beacon rock, which we now observed more accurately than as we descended, stands on the north side of the river, insulated from the hills. The northern side has a partial growth of fir or pine. To the south it rises in an unbroken precipice to the height of seven hundred feet, where it terminates in a sharp point, and may be seen at the distance of twenty miles below. This rock may be considered as the commencement of tide-water, though the influence of the tide is perceptible here in autumn only, at which time the water is low. What the precise difference at those seasons is, we cannot determine; but on examining a rock which we lately passed, and comparing its appearance now with that which we observed last November, we judge the flood of this spring to be twelve feet above the height of the river at that time. From Beacon rock as low as the marshy islands, the general width of the river is from one to two miles, though in many places it is still greater. On landing at the Clahclellahs we found them busy in erecting their huts, which seem to be of a temporary kind only, so that most probably they do not remain longer than the salmon season. Like their country-men, whom we had just left, these people were sulky and ill-humoured, and so much on the alert to pilfer, that we were obliged to keep them at a distance from our baggage. As our large canoes could not ascend the rapids on the north side, we passed to the opposite shore, and entered the narrow channel which separates it from Brant island. The weather was very cold and rainy, and the wind so high, that we were afraid to attempt the rapids this evening, and therefore, finding a safe harbour, we encamped for the night. The wood in this neighbourhood has lately been on fire, and the firs have discharged considerable quantities of pitch, which we collected for some of our boats. We saw to-day some turkey-buzzards, which are the first we have observed on this side of the Rocky mountains.

Thursday, 10. Early in the morning we dropped down the channel to the lower end of Brant island, and then drew our boats up the rapid. At the distance of a quarter of a mile we crossed over to a village of Clahclellahs, consisting of six houses, on the opposite side. The river is here about four hundred yards wide, and the current so rapid, that although we employed five oars for each canoe, we were borne down a considerable distance. While we were at breakfast, one of the Indians offered us two sheep-skins for sale, one, which was the skin of a full grown sheep, was as large as that of a common deer: the second was smaller, and the skin of the head, with the horns remaining, was made into a cap, and highly prized as an ornament by the owner. He however sold the cap to us for a knife, and the rest of the skin for those of two elk; but as they observed our anxiety to purchase the other skin, they would not accept the same price for it, and as we hoped to procure more in the neighbourhood, we did not offer a greater. The horns of the animal were black, smooth, and erect, and they rise from the middle of the forehead, a little above the eyes, in a cylindrical form, to the height of four inches, where they are pointed. The Clahclellahs informed us that the sheep are very abundant on the heights, and among the cliffs of the adjacent mountains; and that these two had been lately killed out of a herd of thirty-six, at no great distance from the village. We were soon joined by our hunters with three black-tailed fallow deer, and having purchased a few white salmon, proceeded on our route. The south side of the river is impassable, and the rapidity of the current as well as the large rocks along the shore, render the navigation of even the north side extremely difficult. During the greater part of the day it was necessary to draw them along the shore, and as we have only a single tow-rope that is strong enough, we are obliged to bring them one after the other. In this tedious and laborious manner, we at length reached the portage on the north side, and carried our baggage to the top of a hill, about two hundred paces distant, where we encamped for the night. The canoes were drawn on shore and secured, but one of them having got loose, drifted down to the last village, the inhabitants of which brought her back to us; an instance of honesty which we rewarded with a present of two knives. It rained all night and the next morning,

Friday, 11, so that the tents, and skins which covered the baggage, were wet. We therefore determined to take the canoes first over the portage, in hopes that by the afternoon the rain would cease, and we might carry our baggage across without injury. This was immediately begun by almost the whole party, who in the course of the day dragged four of the canoes to the head of the rapids, with great difficulty and labour. A guard, consisting of one sick man and three who had been lamed by accidents, remained with captain Lewis to guard the baggage. This precaution was absolutely necessary to protect it from the Wahclellahs, whom we discovered to be great thieves, notwithstanding their apparent honesty in restoring our boat: indeed, so arrogant and intrusive have they become, that nothing but our numbers, we are convinced, saves us from attack. They crowded about us while we were taking up the boats, and one of them had the insolence to throw stones down the bank at two of our men. We now found it necessary to depart from our mild and pacific course of conduct. On returning to the head of the portage, many of them met our men, and seemed very ill disposed. Shields had stopped to purchase a dog, and being separated from the rest of the party, two Indians pushed him out of the road, and attempted to take the dog from him. He had no weapon but a long knife, with which he immediately attacked them both, hoping to put them to death before they had time to draw their arrows, but as soon as they saw his design, they fled into the woods. Soon afterwards we were told by an Indian who spoke Clatsop, which we had ourselves learnt during the winter, that the Wahclellahs had carried off captain Lewis's dog to their village below. Three men well armed were instantly despatched in pursuit of them, with orders to fire if there was the slightest resistance or hesitation. At the distance of two miles, they came within sight of the thieves, who finding themselves pursued, left the dog and made off. We now ordered all the Indians out of our camp, and explained to them, that whoever stole any of our baggage, or insulted our men, should be instantly shot; a resolution which we were determined to enforce, as it was now our only means of safety. We were visited during the day by a chief of the Clahclellahs, who seemed mortified at the behaviour of the Indians, and told us that the persons at the head of their outrages were two very bad men, who belonged to the Wahclellah tribe, but that the nation did not by any means wish to displease us. This chief seemed very well disposed, and we had every reason to believe was much respected by the neighbouring Indians. We therefore gave him a small medal, and showed him all the attentions in our power, with which he appeared very much gratified, and we trust his interposition may prevent the necessity of our resorting to force against his countrymen.

Many Indians from the villages above, passed us in the course of the day, on their return from trading with the natives of the valley, and among others, we recognised an Eloot, who with ten or twelve of his nation were on their way home to the long narrows of the Columbia. These people do not, as we are compelled to do, drag their canoes up the rapids, but leave them at the head, as they descend, and carrying their good across the portage, hire or borrow others from the people below. When the trade is over they return to the foot of the rapids, where they leave these boats and resume their own at the head of the portage. The labour of carrying the goods across is equally shared by the men and women, and we were struck by the contrast between the decent conduct of all the natives from above, and the profligacy and ill manners of the Wahclellahs. About three quarters of a mile below our camp is a burial ground, which seems common to the Wahclellahs, Clahclellahs, and Yehhuhs. It consists of eight sepulchres on the north bank of the river.

Saturday 12. The rain continued all night and this morning. Captain Lewis now took with him all the men fit for duty, and began to drag the remaining periogue over the rapids. This has become much more difficult than when we passed in the autumn; at that time there were in the whole distance of seven miles only three difficult points; but the water is now very considerably higher, and during all that distance the ascent is exceedingly laborious and dangerous, nor would it be practicable to descend, except by letting down the empty boats by means of ropes. The route over this part, from the head to the foot of the portage, is about three miles: the canoes which had been already dragged up were very much injured, by being driven against the rocks, which no precautions could prevent. This morning as we were drawing the fifth canoe round a projecting rock, against which the current sets with great violence, she unfortunately offered too much of her side to the stream. It then drove her with such force, that with all the exertions of the party we were unable to hold her, and were forced to let go the cord, and see her drift down the stream, and be irrecoverably lost. We then began to carry our effects across the portage, but as all those who had short rifles took them in order to repel any attack from the Indians, it was not until five o'clock in the afternoon that the last of the party reached the head of the rapids, accompanied by our new friend the Wahclellah chief. The afternoon being so far advanced, and the weather rainy and cold, we determined to halt for the night, though very desirous of going on, for during the three last days we have not advanced more than seven miles. The portage is two thousand eight hundred yards, along a narrow road, at all times rough, and now rendered slippery by the rain. About half way is an old village which the Clahclellah chief informs us is the occasional residence of his tribe.

These houses are uncommonly large, one of them measured one hundred and sixty by forty feet, and the frames are constructed in the usual manner, except that it is double so as to appear like one house within another. The floors are on a level with the ground, and the roofs have been taken down and sunk in a pond behind the village. We find that our conduct yesterday has made the Indians much more respectful; they do not crowd about us in such numbers, and behave with much more propriety. Among those who visited us were about twenty of the Yehhuhs, a tribe of Shahalas, whom we had found on the north side of the river, immediately above the rapids, but who had now emigrated to the opposite shore, where they generally take salmon. Like their relations, the Wahclellahs, they have taken their houses with them, so that only one is now standing where the old village was. We observe generally, that the houses which have the floor on a level with the earth, are smaller, and have more the appearance of being temporary than those which are sunk in the ground, whence we presume that the former are the dwellings during spring and summer, while the latter are reserved for the autumn and winter. Most of the houses are built of boards and covered with bark, though some of the more inferior kind are constructed wholly of cedar bark, kept smooth and flat by small splinters fixed crosswise through the bark, at the distance of twelve or fourteen inches apart. There is but little difference in appearance between these Yehhuhs, Wahclellahs, Clahclellahs, and Neerchokioos, who compose the Shahala nation. On comparing the vocabulary of the Wahclellahs with that of the Chinnooks, we found that the names for numbers were precisely the same, though the other parts of the language were essentially different. The women of all these tribes braid their hair, pierce the nose, and some of them have lines of dots reaching from the ancle as high as the middle of the leg. These Yehhuhs behaved with great propriety, and condemned the treatment we had received from the Wahclellahs. We purchased from one of them the skin of a sheep killed near this place, for which we gave in exchange the skins of a deer and an elk. These animals, he tells us, usually frequent the rocky parts of the mountains, where they are found in great numbers. The bighorn is also an inhabitant of these mountains, and the natives have several robes made of their skins. The mountains near this place are high, steep, and strewed with rocks, which are principally black. Several species of fir, white pine, and white cedar, forms their covering, while near the river we see the cottonwood, sweet-willow, a species of maple, the broad-leafed ash, the purple haw, a small species of cherry, the purple currant, gooseberry, red willow, the vining and whiteberry honey-suckle, the huckleberry, sacacommis, two kinds of mountain holly, and the common ash.

Sunday 13. The loss of our periogue yesterday obliges us to distribute our loading between the two canoes, and the two remaining periogues. This being done, we proceeded along the north side of the river, but soon finding that the increased loading rendered our vessels difficult to manage, if not dangerous in case of high wind, the two periogues only continued on their route, while captain Lewis with the canoes crossed over to the Yehhuh village, with a view of purchasing one or two more canoes. The village now consisted of eleven houses, crowded with inhabitants, and about sixty fighting men. They were very well disposed, and we found no difficulty in procuring two small canoes, in exchange for two robes and four elk skins. We also purchased with deer skins, three dogs, an animal which has now become a favourite food, for it is found to be a strong healthy diet, preferable to lean deer or elk, and much superior to horseflesh in any state. With these he proceeded along the south side of the river, and joined us in the evening. We had gone along the north shore as high as Cruzatte's river, to which place we had sent some hunters the day before yesterday, and where we were detained by the high winds. The hunters however did not join us, and we therefore, as soon as the wind had abated, proceeded on for six miles, where we halted for captain Lewis, and in the meantime went out to hunt. We procured two black-tailed fallow deer, which seem to be the only kind inhabiting these mountains. Believing that the hunters were still below us, we despatched a small canoe back for them, and in the morning,

April 14, they all joined us with four more deer. After breakfast we resumed our journey, and though the wind was high during the day, yet by keeping along the northern shore, we were able to proceed without danger. At one o'clock we halted for dinner at a large village situated in a narrow bottom, just above the entrance of Canoe creek. The houses are detached from each other, so as to occupy an extent of several miles, though only twenty in number. Those which are inhabited are on the surface of the earth, and built in the same shape as those near the rapids; but there were others at present evacuated, which are completely under ground. They are sunk about eight feet deep, and covered with strong timbers, and several feet of earth in a conical form. On descending by means of a ladder through a hole at the top, which answers the double purpose of a door and a chimney, we found that the house consisted of a single room, nearly circular and about sixteen feet in diameter.

The inhabitants, who call themselves Weocksockwillacum, differ but little from those near the rapids, the chief distinction in dress, being a few leggings and moccasins, which we find here like those worn by the Chopunnish. These people have ten or twelve very good horses, which are the first we have seen since leaving this neighbourhood last autumn. The country below is, indeed, of such a nature, as to prevent the use of this animal, except in the Columbian valley, and there they would be of great service, for the inhabitants reside chiefly on the river side, and the country is too thickly wooded to suffer them to hunt game on horseback. Most of these, they inform us, have been taken in a warlike excursion, which was lately made against the Towanahiooks, a part of the Snake nation living in the upper part of the Multnomah, to the southeast of this place. Their language is the same with that of the Chilluckittequaws. They seemed inclined to be very civil, and gave us in exchange, some roots, shapelell, filberts, dried berries, and five dogs.

After dinner we proceeded, and passing at the distance of six miles, the high cliffs on the left, encamped at the mouth of a small run on the same side. A little above us is a village, consisting of about one hundred fighting men of a tribe called Smackshops, many of whom passed the evening with us. They do not differ in any respect from the inhabitants of the village below. In hopes of purchasing horses we did not set out the next morning,

Tuesday 15, till after breakfast, and in the meantime exposed our merchandise, and made them various offers; but as they declined bartering, we left them and soon reached the Sepulchre rock, where we halted a few minutes. The rock itself stands near the middle of the river, and contains about two acres of ground above high water. On this surface are scattered thirteen vaults, constructed like those below the Rapids, and some of them more than half filled with dead bodies. After satisfying our curiosity with these venerable remains, we returned to the northern shore, and proceeded to a village at the distance of four miles: on landing, we found that the inhabitants belonged to the same nation we had just left, and as they also had horses, we made a second attempt to purchase a few of them: but with all our dexterity in exhibiting our wares, we could not induce them to sell, as we had none of the only articles which they seemed desirous of procuring, a sort of war hatchet, called by the northwest traders an eye-dog. We therefore purchased two dogs, and taking leave of these Weocksockwillacums, proceeded to another of their villages, just below the entrance of Cataract river. Here too, we tried in vain to purchase some horses, nor did we meet with more success at the two villages of Chilluckittequaws, a few miles farther up the river. At three in the afternoon, we came to the mouth of Quinett creek, which we ascended a short distance and encamped for the night, at the spot we had called Rock fort. Here we were soon visited by some of the people from the great narrows and falls: and on our expressing a wish to purchase horses, they agreed to meet us to-morrow on the north side of the river, where we would open a traffic. They then returned to their villages to collect the horses, and in the morning,

Wednesday 16, captain Clarke crossed with nine men, and a large part of the merchandise, in order to purchase twelve horses to transport our baggage, and some pounded fish, as a reserve during the passage of the Rocky mountains. The rest of the men were employed in hunting and preparing saddles.

From the rapids to this place, and indeed as far as the commencement of the narrows, the Columbia is from half a mile to three quarters in width, and possesses scarcely any current: its bed consists principally of rock, except at the entrance of Labiche river, which takes its rise in mount Hood, from which, like Quicksand river, it brings down vast quantities of sand. During the whole course of the Columbia from the Rapids to the Chilluckittequaws are the trunks of many large pine trees standing erect in water, which is thirty feet deep at present, and never less than ten. These trees could never have grown in their present state, for they are all very much doated, and none of them vegetate; so that the only reasonable account which can be given of this phenomenon, is, that at some period, which the appearance of the trees induces us to fix within twenty years, the rocks from the hill sides have obstructed the narrow pass at the rapids, and caused the river to spread through the woods. The mountains which border as far as the Sepulchre rock, are high and broken, and its romantic views accasionally enlivened by beautiful cascades rushing from the heights, and forming a deep contrast with the firs, cedar and pines, which darken their sides. From the Sepulchre rock, where the low country begins, the long-leafed pine is the almost exclusive growth of timber; but our present camp is the last spot where a single tree is to be seen on the wide plains, which are now spread before us to the foot of the Rocky mountains. It is, however, covered with a rich verdure of grass and herbs, some inches in height, which forms a delightful and exhilarating prospect, after being confined to the mountains and thick forests on the seacoast. The climate too, though only on the border of the plains, is here very different from that we have lately experienced. The air is drier and more pure, and the ground itself is as free from moisture as if there had been no rain for the last ten days. Around this place are many esculent plants used by the Indians: among which is a currant, now in bloom, with a yellow blossom like that of the yellow currant of the Missouri, from which however it differs specifically. There is also a species of hyacinth growing in the plains, which presents at this time a pretty flower of a pale blue colour, and the bulb of which is boiled or baked, or dried in the sun, and eaten by the Indians. This bulb, of the present year, is white, flat in shape and not quite solid, and it overlays and presses closely that of the last year, which, though much thinner and withered, is equally wide, and sends forth from its sides a number of small radicles.

Our hunters obtained one of the long-tailed deer with the young horns, about two inches, and a large black or dark brown pheasant, such as we had seen on the upper part of the Missouri. They also brought in a large gray squirrel, and two others resembling it in shape, but smaller than the common gray squirrel of the United States, and of a pied gray and yellowish brown colour. In addition to this game, they had seen some antelopes, and the tracks of several black bear, but no appearance of elk. They had seen no birds, but found three eggs of the party-coloured corvus. Though the salmon has not yet appeared, we have seen less scarcity than we apprehended from the reports we had heard below. At the rapids, the natives subsist chiefly on a few white salmon trout, which they take at this time, and considerable quantities of a small indifferent mullet of an inferior quality. Beyond that place we see none except dried fish of the last season, nor is the sturgeon caught by any of the natives above the Columbia, their whole stores consisting of roots, and fish either dried or pounded.

Captain Clarke had, in the meantime, been endeavouring to purchase horses, without success, but they promised to trade with him if he would go up to the Skilloot village, above the long narrows. He therefore sent over to us for more merchandise, and then accompanied them in the evening to that place, where he passed the night. The next day,

Thursday 17, he sent to inform us that he was still unable to purchase any horses, but intended going as far as the Eneeshur village to-day, whence he would return to meet us to-morrow at the Skilloot village. In the evening the principal chief of the Chilluckittequaws came to see us, accompanied by twelve of his nation, and hearing that we wanted horses, he promised to meet us at the narrows with some for sale.

CHAPTER XXVII.

Captain Clarke procures four horses for the transportation of the baggage—some further account of the Skilloot tribe—their joy at the first appearance of salmon in the Columbia—their thievish propensities—the party arrive at the village of the Eneeshurs, where the natives are found alike unfriendly—the party now provided with horses—the party prevented from the exercise of hostility against this nation by a friendly adjustment—the scarcity of timber so great that they are compelled to buy wood to cook their provisions—arrive at the Wahhowpum village—dance of the natives—their ingenuity in declining to purchase the canoes, on the supposition that the party would be compelled to leave them behind defeated—the party having obtained a complement of horses, proceed by land—arrive at the Pishquitpah village, and some account of that people—their frank and hospitable treatment from the Wollawollahs—their mode of dancing described—their mode of making fishweirs—their amiable character, and their unusual affection for the whites.

FRIDAY, 18. We set out this morning after an early breakfast, and crossing the river, continued along the north side for four miles, to the foot of the first rapid. Here it was necessary to unload and make a portage of seven paces over a rock, round which we then drew the empty boats by means of a cord, and the assistance of setting poles. We then reloaded, and at the distance of five miles, reached the basin at the foot of the long narrows. After unloading and arranging the camp, we went up to the Skilloot village, where we found captain Clarke. He had not been able to procure more than four horses, for which he was obliged to give double the price of those formerly purchased from the Shoshonees and the first tribe of Flatheads. These, however, we hoped might be sufficient with the aid of the small canoes to convey our baggage as far as the villages near the Musscleshell rapid, where horses are cheaper and more abundant, and where we may probably exchange the canoes for as many horses as we want. The Skilloots, indeed, have a number of horses, but they are unwilling to part with them, though at last we laid out three parcels of merchandise, for each of which they promised to bring us a horse in the morning. The long narrows have a much more formidable appearance than when we passed them in the autumn, so that it would, in fact, be impossible either to descend or go up them in any kind of boat. As we had therefore no further use for the two periogues we cut them up for fuel, and early in the morning,

Saturday 19, all the party began to carry the merchandise over the portage. This we accomplished with the aid of our four horses, by three o'clock in the afternoon, when we formed our camp a little above the Skilloot village. Since we left them in the autumn they have removed their village a few hundred yards lower down the river, and have exchanged the cellars in which we then found them, for more pleasant dwellings on the surface of the ground. These are formed by sticks, and covered with mats and straw, and so large, that each is the residence of several families. They are also much better clad than any of the natives below, or than they were themselves last autumn; the dress of the men consists generally of leggings, moccasins, and large robes, and many of them wear shirts in the same form used by the Chopunnish and Shoshonees, highly ornamented, as well as the leggings and moccasins, with porcupine quills. Their modesty is protected by the skin of a fox or some other animal, drawn under a girdle and hanging in front like a narrow apron. The dress of the women differs but little from that worn near the rapids; and both sexes wear the hair over the forehead as low as the eyebrows, with large locks cut square at the ears, and the rest hanging in two queues in front of the body. The robes are made principally of the skins of deer, elk, bighorn, some wolf and buffaloe, while the children use the skins of the large gray squirrel. The buffaloe is procured from the nations higher up the river, who occasionally visit the Missouri; indeed, the greater proportion of their apparel is brought by the nations to the northwest, who come to trade for pounded fish, copper, and beads. Their chief fuel is straw, southernwood, and small willows. The bear-grass, the bark of the cedar, and the silk-grass are employed in various articles of manufacture.

The whole village was filled with rejoicing to-day, at having caught a single salmon, which was considered as the harbinger of vast quantities in four or five days. In order to hasten their arrival, the Indians according to custom, dressed fish and cut it into small pieces, one of which was given to each child in the village. In the good humour excited by this occurrence, they parted, though reluctantly, with four other horses, for which we gave them two kettles, reserving only a single small one for a mess of eight men. Unluckily, however, we lost one of the horses by the negligence of the person to whose charge he was committed. The rest were therefore hobbled and tied; but as the nations here do not understand gelding, all the horses but one were stallions, and this being the season when they are most vicious, we had great difficulty in managing them, and were obliged to keep watch over them all night. In the afternoon captain Clarke set out with four men for the Eneeshur village at the grand falls, in order to make further attempts to procure horses.

Sunday, 20. As it was obviously our interest to preserve the good will of these people, we passed over several small thefts which they have committed, but this morning we learnt that six tomahawks and a knife had been stolen during the night. We addressed ourselves to the chief, who seemed angry with his people and made a harangue to them, but we did not recover the articles, and soon after, two of our spoons were missing. We therefore ordered them from our camp, threatning to beat severely any one detected in purloining. This harshness irritated them so much that they left us in an ill-humour, and we therefore kept on our guard against any insult. Besides this knavery, the faithlessness of the people is intolerable, frequently after receiving goods in exchange for a horse, they return in a few hours and insist on revoking the bargain, or receiving some additional value. We discovered too, that the horse which was missing yesterday, had been gambled away by the fellow from whom we had purchased him, to a man of a different nation, who had carried him off.

Besides these, we bought two more horses, two dogs, and some chapelell, and also exchanged a couple of elk skins for a gun belonging to the chief. This was all we could obtain, for though they had a great abundance of dried fish, they would not sell it, except at a price too exorbitant for our finances. We now found that no more horses could be procured, and therefore prepared for setting out tomorrow. One of the canoes, for which the Indians would give us very little, was cut up for fuel, two others, together with some elk skins and pieces of old iron, we bartered for beads, and the remaining two small canoes were despatched early next morning,

Monday, 21, with all the baggage which could not be carried on horseback. We had intended setting out at the same time, but one of our horses broke loose during the night, and we were under the necessity of sending several men in search of him. In the meantime, the Indians, who were always on the alert, stole a tomahawk, which we could not recover, though several of them were searched. Another fellow was detected in carrying off a piece of iron, and kicked out of camp: captain Lewis then, addressing the Indians, declared that he was not afraid to fight them; for if he chose, he might easily put them to death, and burn their village; that he did not wish to treat them ill if they did not steal; and that although if he knew who had the tomahawks he would take away the horses of the thieves, yet he would rather loose the property altogether than take the horse of an innocent man. The chiefs were present at this harangue, hung their heads and made no reply. At ten o'clock, the men returned with the horse, and soon after, an Indian who had promised to go with us as far as the Chopunnish, came with two horses, one of which he politely offered to carry our baggage. We therefore loaded nine horses, and giving the tenth to Bratton, who was still too sick to walk, about ten o'clock left the village of these disagreeable people. At one o'clock we arrived at the village of the Eneeshurs, where we found captain Clarke, who had been completely unsuccessful in his attempts to purchase horses, the Eneeshurs being quite as unfriendly as the Skilloots. Fortunately, however, the fellow who had sold a horse, and afterwards lost him at gambling, belonged to this village, and we insisted on taking the kettle and knife which had been given to him for the horse, if he did not replace it by one of equal value. He preferred the latter, and brought us a very good horse. Being here joined by the canoes and baggage across the portage, we halted half a mile above the town, and took dinner on some dogs, after which we proceeded on about four miles and encamped at a village of Eneeshurs, consisting of nine mat huts, a little below the mouth of the Towahnahiooks. We obtained from these people a couple of dogs and a small quantity of fuel, for which we were obliged to give a higher price than usual. We also bought a horse with a back so much injured, that he can scarcely be of much service to us, but the price was some trifling articles, which in the United States would cost about a dollar and a quarter. The dress, the manners, and the language of the Eneeshurs differ in no respect from those of the Skilloots. Like them too, these Eneeshurs are inhospitable and parsimonious, faithless to their engagements, and in the midst of poverty and filth, retain a degree of pride and arrogance which render our numbers our only protection against insult, pillage, and even murder. We are, however, assured by our Chopunnish guide, who appears to be a very sincere, honest Indian, that the nations above will treat us with much more hospitality.

Tuesday 22. Two of our horses broke loose in the night and straggled to some distance, so that we were not able to retake them and begin our march before seven o'clock. We had just reached the top of a hill near the village, when the load of one of the horses turned, and the animal taking fright at a robe which still adhered to him, ran furiously towards the village: just as he came there the robe fell, and an Indian hid it in his hut. Two men went back after the horse which they soon took, but the robe was still missing, and the Indians denied having seen it. These repeated acts of knavery now exhausted our patience, and captain Lewis therefore set out for the village, determined to make them deliver up the robe, or to burn the village to the ground. This disagreeable alternative was rendered unnecessary, for on his way he met one of our men, who had found the robe in an Indian hut hid behind some baggage. We resumed our route, and soon after halted at a hill, from the top of which we enjoyed a commanding view of the range of mountains in which mount Hood stands, and which continue south as far as the eye can reach, with their tops covered with snow, mount Hood itself bears south 30° west, and the snowy summit of mount Jefferson south 10° west. Towards the south and at no great distance we discern some woody country, and opposite this point of view is the mouth of the Towahnahiooks. This river receives, at the distance of eighteen or twenty miles, a branch from the right, which takes its rise in mount Hood, while the main stream comes in a course from the southeast, and ten or fifteen miles is joined by a second branch from mount Jefferson. From this place we proceeded with our baggage in the centre, escorted both before and behind by those of the men who were without the care of horses, and having crossed a plain eight miles in extent, reached a village of Eneeshurs, consisting of six houses. Here we bought some dogs on which we dined near the village, and having purchased another horse, went up the river four miles further, to another Eneeshur village of seven mat houses. Our guide now informed us that the next village was at such a distance that we should not reach it this evening, and as we should be able to procure both dogs and wood at this place, we determined to encamp. We here purchased a horse, and engaged for a second in exchange for one of our canoes, but as they were on the opposite side of the river, and the wind very high, they were not able to cross before sunset, at which time the Indian had returned home to the next village above. This evening, as well as at dinnertime, we were obliged to buy wood to cook our meat, for there is no timber in the country, and all the fuel is brought from a great distance. We obtained as much as answered our purposes on moderate terms, but as we are too poor to afford more than a single fire, and lie without any shelter, we find the nights disagreeably cold, though the weather is warm during the daytime. The next morning,

Wednesday 23, two of the horses strayed away in consequence of neglecting to tie them as had been directed. One of them was recovered, but as we had a long ride to make before reaching the next village, we could wait no longer than eleven o'clock for the other. Not being found at that time we set out, and after marching for twelve miles over the sands of a narrow rocky bottom on the north side of the river, came to a village near the Rock rapid, at the mouth of a large creek, which we had not observed in descending. It consisted of twelve temporary huts of mat, inhabited by a tribe called Wahhowpum, who speak a language very similar to that of the Chopunnish, whom they resemble also in dress, both sexes being clad in robes and shirts as well as leggings and moccasins. These people seemed much pleased to see us, and readily gave us four dogs and some chapelell and wood in exchange for small articles, such as pewter-buttons, strips of tin, iron, and brass, and some twisted wire, which we had previously prepared for our journey across the plains. These people, as well as some more living in five huts a little below them, were waiting the return of the salmon. We also found a Chopunnish returning home with his family and a dozen young horses, some of which he wanted us to hire, but this we declined, as in that case we should be obliged to maintain him and his family on the route. After arranging the camp we assembled all the warriors, and having smoked with them, the violins were produced, and some of the men danced. This civility was returned by the Indians in a style of dancing such as we had not yet seen. The spectators formed a circle round the dancers, who with their robes drawn tightly round the shoulders, and divided into parties of five or six men, perform by crossing in a line from one side of the circle to the other. All the parties, performers as well as spectators, sang, and after proceeding in this way for some time, the spectators join, and the whole concludes by a promiscuous dance and song. Having finished, the natives retired at our request, after promising to barter horses with us in the morning. The river is by no means so difficult of passage nor obstructed by so many rapids as it was in the autumn, the water being now sufficiently high to cover the rocks in the bed. In the morning,

Thursday 24, we began early to look for our horses, but they were not collected before one o'clock. In the meantime we prepared saddles for three new horses which we purchased from the Wahhowpums, and agreed to hire three more from the Chopunnish Indian who was to accompany us with his family. The natives also had promised to take our canoes in exchange for horses; but when they found that we were resolved on travelling by land, they refused giving us any thing, in hopes that we would be forced to leave them. Disgusted at this conduct, we determined rather to cut them to pieces than suffer these people to enjoy them, and actually began to split them, on which they gave us several strands of beads for each canoe. We had now a sufficient number of horses to carry our baggage, and therefore proceeded wholly by land. At two o'clock we set out, and passing between the hills and the northern shore of the river, had a difficult and fatiguing march over a road alternately sandy and rocky. At the distance of four miles, we came to four huts of the Metcowwee tribe, two miles further the same number of huts, and after making twelve miles from our last night's camp, halted at a larger village of five huts of Metcowwees.

As we came along many of the natives passed and repassed without making any advances to converse, though they behaved with distant respect. We observed in our route no animals except the killdeer, the brown lizards, and a moonax, which the people had domesticated as a favourite. Most of the men complain of a soreness in their feet and legs, occasioned by walking on rough stones and deep sands, after being accustomed for some months past to a soft soil. We therefore determined to remain here this evening, and for this purpose bought three dogs and some chapelell, which we cooked with dry grass and willow boughs. The want of wood is a serious inconvenience, on account of the coolness of the nights, particularly when the wind sets from mount Hood, or in any western direction: those winds being much colder than the winds from the Rocky mountains. There are no dews in the plains, and from the appearance, we presume, that no rain has fallen for several weeks. By nine o'clock the following morning,

Friday 25, we collected our horses and proceeded eleven miles to a large village of fifty-one mat houses, where we purchased some wood and a few dogs, on which we made our dinner. The village contained about seven hundred persons of a tribe called Pishquitpah, whose residence on the river is only during the spring and summer, the autumn and winter being passed in hunting through the plains, and along the borders of the mountains. The greater part of them were at a distance from the river as we descended, and never having seen white men before, they flocked round us in great numbers; but although they were exceedingly curious they treated us with great respect, and were very urgent that we should spend the night with them. Two principal chiefs were pointed out by our Chopunnish companion, and acknowledged by the tribe, and we therefore invested each of them with a small medal. We were also very desirous of purchasing more horses; but as our principal stock of merchandise consists of a dirk, a sword, and a few old clothes, the Indians could not be induced to traffic with us. The Pishquitpahs are generally of a good stature and proportion, and as the heads of neither males nor females are so much flattened as those lower down the river, their features are rather pleasant. The hair is braided in the manner practised by their western neighbours; but the generality of the men are dressed in a large robe, under which is a shirt reaching to the knees, where it is met by long leggings, and the feet covered with moccasins: others, however, wear only the truss and robe. As they unite the occupations of hunting and fishing life, both sexes ride very dexterously, their caparison being a saddle or pad of dressed skin, stuffed with goats' hair, and from which wooden stirrups are suspended; and a hair rope tied at both ends to the under jaw of the animal.

The horses, however, though good, suffer much, as do in fact all Indian horses, from sore backs. Finding them not disposed to barter with us, we left the Pishquitpahs at four o'clock, accompanied by eighteen or twenty of their young men on horseback. At the distance of four miles, we passed without halting, five houses belonging to the Wollawollahs; and five miles further, observing as many willows as would answer the purpose of making fires, availed ourselves of the circumstance, by encamping near them. The country through which we passed bore the same appearance as that of yesterday. The hills on both sides of the river are about two hundred and fifty feet high, generally abrupt and craggy, and in many places presenting a perpendicular face of black, hard, and solid rock. From the top of these hills, the country extends itself in level plains to a very great distance, and though not as fertile as the land near the falls, produces an abundant supply of low grass, which is an excellent food for horses. This grass must indeed be unusually nutritious, for even at this season of the year, after wintering on the dry grass of the plains, and being used with greater severity than is usual among the whites, many of these horses are perfectly fat, nor have we, indeed, seen a single one who was poor. In the course of the day we killed several rattlesnakes, like those of the United States, and saw many of the common as well as the horned-lizard. We also killed six ducks, one of which proved to be of a different species from any we had yet seen, being distinguished by yellow legs, and feet webbed like those of the duckinmallard. The Pishquitpahs passed the night with us, and at their request, the violin was played, and some of the men amused themselves with dancing. At the same time we succeeded in obtaining two horses at nearly the same prices which had already been refused in the village. In the morning,

Saturday 26, we set out early. At the distance of three miles, the river hills become low, and retiring to a great distance, leave a low, level, extensive plain, which on the other side of the river, had begun thirteen miles lower. As we were crossing this plain, we were overtaken by several families travelling up the river with a number of horses, and although their company was inconvenient, for the weather was warm, the roads dusty, and their horses crowded in and broke our line of march, yet we were unwilling to displease the Indians by any act of severity. The plain possesses much grass and a variety of herbaceous plants and shrubs; but after going twelve miles, we were fortunate enough to find a few willows, which enabled us to cook a dinner of jerked elk, and the remainder of the dogs purchased yesterday. We then went on sixteen miles further, and six miles above our camp of the nineteenth of October, encamped in the rain, about a mile below three houses of Wollawollahs. Soon after we halted, an Indian boy took a piece of bone, which he substituted for a fish-hook, and caught several chub, nine inches long.

Sunday, 27. We were detained till nine o'clock, before a horse, which broke loose in the night, could be recovered. We then passed, near our camp, a small river, called Youmalolam, proceeded through a continuation, till at the distance of fifteen miles, the abrupt and rocky hills three hundred feet high, return to the river. These we ascended, and then crossed a higher plain for nine miles, when we again came to the water side. We had been induced to make this long march because we had but little provisions, and hoped to find a Wollawollah village, which our guide had told us we should reach when next we met the river. There was, however, no village to be seen, and as both the men and horses were fatigued, we halted, and collecting some dry stalks of weeds and the stems of a plant resembling southern wood, cooked a small quantity of jerked meat for dinner. Soon after we were joined by seven Wollawollahs, among whom we recognised a chief by the name of Yellept, who had visited us on the nineteenth of October, when we gave him a medal with the promise of a larger one on our return. He appeared very much pleased at seeing us again, and invited us to remain at his village three or four days, during which he would supply us with the only food they had, and furnish us with horses for our journey. After the cold, inhospitable treatment we have lately received, this kind offer was peculiarly acceptable, and after a hasty meal, we accompanied him to his village, six miles above, situated on the edge of the low country, and about twelve miles below the mouth of Lewis's river. Immediately on our arrival, Yellept, who proved to be a man of much influence, not only in his own, but in the neighbouring nations, collected the inhabitants, and after having made an harangue, the purport of which was to induce the nations to treat us hospitably, set them an example, by bringing himself an armful of wood, and a platter containing three roasted mullets. They immediately assented to one part, at least of the recommendation, by furnishing us with an abundance of the only sort of fuel they employ, the stems of shrubs growing in the plains. We then purchased four dogs, on which we supped heartily, having been on short allowance for two days past. When we were disposed to sleep, the Indians retired immediately on our request, and indeed, uniformly conducted themselves with great propriety. These people live on roots, which are very abundant in the plains, and catch a few salmon-trout; but at present they seem to subsist chiefly on a species of mullet, weighing from one to three pounds. They now informed us that opposite to the village, there was a route which led to the mouth of the Kooskooskee, on the south side of Lewis's river, that the road itself was good, and passed over a level country, well supplied with water and grass, and that we should meet with plenty of deer and antelope. We knew that a road in that direction would shorten the distance at least eighty miles, and as the report of our guide was confirmed by Yellept and other Indians, we did not hesitate to adopt that course; they added, however, that there were no houses or permanent residence of Indians on the road, and it was therefore deemed prudent not to trust wholly to our guns, but to lay in a stock of provisions. In the morning,

Monday, 28, therefore we purchased ten dogs. While this trade was carrying on by our men, Yellept brought a fine white horse, and presented him to captain Clarke, expressing at the same time, a wish to have a kettle; but on being informed that we had already disposed of the last kettle we could spare, he said he would be content with any present we should make in return. Captain Clarke therefore gave his sword, for which the chief had before expressed a desire, adding one hundred balls, some powder, and other small articles, with which he appeared perfectly satisfied. We were now anxious to depart, and requested Yellept to lend us canoes for the purpose of crossing the river. But he would not listen to any proposal of leaving the village. He wished us to remain two or three days; but would not let us go to-day, for he had already sent to invite his neighbours, the Chimnapoos, to come down this evening and join his people in a dance for our amusement. We urged, in vain, that by setting out sooner, we would the earlier return with the articles they desired;

for a day, he observed, would make but little difference. We at length mentioned, that as there was no wind, it was now the best time to cross the river, and would merely take the horses over, and return to sleep at their village. To this he assented, and we then crossed with our horses, and having hobbled them, returned to their camp. Fortunately there was among these Wollawollahs, a prisoner belonging to a tribe of Shoshonee or Snake Indians, residing to the south of the Multnomah, and visiting occasionally the heads of the Wollawollah creek. Our Shoshonee woman, Sacajaweah, though she belonged to a tribe near the Missouri, spoke the same language as this prisoner, and by their means we were able to explain ourselves to the Indians, and answer all their inquiries with respect to ourselves and the object of our journey. Our conversation inspired them with much confidence, and they soon brought several sick persons, for whom they requested our assistance. We splintered the broken arm of one, gave some relief to another, whose knee was contracted by rheumatism, and administered what we thought beneficial for ulcers and eruptions of the skin, on various parts of the body, which are very common disorders, among them. But our most valuable medicine was eye-water, which we distributed, and which, indeed, they required very much: the complaint of the eyes, occasioned by living on the water, and increased by thc fine sand of the plains, being now universal.

A little before sunset, the Chimnapoos, amounting to one hundred men, and a few women, came to the village, and joining the Wollawollahs, who were about the same number of men, formed themselves in a circle round our camp, and waited very patiently till our men were disposed to dance, which they did for about an hour, to the tune of the violin. They then requested to see the Indians dance. With this they readily complied, and the whole assemblage, amounting, with the women and children of the village, to several hundred, stood up, and sang and danced at the same time. The exercise was not, indeed, very violent nor very graceful, for the greater part of them were formed into a solid column, round a kind of hollow square, stood on the same place, and merely jumped up at intervals, to keep time to the music. Some, however, of the more active warriors, entered the square, and danced round it sidewise, and some of our men joined in the dance, to the great satisfaction of the Indians. The dance continued till ten o'clock. The next morning,

Tuesday 29, Yellept supplied us with two canoes in which we crossed with all our baggage by eleven o'clock, but the horses having strayed to some distance, we could not collect them in time to reach any fit place to encamp if we began our journey, as night would overtake us before we came to water. We therefore thought it adviseable to encamp about a mile from the Columbia, on the mouth of the Wollawollah river. This is a handsome stream, about fifty yards wide, and four and a half feet in depth: its waters, which are clear, roll over a bed composed principally of gravel, intermixed with some sand and mud, and though the banks are low they do not seem to be overflowed. It empties into the Columbia, about twelve or fifteen miles from the entrance of Lewis's river, and just above a range of high hills crossing the Columbia. Its sources, like those of the Towahnahiooks, Lapage, Youmalolam, and Wollawollah, come, as the Indians inform us, from the north side of a range of mountains which we see to the east and southeast, and which, commencing to the south of mount Hood, stretch in a northeastern direction to the neighbourhood of a southern branch of Lewis's river, at some distance from the Rocky mountains. Two principal branches however of the Towahnahiooks take their rise in mount Jefferson and mount Hood, which in fact appear to separate the waters of the Multnomah and Columbia. They are now about sixty-five or seventy miles from this place, and although covered with snow, do not seem high. To the south of these mountains the Indian prisoner says there is a river, running towards the northwest, as large as the Columbia at this place, which is nearly a mile. This account may be exaggerated, but it serves to show that the Multnomah must be a very large river, and that with the assistance of a southeastern branch of Lewis's river, passing round the eastern extremity of that chain of mountains in which mounts Hood and Jefferson are so conspicuous, waters the vast tract of country to the south, till its remote sources approach those of the Missouri and Rio del Norde.

Near our camp is a fish-weir, formed of two curtains of small willow switches, matted together with wythes of the same plant, and extending across the river in two parallel lines, six feet asunder. These are supported by several parcels of poles, in the manner already described, as in use among the Shoshonees, and are either rolled up or let down at pleasure for a few feet, so as either to suffer the fish to pass or detain them. A seine of fifteen or eighteen feet in length is then dragged down the river by two persons, and the bottom drawn up against the curtain of willows. They also employ a smaller seine like a scooping net, one side of which is confined to a semicircular bow five feet long, and half the size of a man's arm, and the other side is held by a strong rope, which being tied at both ends to the bow, forms the chord to the semicircle. This is used by one person, but the only fish which they can take at this time is a mullet of from four to five pounds in weight, and this is the chief subsistence of a village of twelve houses of Wollawollahs, a little below us on this river, as well as of others on the opposite side of the Columbia. In the course of the day we gave small medals to two inferior chiefs, each of whom made us a present of a fine horse. We were in a poor condition to make an adequate acknowledgment for this kindness, but gave several articles, among which was a pistol, with some hundred rounds of ammunition. We have indeed been treated by these people with an unusual degree of kindness and civility. They seem to have been successful in their hunting during the last winter, for all of them, but particularly the women, are much better clad than when we saw them last; both sexes among the Wollawollahs, as well as the Chimnapoos, being provided with good robes, moccasins, long shirts, and leggings. Their ornaments are similar to those used below, the hair cut in the forehead, and queues falling over the shoulders in front of the body: some have some small plaits at the earlocks, and others tie a bundle of the docked foretop in front of the forehead.

They were anxious that we should repeat our dance of last evening, but as it rained a little and the wind was high, we found the weather too cold for such amusement.

Wednesday 30. Although we had hobbled and secured our new purchases, we found some difficulty in collecting all our horses. In the meantime we purchased several dogs, and two horses, besides exchanging one of our least valuable horses for a very good one belonging to the Chopunnish who is accompanying us with his family. The daughter of this man is now about the age of puberty, and being incommoded by the disorder incident to that age, she is not permitted to associate with the family, but sleeps at a distance from her father's camp, and on the route always follows at some distance alone. This delicacy or affectation is common to many nations of Indians, among whom a girl in that state is separated from her family, and forbidden to use any article of the household or kitchen furniture, or to engage in any occupation. We have now twenty-three horses, many of whom are young and excellent animals, but the greater part of them are afflicted with sore backs. The Indians in general are cruel masters; they ride very hard, and as the saddles are so badly constructed that it is almost impossible to avoid wounding the back, yet they continue to ride when the poor creatures are scarified in a dreadful manner. At eleven o'clock we left these honest, worthy people, accompanied by our guide and the Chopunnish family, and directed our course north 30° east, across an open level sandy plain, unbroken except by large banks of pure sand, which have drifed in many parts of the plain to the height of fifteen or twenty feet. The rest of the plain is poor in point of soil, but throughout is generally short grass interspersed with aromatic shrubs, and a number of plants, the roots of which supply the chief sustenance of the natives. Among these we observe a root something like the sweet potatoe. At the distance of fourteen miles we reached a branch of Wollawollah river, rising in the same range of mountains, and empties itself six miles above the mouth of the latter. It is a bold deep stream, about ten yards wide, and seems to be navigable for canoes. The hills of this creek are generally abrupt and rocky, but the narrow bottom is very fertile, and both possess twenty times as much timber as the Columbia itself; indeed, we now find, for the first time since leaving Rockfort, an abundance of firewood. The growth consists of cotton-wood, birch, the crimson haw, red and sweet willow, choke-cherry, yellow currants, gooseberry, the honeysuckle with a white berry, rosebushes, sevenbark, sumac, together with some corn-grass and rushes. The advantage of a comfortable fire induced us, as the night was come, to halt at this place. We were soon supplied by Drewyer with a beaver and an otter, of which we took only a part of the beaver, and gave the rest to the Indians. The otter is a favourite food, though much inferior, at least in our estimation, to the dog, which they will not eat. The horse too is seldom eaten, and never except when absolute necessity compels them to cat it, as the only alternative to prevent their dying of hunger. This fastidiousness does not, however, seem to proceed so much from any dislike to the food, as from attachment to the animal itself, for many of them eat very heartily of the horse-beef which we give them. At an early hour in the morning,

Thursday, May 1, 1805, we collected our horses, and after breakfast set out about seven o'clock, and followed the road up the creek. The low grounds and plains presented the same appearance as that of yesterday, except that the latter were less sandy. At the distance of nine miles, the Chopunnish Indian, who was in front, pointed out an old unbeaten road to the left, which he informed us was our shortest route. Before venturing, however, to quit our present road, which was level, and not only led us in the proper direction, but was well supplied with wood and water, we halted to let our horses graze till the arrival of our other guide, who happened to be at some distance behind. On coming up he seemed much displeased with the other Indian, and declared that the road we were pursuing was the proper one; that if we decided on taking the left road, it would be necessary to remain till to-morrow morning, and then make an entire day's march before we could reach either water or wood. To this the Chopunnish assented, but declared that he himself meant to pursue that route, and we therefore gave him some powder and lead which he requested.

Four hunters whom we had sent out in the morning, joined us while we halted, and brought us a beaver for dinner. We then took our leave of the Chopunnish at one o'clock, and pursued our route up the creek, through a country similar to that we had passed in the morning. But at the distance of three miles, the hills on the north side became lower, and the bottoms of the creek widened into a pleasant country, two or three miles in extent. The timber too, is now more abundant, and our guide tells us that we shall not want either wood or game from this place as far as the Kooskooskee. We have already seen a number of deer, of which we killed one, and observed great quantities of the curlew, as well as some cranes, ducks, prairie larks, and several species of sparrow, common to the prairies. There is, in fact, very little difference in the general face of the country here from that of the plains on the Missouri, except that the latter are enlivened by vast herds of buffaloe, elk and other animals, which give it an additional interest. Over these wide bottoms we continued on a course north, 75° east, till, at the distance of seventeen miles from where we dined, and twenty-six from our last encampment, we halted for the night. We had scarcely encamped, when three young men came up from the Wollawollah village, with a steel trap, which had been left behind inadvertently, and which they had come a whole day's journey in order to restore. This act of integrity was the more pleasing, because, though very rare among Indians, it corresponds perfectly with the general behaviour of the Wollawollahs, among whom we had lost carelessly several knives, which were always returned as soon as found. We may, indeed, justly affirm, that of all the Indians whom we have met since leaving the United States, the Wollawollahs were the most hospitable, honest and sincere.

CHAPTER XXVIII.

The party still pursue their route towards the Kooskooskee on horseback with Wollawollah guides—character of the country—the quamash and other flowering shrubs in bloom—the party reach the Kinnooenim creek—they meet with an old acquaintance called the Bighorn Indian—they arrive at the mouth of the Kooskooskee—singular custom among the Chopunnish women—difficulty of purchasing provisions from the natives, and the new resort of the party to obtain them—the Chopunnish style of architecture—captain Clarke turns physician, and performs several experiments with success upon the natives, which they reward—an instance of their honesty—the distress of the Indians for want of provisions during the winter—the party finally meet the Twistedhair, to whom was entrusted their horses during their journey down—the quarrel between that chief and another of his nation, on the subject of his horses—the causes of this controversy stated at large—the two chiefs reconciled by the interference of the party, and the horses restored—extraordinary instance of Indian hospitality towards strangers—a council held with the Chopunnish, and the object of the expedition explained in a very circuitous route of explanation—the party again perform medical cures—the answer of the Chopunnish to the speech delivered at the council, confirmed by a singular ceremony of acquiescence—they promise faithfully to follow the advice of their visiters.

FRIDAY, May 2. We despatched two hunters ahead; but the horse we had yesterday purchased from the Chopunnish, although closely hobbled, contrived to break loose in the night, and went back to rejoin his companions. He was however overtaken and brought to us about one o'clock, and we then set forward. For three miles we followed a hilly road on the north side of the creek, opposite to a wide bottom, where a branch falls in from the southwest mountains, which, though covered with snow, are about twenty-five miles distant, and do not appear high. We then entered an extensive level bottom, with about fifty acres of land well covered with pine near the creek, and the long-leafed pine occasionally on the sides of the hills along its banks. After crossing the creek at the distance of seven miles from our camp, we repassed it seven miles further, near the junction of one of its branches from the northeast. The main stream here bears to the south, towards the mountains where it rises, and its bottoms then become narrow, as the hills are higher. We followed the course of this northeast branch in a direction N. 45° E. for eight and three quarter miles, when having made nineteen miles, we halted in a little bottom on the north side. The creek is here about four yards wide, and as far as we can perceive, it comes from the east, but the road here turns from it into the high open plain. The soil of the country seems to improve as we advance, and this afternoon we see, in the bottoms, an abundance of quamash now in bloom. We killed nothing but a duck, though we saw two deer at a distance, as well as many sandhill crows, curlews, and other birds common to the prairies, and there is much sign of both beaver and otter, along the creeks. The three young Wollawollahs continued with us. During the day we observed them eating the inner part of the young succulent stem of a plant very common in the rich lands on the Mississippi, Ohio and its branches. It is a large coarse plant, with a ternate leaf, the leaflets of which are three-lobed, and covered with a woolly pubescence, while the flower and fructification resemble that of the parsnip. On tasting this plant, we found it agreeable, and eat heartily of it without any inconvenience.

Saturday, 3. We set out at an early hour, and crossed the high plains, which we found more fertile and less sandy than below; yet, though the grass is taller, there are very few aromatic shrubs. After pursuing a course N. 25° E. for twelve miles, we reached the Kinnooenim. This creek rises in the southwest mountains, and though only twelve yards wide, discharges a considerable body of water into Lewis's river, a few miles above the narrows. Its bed is pebbled, its banks low, and the hills near its sides high and rugged; but in its narrow bottoms are found some cottonwood, willow, and the underbrush, which grows equally on the east branch of the Wollawollah.

After dining at the Kinnooenim, we resumed our journey over the high plains, in the direction of N. 45° E. and reached, at the distance of three miles, a small branch of that creek about five yards wide. The lands in its neighbourhood are composed of a dark rich loam; its hill sides, like those of the Kinnooenim, are high, its bottoms narrow, and possess but little timber. It increased however in quantity as we advanced along the north side of the creek for eleven miles. At that distance we were agreeably surprised by the appearance of Weahkoonut, or the Indian whom we had called the Bighorn from the circumstance of his wearing a horn of that animal, suspended from his left arm. He had gone down with us last year along Lewis's river, and was highly serviceable in preparing the minds of the natives for our reception. He is, moreover, the first chief of a large band of Chopunnish; and hearing that we are on our return, he had come with ten of his warriors to meet us. He now turned back with us, and we continued up the bottoms of the creek for two miles, till the road began to leave the creek, and cross the hill to the plains. We therefore encamped for the night in a grove of cottonwood, after we had made a disagreeable journey of twenty-eight miles. During the greater part of the day the air was keen and cold, and it alternately rained, hailed and snowed; but, though the wind blew with great violence, it was fortunately from the southwest, and on our backs. We had consumed at dinner the last of our dried meat, and nearly all that was left of the dogs; so that we supped very scantily on the remainder, and had nothing for to-morrow. Weahkoonut, however, assured us that there was a house on the river at no great distance, where we might supply ourselves with provisions. We now missed our guide and the Wollawollahs, who left us abruptly this morning, and never returned. After a disagreeable night, we collected our horses at an early hour,

Sunday, 4, and proceeded with a continuation of the same weather. We are now nearer to the southwest mountains, which appear to become lower as they advance towards the northeast. We followed the road over the plains, north 60° east, for four miles to a ravine, where was the source of a small creek, down the hilly and rocky sides of which we proceeded for eight miles to its entrance into Lewis's river, about seven miles and a half above the mouth of the Kooskooskee. Near this place we found the house of which Weahkoonut had mentioned, and where we now halted for breakfast. It contained six families, but so miserably poor that all we could obtain from them were two lean dogs and a few large cakes of half cured bread, made of a root resembling the sweet potatoe, of all which we contrived to form a kind of soup. The soil of the plain is good, but it has no timber. The range of southwest mountains is about fifteen miles above us, but continues to lower, and is still covered with snow to its base. After giving a passage to Lewis's river, near their northeastern extremity, they terminate in a high level plain between that river and the Kooskooskee. The salmon not having yet called them to the rivers, the greater part of the Chopunnish are now dispersed in villages through this plain, for the purpose of collecting quamash and cows, which here grow in great abundance, the soil being extremely fertile, and in many places covered with the long-leafed pine, the larch, and balsam-fir, which contribute to render it less thirsty than the open unsheltered plains. After our repast we continued our route along the west side of the river, where as well as on the opposite shore, the high hills approach it closely, till at the distance of three miles we halted opposite to two houses: the inhabitants consisted of five families of Chopunnish, among whom were Tetoh, or Sky, the younger of the two chiefs who accompanied us in the autumn to the great falls of the Columbia, and also our old pilot who had conducted us down the river to the Columbia. They both advised us to cross here, and ascend the Kooskooskee on the northeast side, this being the shortest and best route to the forks of that river, where we should find the Twistedhair, in whose charge we left our horses, and to which place they promised to show us the way. We did not hesitate to accept this offer, and therefore crossed with the assistance of three canoes; but as the night was coming on, we purchased a little wood and some roots of cows, and encamped, though we had made only fifteen miles to-day. The evening proved cold and disagreeable, and the natives crowded round our fire in such numbers that we could scarcely cook or even keep ourselves warm. At these houses of Chopunnish we observed a small hut with a single fire, which we are informed is appropriated for women who are undergoing the operation of the menses; there they are obliged to retreat; the men are not permitted to approach within a certain distance of them, and when any thing is to be conveyed to those deserted females, the person throws it to them forty or fifty paces off, and then retires. It is singular, indeed, that amongst the nations of the wilderness, there should be found customs and rites so nearly resembling those of the Jews. It is scarcely necessary to allude more particularly to the uncleanness of Jewish females and the rites of purification.

Monday 5. We collected our horses, and at seven o'clock set forward alone; for Weahkoonut, whose people resided above on the west side of Lewis's river, continued his route homeward when we crossed to the huts. Our road was across the plains for four and a half miles, to the entrance of the Kooskooskee. We then proceeded up that river, and at five miles reached a large mat house, but could not procure any provisions from the inhabitants, but on reaching another three miles beyond, we were surprised at the liberality of an Indian, who gave captain Clarke a very elegant gray mare, for which, all he requested was a phial of eye-water. Last autumn, while we were encamped at the mouth of the Chopunnish river, a man who complained of a pain in his knee and thigh, was brought to us in hopes of receiving relief. The man was to appearance recovered from his disorder, though he had not walked for some time. But that we might not disappoint them, captain Clarke, with much ceremony, washed and rubbed his sore limb, and gave him some volatile liniment to continue the operation, which either caused, or rather did not prevent his recovery. The man gratefully circulated our praises, and our fame as physicians was increased by the efficacy of some eye-water which we gave them at the same time. We are by no means displeased at this new resource for obtaining subsistence, as they will give us no provisions without merchandise, and our stock is now very much reduced: we cautiously abstain from giving them any but harmless medicines, and as we cannot possibly do harm, our prescriptions, though unsanctioned by the faculty, may be useful, and are entitled to some remuneration. Four miles beyond this house we came to another large one, containing ten families, where we halted, and made our dinner on two dogs and a small quantity of roots, which we did not procure without much difficulty. Whilst we were eating, an Indian standing by, and looking with great derision at our eating dogs, threw a poor half-starved puppy almost into captain Lewis's plate, laughing heartily at the humour of it. Captain Lewis took up the animal and flung it with great force into the fellow's face, and seizing his tomahawk, threatened to cut him down if he dared to repeat such insolence. He immediately withdrew, appently much mortified, and we continued our repast of dog very quietly. Here we met our old Chopunnish guide, with his family, and soon afterwards one of our horses, which had been separated from the rest in the charge of the Twistedhair, and been in this neighbourhood for several weeks, was caught and restored to us. After dinner we proceeded to the entrance of Colter's creek, at the distance of four miles, and having made twenty and a half miles, encamped on the lower side of it. Colter's creek rises not far from the Rocky mountains, and passing in the greater part of its course through a country well supplied with pine, discharges a large body of water. It is about twenty-five yards wide, with a pebbled bed and low banks. At a little distance from us are two Chopunnish houses, one of which contains eight families, and the other, which is by much the largest we have ever seen, inhabited by at least thirty. It is rather a kind of shed, built like all the other huts, of straw and mats in the form of the roof of a house, one hundred and fifty-six feet long, and about fifteen wide, closed at the ends, and having a number of doors on each side. The vast interior is without partitions, but the fire of each family is kindled in a row along the middle of the building, and about ten feet apart. This village is the residence of one of the principal chiefs of the nation, who is called Neeshnepahkeook, or *Cutnose,* from the circumstance of having his nose cut from the stroke of a lance in battle with the Snake Indians. We gave him a small medal, but though he is a great chief, his influence among his own people does not seem to be considerable, and his countenance possesses very little intelligence. We arrived very hungry and weary, but could not purchase any provisions, except a small quantity of the roots and bread of the cows. They had, however, heard of our medical skill, and made many applications for assistance, but we refused to do anything unless they gave us either dogs or horses to eat. We had soon nearly fifty patients. A chief brought his wife with an abcess on her back, and promised to furnish us with a horse to-morrow if we would relieve her. Captain Clarke, therefore, opened the abcess, introduced a tent, and dressed it with basilicon. We prepared also, and distributed some doses of the flour of sulphur and cream of tarter, with directions for its use. For these we obtained several dogs, but too poor for use, and we therefore postponed our medical operations till the morning. In the meantime a number of Indians, beside the residents of the village, gathered about us or encamped in the woody bottom of the creek.

In the evening, we learnt by means of a Snake Indian, who happens to be at this place, that one of the old men has been endeavouring to excite prejudices against us, by observing that he thought we were bad men, and came here, most probably, for the purpose of killing them. In order to remove such impressions, we made a speech, in which, by means of the Snake Indian, we told them our country and all the purposes of our visit. While we were engaged in this occupation, we were joined by Weahkoonut, who assisted us in effacing all unfavourable impressions from the minds of the Indians. The following morning,

Tuesday 6, our practice became more valuable. The woman declared that she had slept better than at any time since her illness. She was therefore dressed a second time, and her husband, according to promise, brought us a horse, which we immediately killed. Besides this woman, we had crowds of other applicants, chiefly afflicted with sore eyes, and after administering to them for several hours, found ourselves once more in possession of a plentiful meal, for the inhabitants began to be more accommodating, and one of them even gave us a horse for our remedies to his daughter, a little girl, who was afflicted with the rheumatism. We moreover, exchanged one of our horses with Weahkoonut, by the addition of a small flag, which procured us an excellent sorrel horse. We here found three men, of a nation called Skeetsomish, who reside at the falls of a large river, emptying itself into the north side of the Columbia. This river takes its rise from a large lake in the mountains, at no great distance from the falls where these natives live. We shall designate this river, hereafter, by the name of Clarke's river, as we do not know its Indian appellation, and we are the first whites who have ever visited its principal branches; for the Great Lake river mentioned by Mr. Fidler, if at all connected with Clarke's river, must be a very inconsiderable branch. To this river, moreover, which we have hitherto called Clarke's river, which rises in the southwest mountains, we restored the name of Towahnahiooks, the name by which it is known to the Eneeshurs. In dress and appearance these Skeetsomish were not to be distinguished from the Chopunnish, but their language is entirely different, a circumstance which we did not learn till their departure, when it was too late to procure from them a vocabulary.

About two o'clock we collected our horses and set out, accompanied by Weahkoonut, with ten or twelve men, and a man who said he was the brother of the Twistedhair. At four miles we came to a single house of three families, but we could not procure provisions of any kind; and five miles further we halted for the night near another house, built like the rest, of sticks, mats and dried hay, and containing six families. It was now so difficult to procure any thing to eat that our chief dependence was on the horse which we received yesterday for medicine; but to our great disappointment, he broke the rope by which he was confined, made his escape, and left us supperless in the rain. The next morning,

Wednesday 7, Weahkoonut and his party left us, and we proceeded up the river with the brother of the Twistedhair as a guide. The Kooskooskee is now rising fast, the water is clear and cold, and as all the socks and shoals are now covered, the navigation is safe, notwithstanding the rapidity of the current. The timber begins about the neighbourhood of Colter's creek, and consists chiefly of long-leafed pine. After going four miles, we reached a house of six families, below the entrance of a small creek, where our guide advised us to cross the river, as the route was better, and the game more abundant near the mouth of the Chopunnish. We therefore unloaded, and by means of a single canoe, passed to the south side in about four hours, during which time we dined. An Indian of one of the houses now brought two canisters of powder, which his dog had discovered under ground in a bottom some miles above. We immediately knew them to be the same we had buried last autumn, and as he had kept them safely, and had honesty enough to return them, we rewarded him inadequately, but as well as we could, with a steel for striking fire. We set out at three o'clock, and pursued a difficult and stony road for two miles, when we left the river and ascended the hills on the right, which begin to resemble mountains. But when we reached the heights, we saw before us a beautiful level country, partially ornamented with the long-leafed pine, and supplied with an excellent pasture of thick grass, and a variety of herbaceous plants, the abundant productions of a dark rich soil. In many parts of the plain, the earth is thrown up into little mounds, by some animal, whose habits most resemble those of the salamander; but although these tracks are scattered over all the plains from the Mississippi to the Pacific, we have never yet been able to obtain a sight of the animal itself.

As we entered the plain Neeshnepahkee, the Cutnose, overtook us, and after accompanying us a few miles, turned to the right to visit some of his people, who were now gathering roots in the plain. Having crossed the plain a little to the south of east, we descended a long steep hill, at the distance of five miles, to a creek six yards wide, which empties itself into the Kooskooskee. We ascended this little stream for a mile, and encamped at an Indian establishment of six houses, which seem to have been recently evacuated. Here we were joined by Neeshnepahkee, and the Shoshonee who had interpreted for us on the fifth.

From the plain we observed that the spurs of the Rocky mountains are still perfectly covered with snow, which the Indians inform us is so deep that we shall not be able to pass before the next full moon, that is, the first of June: though others place the time for crossing at a still greater distance. To us, who are desirous of reaching the plains of the Missouri, if for no other reason, for the purpose of enjoying a good meal, this intelligence was by no means welcome, and gave no relish to the remainder of the horse killed at Colter's creek, which formed our supper, part of which had already been our dinner. Observing, however, some deer, and a great appearance of more, we determined to make an attempt to get some of them, and therefore, after a cold night's rest,

Thursday, 8, most of the hunters set out at daylight. By eleven o'clock they all returned, with four deer, and a duck of an uncommon kind, which, with the remains of our horse, formed a stock of provisions such as we had not lately possessed. Without our facilities of procuring subsistence with guns, the natives of this country must often suffer very severely. During last winter they were so much distressed for food, that they were obliged to boil and eat the moss growing on the pine trees. At the same period they cut down nearly all the long-leafed pines, which we observed on the ground, for the purpose of collecting its seed, which resemble in size and shape that of the large sunflower, and when roasted or boiled, is nutritious and not disagreeable to the taste. At the present season they peal this pine tree, and eat the inner and succulent bark. In the creek near us, they also procure trout by means of a falling trap, constructed on the same plan with those common to the United States. We gave Neeshnepahkee and his people some of our game and horse-beef, besides the entrails of the deer, and four fawns which we found inside of two of them. They did not eat any of it perfectly raw, but the entrails had very little cooking, and the fawns were boiled whole, and the hide, hair, and entrails all consumed. The Shoshonee was offended at not having as much venison as he wished, and refused to interpret; but as we took no notice of him, he became very officious in the course of a few hours, and made many efforts to reinstate himself in our favour. The mother of the Twistedhair, and Neeshnepahkeeook now drew a sketch, which we preserved, of all the waters west of the Rocky mountains. They make the main southern branch of Lewis's river, much more extensive than the other, and place a great number of Shoshonee villages on its western side. Between three and four o'clock in the afternoon we set out, in company with Neeshnepahkeeook and other Indians, the brother of the Twistedhair having left us. Our route was up a high steep hill to a level plain, with little wood, through which we passed in a direction parallel to the river, for four miles, when we met the Twistedhair and six of his people. To this chief we had confided our horses and a part of our saddles, last autumn, and we therefore formed very unfavourable conjectures on finding that he received us with great coldness. Shortly after he began to speak in a very loud, angry manner, and was answered by Neeshnepahkeeook. We now discovered that a violent quarrel had arisen between these chiefs, on the subject, as we afterwards understood, of our horses. But as we could not learn the cause, and were desirous of terminating the dispute, we interposed, and told them we should go on to the first water and encamp. We therefore set out, followed by all the Indians, and having reached, at two miles distance, a small stream, running to the right, we encamped with the two chiefs and their little bands, forming separate camps, at a distance from each other. They all appeared to be in an ill humour, and as we had already heard reports that the Indians had discovered and carried off our saddles, and that the horses were very much scattered, we began to be uneasy, lest there should be too much foundation for the report. We were therefore anxious to reconcile the two chiefs as soon as possible, and desired the Shoshonee to interpret for us, while we attempted a mediation; but he peremptorily refused to speak a word: he observed that it was a quarrel between the two chiefs, and he had therefore no right to interfere; nor could all our representations, that by merely repeating what we said, he could not possibly be considered as meddling between the chiefs, induce him to take any part in it. Soon afterwards

Drewyer returned from hunting, and was sent to invite the Twisted-hair to come and smoke with us. He accepted the invitation, and as we were smoking the pipe over our fire, he informed us, that according to his promise, on leaving us at the falls of the Columbia, he had collected our horses and taken charge of them, as soon as he had reached home. But about this time Neeshnepahkeeooks and Tunnachemootoolt (the Brokenarm) who, as we passed, had been on a war party against the Shoshonees on the south branch of Lewis's river, returned, and becoming jealous of him, because the horses had been confided to his care, were constantly quarrelling with him. At length, being an old man, and unwilling to live in perpetual dispute with the two chiefs, he had given up the care of the horses, which had consequently become very much scattered. The greater part of them were, however, still in this neighbourhood; some in the forks between the Chopunnish and Kooskooskee, and three or four at the village of the Brokenarm, about half a day's march higher up the river. He added, that on the rise of the river in the spring, the earth had fallen from the door of the cache and exposed the saddles, some of which had probably been lost; but as soon as he was acquainted with the situation of them, he had them buried in another deposit, where they now are. He now promised that if we would stay to-morrow at his house, a few miles from this place, he would collect such of the horses as were in the neighbourhood, and send his young men for those in the forks over the Kooskooskee. He moreover advised us to visit the Brokenarm, who was a chief of great eminence, and that he would himself guide us to his dwelling. We told him that we meant to follow his advice in every respect; that we had confided our horses to his charge, and expected that he would deliver them to us, on which we should willingly pay him the two guns and ammunition, as we had promised. With this he seemed very much pleased, and declared that he would use every exertion to restore our horses. We now sent for the Cutnose, and after smoking for some time, took occasion to express to the two chiefs, our regret at seeing a misunderstanding between them. Neeshnepahkeeook told us that the Twistedhair was a bad old man, and wore two faces; for instead of taking care of our horses, he had suffered his young men to hunt with them, so that they had been very much injured, and that it was for this reason that the Brokenarm and himself had forbidden him to use them. The Twistedhair made no reply to this speech, after which we told Neeshnepahkeeook of our arrangement for to-morrow. He appeared very well satisfied, and said that he would himself go with us to the Brokenarm, who expected that we would see him, and who had *two bad horses for us*, an expression by which was meant that he intended making us a present of two valuable horses. That chief, he also informed us, had been apprised of our want of provisions, and sent four young men to meet us with a supply; but having taken a different road, they had missed us. After this interview we retired to rest at a late hour, and in the morning,

Friday 9, after sending out several hunters, we proceeded through a level rich country, similar to that of yesterday, for six miles, when we reached the house of the Twistedhair, situated near some larch trees, and a few bushes of balsam fir. It was built in the usual form, of sticks, mats, and dried hay; and although it contained no more than two fires and twelve persons, was provided with the customary appendage of a small hut, to which females in certain situations were to retreat. As soon as we halted at this place, we went with the Twistedhair to the spot where he had buried our saddles, and two other young Indians were despatched after the horses. Our hunters joined us with nothing but a few pheasants, the only deer which they killed being lost in the river. We therefore dined on soup, made of the roots of cows, which we purchased of the Indians. Late in the afternoon, the Twistedhair returned with about half the saddles we had left in the autumn, and some powder and lead which was buried at the same place. Soon after, the Indians brought us twenty-one of our horses, the greater part of whom were in excellent order, though some had not yet recovered from hard usage, and three had sore backs. We were however very glad to procure them in any condition. Several Indians came down from the village of Tunnachemootoolt, and passed the night with us. The Cutnose and Twistedhair seem now perfectly reconciled, for they both slept in the house of the latter. The man who had imposed himself upon us as a brother of the Twistedhair, also came and renewed his advances, but we now found that he was an impertinent proud fellow, of no respectability in the nation, and we therefore felt no inclination to cultivate his intimacy. Our camp was in an open plain, and soon became very uncomfortable, for the wind was high and cold, and the rain and hail which began about seven o'clock, changed in about two hours to a heavy fall of snow, which continued till after six o'clock.

Saturday, 10, the next morning, when it ceased, after covering the ground eight inches deep, and leaving the air keen and cold. We soon collected our horses, and after a scanty breakfast of roots, set out on a course S. 35° E. across the plains, the soil of which being covered with snow, we could only judge from observing that near the ravines, where it had melted, the mud was deep, black, and well supplied with quamash. The road was very slippery, and the snow stuck to the horses' feet and made them slip down very frequently. After going about sixteen miles, we came to the hills of Commearp creek, which are six hundred feet in height, but the tops of which only are covered with snow, the lower parts as well as the bottoms of the creek having had nothing but rain while it snowed in the high plains. On descending these hills to the creek, we reached about four o'clock, the house of Tunnachemootoolt, where was displayed the flag which we had given him, raised on a staff: under this we were received with due form, and then conducted a short distance to a good spot for an encampment, on Commearp creek. We soon collected the men of consideration, and after smoking, explained how destitute we were of provisions. The chief spoke to the people, who immediately brought about two bushels of dried quamash roots, some cakes of the roots of cows, and a dried salmon trout: we thanked them for this supply, but observed that, not being accustomed to live on roots alone, we feared that such diet might make our men sick, and therefore proposed to exchange one of our good horses, which was rather poor, for one that was fatter, and which we might kill. The hospitality of the chief was offended at the idea of an exchange; he observed that his people had an abundance of young horses, and that if we were disposed to use that food, we might have as many as we wanted. Accordingly, they soon gave us two fat young horses, without asking any thing in return, an act of liberal hospitality much greater than any we have witnessed since crossing the Rocky mountains, if it be not in fact the only really hospitable treatment we have received in this part of the world. We killed one of the horses, and then telling the natives that we were fatigued and hungry, and that as soon as we were refreshed, we would communicate freely with them, began to prepare our repast. During this time, a principal chief, called Hohastillpilp, came from his village about six miles distant, with a party of fifty men, for the purpose of visiting us. We invited him into our circle, and he alighted and smoked with us, while his retinue, who had five elegant horses, continued mounted at a short distance. While this was going on, the chief had a large leathern tent spread for us, and desired that we would make that our home whilst we remained at his village. We removed there, and having made a fire, and cooked a supper of horse-beef and roots, collected all the distinguished men present, and spent the evening in explaining who we were, the objects of our journey, and giving answers to their inquiries. To each of the chiefs, Tunnachemootoolt, and Hohastillpilp, we gave a small medal, explaining their use and importance, as honorary distinctions both among the whites and red men. Our men are delighted at once more having made a hearty meal. They have generally been in the habit of crowding the houses of the Indians, and endeavouring to purchase provisions on the best terms they could; for the inhospitality of the country was such, that in the extreme of hunger they were often obliged to treat the natives with but little ceremony, but this the Twistedhair had told us was disagreeable. Finding that these people are so kind and liberal, we ordered our men to treat them with great respect and not to throng round their fires, so that they now agree perfectly well together. After our council, the Indians felt no disposition to retire, and our tent was crowded with them all night. The next morning,

Sunday 11, we arose early and breakfasted again on horse-flesh. This village of Tunnachemootoolt, is in fact only a single house, one hundred and fifty feet long, built after the Chopunnish fashion, with sticks, straw, and dried grass. It contains twenty-four fires, about double that number of families, and might perhaps muster one hundred fighting men. The usual outhouse, or retiring hut for females, is not omitted. Their chief subsistence is roots, and the noise made by the women in pounding them, gives the hearer the idea of a nail factory. Yet, notwithstanding so many families are crowded together, the Chopunnish are much more cleanly in their persons and habitations, than any people we have met since we left the Ottoes on the river Platte. In the course of the morning, a chief named Yoompahkatim, a stout good looking man, of about forty years of age, who had lost his left eye, arrived from his village on the south side of Lewis's river. We gave him a small medal, and finding that there were now present the principal chiefs of the Chopunnish nation, Tunnachemootoolt (the Brokenarm) Neeshnepahkeeook, Yoompahkatim, and Hohastilpilp, whose rank is in the order they are mentioned, we thought this a favourable moment to explain to them the intentions of our government. We therefore collected the chiefs and warriors, and having drawn a map of the relative situation of our country, on a mat, with a piece of coal, detailed the nature and power of the American nation, its desire to preserve harmony between all its red brethren, and its intonation of establishing trading houses for their relief and support. It was not without difficulty, nor till after nearly half the day was spent, that we were able to convey all this information to the Chopunnish, much of which might have been lost or distorted, in its circuitous route through a variety of languages; for in the first place, we spoke in English to one of our men, who translated it into French to Chaboneau; he interpreted it to his wife in the Minnetaree language, and she then put it into Shoshonee, and the young Shoshonee prisoner explained it to the Chopunnish in their own dialect. At last we succeeded in communicating the impression they wished, and then adjourned the council; after which we amused them by showing the wonders of the compass, the spy-glass, the magnet, the watch and air-gun, each of which attracted its share of admiration. They said that after we had left the Minnetarees last autumn, three young Chopunnish had gone over to that nation, who had mentioned our visit and the extraordinary articles we had with us, but they placed no confidence in it until now. Among other persons present, was a youth, son of the Chopunnish chief, of much consideration, killed not long since by the Minnetarees of Fort de Prairie. As soon as the council was over, he brought a very fine mare with a colt, and begged us to accept them as a proof that he meant to pursue our advice, for he had opened his ears to our councils, which had made his heart glad. We now resumed our medical labours, and had a number of patients afflicted with scrophula, rheumatism and sore eyes, to all which we administered very cheerfully as far as our skill and supplies of medicine would permit. We also visited a chief who has for three years past so completely lost the use of his limbs, that he lies like a perfect corpse in whatever position he is placed, yet he eats heartily, digests his food very well, has a regular pulse, and retains his flesh; in short, were he not somewhat pale from lying so long out of the sun, he might be mistaken for a man in perfect health. This disease does not seem to be common; indeed, we have seen only three cases of it among the Chopunnish, who alone are afflicted with it. The scrophulous disorders we may readily conjecture to originate in the long confinement to vegetable diet; which may perhaps also increase the soreness of the eyes; but this strange disorder baffles at once our curiosity and our skill. Our assistance was again demanded early the next morning,

Monday 12, by a crowd of Indians, to whom we gave eye-water. Shortly after, the chiefs and warriors held a council among themselves, to decide on the answer to our speech; and the result was, as we were informed, that they confided in what we had told them, and resolved to follow our advice. This resolution once made, the principal chief, Tunnachemootoolt, took a quantity of flour of the roots of cows, and going round to all the kettles and baskets, in which his people were cooking, thickened the soup into a kind of mush. He then began a harangue, making known the result of the deliberations among the chiefs, and after exhorting them to unanimity, concluded by an invitation to all who agreed to the proceedings of the council, to come and eat, while those who would not abide by the decision of the chiefs were requested to show their dissent by not partaking in the feast. During this animated harangue, the women, who were probably uneasy at the prospect of forming this new connexion with strangers, tore their hair, and wrung their hands with the greatest appearance of distress. But the concluding appeal of the orator effectually stopped the mouths of every malcontent, and the proceedings were ratified, and the mush devoured with the most zealous unanimity. The chiefs and warriors then came in a body to visit us, as we were seated near our tent, and at their instance, two young men, one of whom was the son of Tunnachemootoolt, and the other the youth whose father had been killed by the Pahkees, presented to each of us a fine horse. We caused the chiefs to be seated, and gave every one of them a flag, a pound of powder, and fifty balls, and a present of the same kind to the young men from whom we had received the horses. They then invited us into the tent, and told us that they now wished to answer what we had told them yesterday; but that many of their people were at that moment waiting in great pain for our medical assistance. It was therefore agreed that captain Clarke, who is the favourite physician, should visit the sick, while captain Lewis would hold the council; which was accordingly opened by an old man, the father of Hohastilpilp. He began by declaring that the nation had listened with attention to our advice, and had only one heart and one tongue in declaring their determination to follow it. They knew well the advantages of peace, for they valued the lives of their young men too much to expose them to the dangers of war; and their desire to live quietly with their neighbours, had induced them last summer to send three warriors with a pipe to the Shoshonees, in the plains of Columbia, south of

Lewis's river. These ministers of peace had been killed by the Shoshonees, against whom the nation immediately took up arms. They had met them last winter, and killed forty-two men, with the loss of only three of their own party; so that having revenged their deceased brethren, they would no longer make war on the Shoshonees, but receive them as friends. As to going with us to the plains of the Missouri, they would be very willing to do so, for though the Blackfoot Indians and the Pahkees had shed much of their blood, they still wished to live in peace with them. But we had not yet seen either of these nations, and it would therefore be unsafe for them to venture, till they were assured of not being attacked by them. Still, however, some of their young men would accompany us across the mountains, and if they could effect a peace with their enemies, the whole nation would go over to the Missouri in the course of next summer. On our proposal that one of the chiefs should go with us to the country of the whites, they had not yet decided, but would let us know before we left them. But that, at all events, the whites might calculate on their attachment and their best services, for though poor, their hearts were good. The snow was, however, still so deep on the mountains, that we should perish in attempting the passage, but if we waited till after the next full moon, the snows would have sufficiently melted to enable our horses to subsist on the grass. As soon as this speech was concluded, captain Lewis replied at some length: with this they appeared highly gratified, and after smoking the pipe, made us a present of another fat horse for food. We, in turn, gave the Brokenarm a phial of eyewater, with directions to wash the eyes of all who should apply for it; and as we promised to fill it again when it was exhausted, he seemed very much pleased with our liberality. To the Twistedhair, who had last night collected six more horses, we gave a gun, an hundred balls, and two pounds of powder, and told him he should have the same quantity when we received the remainder of our horses. In the course of the day three more of them were brought in, and a fresh exchange of small presents put the Indians in excellent humour. On our expressing a wish to cross the river, and form a camp, in order to hunt and fish till the snows had melted, they recommended a position a few miles distant, and promised to furnish us to-morrow with a canoe to cross. We invited the Twisted-hair to settle near our camp, for he has several young sons, one of whom we hope to engage as a guide, and he promised to do so. Having now settled all their affairs, the Indians divided themselves into two parties, and began to play the game of hiding a bone, already described, as common to all the natives of this country, which they continued playing for beads and other ornaments.

CHAPTER XXIX.

The party encamp amongst the Chopunnish, and receive further evidences of their hospitality—the Indian mode of boiling bears-flesh—of gelding horses—their mode of decoying the deer within reach of their arrows—character of the soil and climate in the Rocky mountains—varieties of climate—character of the natives —their dress and ornaments—mode of burying the dead—the party administer medical relief to the natives—one of the natives restored to the use of his limbs by sweating, and the curious process by which perspiration was excited—another proof of Chopunnish hospitality—success of their sweating prescription on the Indian chief—description of the horned lizzard, and a variety of insects—the attachment of the friends of a dying Indian to a tomahawk which he had stolen from the party, and which they desired to bury with the body—description of the river Tommanamah—the Indians return an answer to a proposition made by the party.

TUESDAY, 13. Our medical visits occupied us till a late hour, after which we collected our horses and proceeded for two miles in a southeastern direction, crossing a branch from the right, at the distance of a mile. We then turned nearly north, and crossing an extensive open bottom, about a mile and a half wide, reached the bank of the Kooskooskee. Here we expected the canoe which they had promised; but although a man had been despatched with it at the appointed time, he did not arrive before sunset. We therefore encamped, with a number of Indians who had followed us from the village, and in the morning,

Wednesday 14, after sending out some hunters, transported the baggage by means of the canoe, and then drove our horses into the river, over which they swam without accident, although it is one hundred and fifty yards wide, and the current very rapid. We then descended the river about half a mile, and formed our camp on the spot which the Indians had recommended. It was about forty paces from the river, and formerly an Indian habitation; but nothing remained at present but a circle thirty yards in diameter, sunk in the ground about four feet, with a wall round it of nearly three and a half feet in height. In this place we deposited our baggage, and round its edges formed our tents of sticks and grass. This situation is in many respects advantageous. It is an extensive level bottom, thinly covered with long leafed pine, with a rich soil, affording excellent pasture, and supplied, as well as the high and broken hills on the east and northeast, with the best game in the neighbourhood; while its vicinity to the river makes it convenient for the salmon, which are now expected daily. As soon as we had encamped, Tunnachemootoolt and Hohastilpilp, with about twelve of their nation, came to the opposite side and began to sing, this being the usual token of friendship on similar occasions. We sent the canoe for them, and the two chiefs came over with several of the party, among whom were the two young men who had given us the two horses in behalf of the nation. After smoking some time, Hohastilpilp presented to captain Lewis an elegant gray gelding, which he had brought for the purpose, and was perfectly satisfied at receiving in return a handkerchief, two hundred balls, and four pounds of powder.

The hunters killed some pheasants, two squirrels, and a male and a female bear, the first of which was large and fat, and of a bay colour; the second meagre, grisly, and of smaller size. They were of the species common to the upper part of the Missouri, and might well be termed the variegated bear, for they are found occasionally of a black grisly brown or red colour. There is every reason to believe them to be of precisely the same species. Those of different colours are killed together, as in the case of these two, and as we found the white and bay associated together on the Missouri; and some nearly white were seen in this neighbourhood by the hunters. Indeed, it is not common to find any two bears of the same colour, and if the difference in colour were to constitute a distinction of species, the number would increase to almost twenty. Soon after they killed a female bear with two cubs. The mother was black, with a considerable intermixture of white hairs and a white spot on the breast. One of the cubs was jet black, and the other of a light reddish brown, or bay colour. The foil of these variegated bears, are much finer, longer, and more abundant than that of the common black bear: but the most striking difference between them is, that the former are larger, have longer tusks, and longer as well as blunter talons; that they prey more on other animals; that they lie neither so long nor so closely in winter quarters, and never climb a tree, however closely pressed by the hunters. This variegated bear, though specifically the same with those we met on the Missouri, are by no means so ferocious, probably, because of the scarcity of game, and the habit of living on roots may have weaned them from the practices of attacking and devouring animals. Still, however, they are not so passive as the common black bear, which are also to be found here; for they have already fought with our hunters, though with less fury than those on the other side of the mountain.

A large part of the meat we gave to the Indians, to whom it was a real luxury, as they scarcely taste flesh once in a month. They immediately prepared a large fire of dried wood, on which were thrown a number of smooth stones from the river. As soon as the fire went down, and the stones were heated, they were laid next to each other, in a level position, and covered with a quantity of branches of pine, on which were placed flitches of the bear, and thus placing the boughs and flesh alternately for several courses, leaving a thick layer of pine on the top. On this heap was then poured a small quantity of water, and the whole covered with earth to the depth of four inches. After remaining in this state about three hours, the meat was taken off, and was really more tender than that which we had boiled or roasted, though the strong flavour of the pine, rendered it disagreeable to our palates. This repast gave them much satisfaction, for though they sometimes kill the black bear, yet they attack very reluctantly the furious variegated bear, and only when they can pursue him on horseback, through the plains, and shoot him with arrows.

The stone horses we found so troublesome that we have endeavoured to exchange them for either mares or geldings; but although we offered two for one, they were unwilling to barter. It was therefore determined to castrate them; and being desirous of ascertaining the best method of performing this operation, two were gelded in the usual manner, while one of the natives tried the experiment in the Indian way, without tying the string of the stone (which he assured us was much the better plan) and carefully scraping the string clean and separating it from the adjoining veins before cutting it. All the horses recovered; but we afterwards found that those on which the Indian mode had been tried, although they bled more profusely at first, neither swell nor appear to suffer as much as the others, and recovered sooner, so that we are fully persuaded that the Indian method is preferable to our own.

May 15. As we shall now be compelled to pass some time in this neighbourhood, a number of hunters were sent in different directions, and the rest were employed in completing the camp. From this labour we, however, exempted five of the men, two of whom are afflicted with cholic, and the others complain of violent pains in the head, all which are occasioned, we presume, by the diet of roots, to which they have recently been confined. We secured the baggage with a shelter of grass, and made a kind of bower of the under part of an old sail, the leathern tent being now too rotten for use, while the men formed very comfortable huts in the shape of the awning of a wagon, by means of willow poles and grass. Tunnachemootoolt and his young men left us this morning on their way home; and soon after we were visited by a party of fourteen Indians on horseback, armed with bows and arrows going on a hunting excursion. The chief game is the deer, and whenever the ground will permit, the favourite hunt is on horseback; but in the woodlands, where this is impracticable, they make use of a decoy. This consists of the skin of the head and upper part of the neck of a deer, kept in its natural shape by a frame of small sticks on the inside. As soon as the hunter perceives a deer he conceals himself, and with his hand moves the decoy so as to represent a real deer in the act of feeding, which is done so naturally that the game is seduced within reach of their arrows.

We also exercised our horses by driving them together, so as to accustom them to each other, and incline them the less to separate. The next morning,

Friday 16, an Indian returned with one of them, which had strayed away in the night to a considerable distance, an instance of integrity and kindness by no means singular among the Chopunnish. Hohastilpilp, with the rest of the natives left us to-day. The hunters who have as yet come in, brought nothing, except a few pheasants, so that we still place our chief reliance on the mush made of roots (among these the cows and the quamash are the principal) with which we use a small onion, which grows in great abundance, and which corrects any bad effects they may have on the stomach. The cows and quamash, particularly, incline to produce flatulency, to obviate which we employ a kind of fennel, called by the Shoshonees, yearhah, resembling anniseed in flavour, and a very agreeable food.

In the course of the day two other hunters brought in a deer. The game they said was scarce; but they had wounded three bear as white as sheep. The last hunters who had left us yesterday, also came in to-night, with information, that at the distance of five or six miles, they attempted to cross Collins's creek, on the other side, where game is most abundant, but that they could not ford it with their horses, on account of its depth, and the rapidity of the current.

Saturday, 17. It rained during the greater part of the night, and our flimsy covering being insufficient for our protection, we lay in the water most of the time. What was more unlucky, our chronometer became wet, and, in consequence, somewhat rusty, but by care we hope to restore it. The rain continued nearly the whole day, while on the high plains the snow is falling, and already two or three inches in depth. The bad weather confined us to the camp and kept the Indians from us, so that for the first time since we left the narrows of the Columbia, a day has passed without our being visited by any of the natives.

The country along the Rocky mountains for several hundred miles in length and about fifty wide, is a high level plain; in all its parts extremely fertile, and in many places covered with a growth of tall long-leafed pine. This plain is chiefly interrupted near the streams of water, where the hills are steep and lofty; but the soil is good, being unincumbered by much stone, and possess more timber than the level country. Under shelter of these hills, the bottom lands skirt the margin of the rivers, and though narrow and confined, are still fertile and rarely inundated. Nearly the whole of this wide spread tract is covered with a profusion of grass and plants, which are at this time as high as the knee. Among these are a variety of esculent plants and roots, acquired without much difficulty, and yielding not only a nutritious, but a very agreeable food. The air is pure and dry, the climate quite as mild, if not milder, than the same parallels of latitude in the Atlantic states, and must be equally healthy, for all the disorders which we have witnessed, may fairly be imputed more to the nature of the diet than to any intemperance of climate. This general observation is of course to be qualified, since in the same tract of country, the degrees of the combination of heat and cold obey the influence of situation. Thus the rains of the low grounds near our camp, are snows in the high plains, and while the sun shines with intense heat in the confined bottoms, the plains enjoy a much colder air, and the vegetation is retarded at least fifteen days, while at the foot of the mountains the snows are still many feet in depth; so that within twenty miles of our camp we observe the rigours of winter cold, the cool air of spring, and the oppressive heat of midsummer. Even on the plains, however, where the snow has fallen, it seems to do but little injury to the grass and other plants, which, though apparently tender and susceptible, are still blooming, at the height of nearly eighteen inches through the snow. In short, this district affords many advantages to settlers, and if properly cultivated, would yield every object necessary for the subsistence and comfort of civilized man.

The Chopunnish themselves are in general stout, well formed, and active; they have high, and many of them aqueline noses, and the general appearance of the face is cheerful and agreeable, though without any indication of gayety and mirth. Like most of the Indians they extract their beards; but the women only pluck the hair from the rest of the body. That of the men is very often suffered to grow, nor does there appear to be any natural deficiency in that respect; for we observe several men, who, if they had adopted the practice of shaving, would have been as well supplied as ourselves. The dress of both sexes resembles that of the Shoshonees, and consists of a long shirt reaching to the thigh, leggings as high as the waist, moccasins and robes, all of which are formed of skins.

Their ornaments are beads, shells, and pieces of brass attached to different parts of the dress, or tied round the arms, neck, wrists, and over the shoulders: to these are added pearls and beads, suspended from the ears, and a single shell of wampum through the nose. The head-dress of the men is a bandeau of fox or otter skin, either with or without the fur, and sometimes an ornament is tied to a plait of hair, falling from the crown of the head: that of the women is a cap without rim, formed of bear grass and cedar bark; while the hair itself, of both sexes, falls in two rows down the front of the body. Collars of bears' claws are also common. But the personal ornament most esteemed is a sort of breastplate, formed of a strip of otter skin, six inches wide, cut out of the whole length of the back of the animal, including the head; this being dressed with the hair on, a hole is made at the upper end, through which the head of the wearer is placed, and the skin hangs in front with the tail reaching below the knee, and ornamented with pieces of pearl, red cloth, and wampum; or, in short, any other fanciful decoration. Tippets also are occasionally worn. That of Hohastilpilp was formed of human scalps, and adorned with the thumbs and fingers of several men slain by him in battle.

The Chopunnish are among the most amiable men we have seen. Their character is placid and gentle, rarely moved into passion, yet not often enlivened by gayety. Their amusements consist in running races, shooting with arrows at a target, and they partake of the great and prevailing vice of gambling. They are, however, by no means so much attached to baubles as the generality of Indians, but are anxious to obtain articles of utility, such as knives, tomahawks, kettles, blankets, and awls for moccasins. They have also suffered so much from the superiority of their enemies, that they are equally desirous of procuring arms and ammunition, which they are gradually acquiring, for the band of Tunnachemootoolt have already six guns, which they acquired from the Minnetarees.

The Chopunnish bury their dead in sepulchres, formed of boards, constructed like the roof of a house. The body is rolled in skins and laid one over another, separated by a board only, both above and below. We have sometimes seen their dead buried in wooden boxes, and rolled in skins in the manner above mentioned. They sacrifice their horses, canoes, and every other species of property to their dead; the bones of many horses are seen lying round their sepulchres.

Among the reptiles common to this country are the two species of innocent snakes already described, and the rattlesnake, which last is of the same species as that of the Missouri, and though abundant here, is the only poisonous snake we have seen between the Pacific and the Missouri. Besides these there are the common black lizard and horned lizard. Of frogs there are several kinds, such as the small green tree frog, the small frog common in the United States, which sings in the spring of the year, a species of frog frequenting the water, much larger than the bull-frog, and in shape between the delicate length of the bull-frog, and the shorter and less graceful form of the toad like; the last of which, however, its body is covered with little pustules, or lumps: we have never heard it make a noise of any kind. Neither the toad bull-frog; the moccasin-snake, nor the copperhead-snake are to be found here. Captain Lewis killed a snake near the camp three feet and eleven inches in length, and much the colour of the rattlesnake. There was no poisonous tooth to be found. It had two hundred and eighteen scuta on the abdomen, and fifty-nine squama or half-formed scuta on the tail. The eye was of a moderate size: the iris of a dark yellowish brown, and the pupil black. There was nothing remarkable in the form of the head, which was not so wide across the jaws as that of the poisonous class of snakes usually are.

There is a species of lizard, which we have called the horned lizard, about the size and much resembling in figure the ordinary black lizard. The belly is, notwithstanding, broader, the tail shorter, and the action much slower than the ordinary lizard. It crawls like the toad, is of a brown colour, and interspersed with yellowish brown spots; it is covered with minute shells, interspersed with little horny projections like prickles on the upper part of the body. The belly and throat resemble the frogs, and are of a light yellowish brown. The edge of the belly is regularly beset with these horny projections, which give to those edges a serrate figure; the eye is small and of a dark colour. Above and behind the eyes are several projections of the bone, which being armed at the extremities with a firm black substance, having the appearance of horns sprouting from the head, has induced us to call it the horned lizard. These animals are found in great abundance in the sandy parts of the plains, and after a shower of rain are seen basking in the sun. For the greatest part of the time they are concealed in holes. They are found in great numbers on the banks of the Missouri, and in the plains through which we have passed above the Wollawollahs.

Most of the insects common to the United States are seen in this country: such as the butterfly, the common housefly, the blowingfly, the horsefly, except one species of it, the gold-coloured earfly, the place of which is supplied by a fly of a brown colour, which attaches itself to the same part of the horse, and is equally troublesome. There are likewise nearly all the varieties of beatles known in the Atlantic states, except the large cow beatle, and the black beatle, commonly called the tumblebug. Neither the hornet, the wasp, nor the yellowjacket inhabit this part of the country, but there is an insect resembling the last of these, though much larger, which is very numerous, particularly in the Rocky mountains and on the waters of the Columbia; the body and abdomen are yellow, with transverse circles of black, the head black, and the wings, which are four in number, of a dark brown colour: their nests are built in the ground, and resemble that of the hornet, with an outer covering to the comb. These insects are fierce, and sting very severely, so that we found them very troublesome in frightening our horses as we passed the mountains. The silkworm is also found here, as well as the humble-bee, though the honey-bee is not.

May 18. Twelve hunters set out this morning after the bear, which are now our chief dependence; but as they are now ferocious, the hunters henceforward never go except in pairs. Soon after they left us, a party of Chopunnish erected a hut on the opposite side of the river in order to watch the salmon, which is expected to arrive every day. For this purpose they have constructed with sticks, a kind of wharf, projecting about ten feet into the river, and three feet above its surface, on the extremity of which one of the fishermen exercised himself with a scooping net, similar to that used in our country; but after several hours' labour he was still unsuccessful. In the course of the morning three Indians called at our camp and told us that they had been hunting near the place where we met the Chopunnish last autumn, and which is called by them the quamash grounds, but after roaming about for several days had killed nothing. We gave them a small piece of meat, which they said they would keep for their small children, which they said were very hungry, and then, after smoking, took leave of us. Some of our hunters returned almost equally unsuccessful. They had gone over the whole country between Collins's creek and the Kooskooskee, to their junction, at the distance of ten miles, without seeing either a deer or bear, and at last brought in a single hawk and a salmon dropped by an eagle. This last was not in itself considerable, but gave us hopes of soon seeing that fish in the river, an event which we ardently desire, for though the rapid rise of the river denotes a great decrease of snow on the mountains, yet we shall not be able to leave our camp for some time.

Monday, 19. After a cold rainy night, during a greater part of which we lay in the water, the weather became fair, and we then sent some men to a village above us, on the opposite side, to purchase some roots. They carried with them for this purpose a small collection of alls, knitting pins, and armbands, with which they obtained several bushels of the root of cows, and some bread of the same material. They were followed too by a train of invalids from the village, who came to ask for our assistance. The men were generally afflicted with sore eyes, but the women had besides this a variety of other disorders, chiefly rheumatic, a violent pain and weakness in the loins, which is a common complaint among the females, and one of them seemed much dejected, and as we thought, from the account of her disease, hysterical. We gave her thirty drops of laudanum, and after administering eye-water and rubbing the rheumatic patients with volatile linament, and giving cathartics to others, they all thought themselves much relieved, and returned highly satisfied to the village. We were fortunate enough to retake one of the horses on which we crossed the Rocky mountains in the autumn, and which had become almost wild since that time.

Tuesday, 20. Again it rained during the night, and the greater part of this day. Our hunters were out in different directions, but though they saw a bear and a deer or two, they only killed one of the latter, which proved to be of the muledeer species. The next day,

Wednesday 21, finding the rain still continue we left our ragged sail tent, and formed a hut with willow poles and grass. The rest of the men were occupied in building a canoe for present use, as the Indians promise to give us a horse for it when we leave them. We received nothing from our hunters except a single sandhill crane, which are very abundant in this neighbourhood, and consumed at dinner the last morsel of meat which we have. As there now seems but little probability of our procuring a stock of dried meat, and the fish is as yet an uncertain resource, we made a division of all our stock of merchandise, so as to enable the men to purchase a store of roots and bread for the mountains. We might ourselves collect those roots, but as there are several species of hemlock growing among the cows, and difficult to be distinguished from that plant, we are afraid to suffer the men to collect them, lest the party might be poisoned by mistaking them. On parcelling out the stores, the stock of each man was found to consist of only one awl and one knitting-pin, half an ounce of vermillion, two needles, a few skeins of thread, and about a yard of riband—a slender means of bartering for our subsistence; but the men have been now so much accustomed to privations, that neither the want of meat, nor the scanty funds of the party, excite the least anxiety among them.

Thursday, 22. We availed ourselves of the fair weather to dry our baggage and store of roots, and being still without meat, killed one of our colts, intending to reserve the other three for the mountains. In the afternoon we were amused by a large party of Indians, on the opposite side of the river, hunting on horseback. After riding at full speed down the steep hills, they at last drove the deer into the river, where we shot it, and two Indians immediately pursued it on a raft, and took it. Several hunters, who had gone to a considerable distance near the mountains, returned with five deer. They had purchased also two red salmon trout, which the Indians say remain in this river during the greater part of the winter, but are not good at this season, as it in fact appeared, for they were very meagre. The salmon, we understand, are now arrived at no great distance, in Lewis's river, but some days will yet elapse before they come up to this place. This, as well as the scarcity of game, made us wish to remove lower down; but on examination we found that there was no place in that direction calculated for a camp, and therefore resolved to remain in our present position. Some uneasiness has been excited by a report, that two nights ago a party of Shoshonees had surrounded a Chopunnish house, on the south side of Lewis's river, but the inhabitants having discovered their intentions, had escaped without injury.

Friday, 23. The hunters were sent out to make a last effort to procure provisions, but after examining the whole country between Collins's creek and the Kooskooskee, they found nothing except a few pheasants of the dark brown kind. In the meantime we were visited by four Indians who had come from a village on Lewis's river, at the distance of two days' ride, who came for the purpose of procuring a little eye-water: the extent of our medical fame is not a little troublesome, but we rejoice at any circumstance which enables us to relieve these poor creatures, and therefore willingly washed their eyes, after which they returned home.

Saturday, 24. This proved the warmest day we have had since our arrival here. Some of our men visited the village of the Brokenarm, and exchanged some awls, which they had made of the links of a small chain belonging to one of their steel traps, for a plentiful supply of roots.

Besides administering medical relief to the Indians, we are obliged to devote much of our time to the care of our own invalids. The child of Sacajawea is very unwell; and with one of the men we have ventured an experiment of a very robust nature. He has been for some time sick, but has now recovered his flesh, eats heartily and digests well, but has so great a weakness in the loins that he cannot walk nor even sit upright without extreme pain. After we had in vain exhausted the resources of our art, one of the hunters mentioned that he had known persons in similar situations restored by violent sweats, and at the request of the patient, we permitted the remedy to be applied. For this purpose, a hole about four feet deep and three in diameter was dug in the earth, and heated well by a large fire in the bottom of it. The fire was then taken out, and an arch formed over the hole by means of willow poles, and covered with several blankets, so as to make a perfect awning. The patient being stripped naked, was seated under this on a bench, with a piece of board for his feet, and with a jug of water sprinkled the bottom and sides of the hole, so as to keep up as hot a steam as he could bear. After remaining twenty minutes in this situation, he was taken out, immediately plunged twice in cold water, and brought back to the hole, where he resumed the vapour bath. During all this time he drank copiously a strong infusion of horsemint, which was used as a substitute for the seneca root, which our informant said he had seen employed on these occasions, but of which there is none in this country. At the end of three quarters of an hour, he was again withdrawn from the hole, carefully wrapped, and suffered to cool gradually. This operation was performed yesterday, and this morning he walked about, and is nearly free from pain. About eleven o'clock a canoe arrived with three Indians, one of whom was the poor creature who had lost the use of his limbs, and for whose recovery the natives seem very anxious, as he is a chief of considerable rank among them. His situation is beyond the reach of our skill. He complains of no pain in any peculiar limb, and we therefore think his disorder cannot be rheumatic, as his limbs would have been more diminished if his disease had been a paralytic affection. We had already ascribed it to his diet of roots, and had recommended his living on fish and flesh, and using the cold bath every morning, with a dose of cream of tarter, or flowers of sulphur, every third day. These prescriptions seem to have been of little avail, but as he thinks himself somewhat better for them, we concealed our ignorance by giving him a few drops of laudanum and a little portable soup, with a promise of sweating him, as we had done our own man. On attempting it however, in the morning,

Sunday 25, we found that he was too weak to sit up or be supported in the hole: we therefore told the Indians that we knew of no other remedy except frequent perspirations in their own sweat-houses, accompanied by drinking large quantities of the decoction of horsemint, which we pointed out to them. Three hunters set out to hunt towards the Quamash flats if they could pass Collins's creek. Others crossed the river for the same purpose, and one of the men was sent to a village on the opposite side, about eight miles above us. Nearly all the inhabitants were either hunting, digging roots, or fishing in Lewis's river, from which they had brought several fine salmon. In the course of the day, some of our hunters wounded a female bear with two cubs, one of which was white and the other perfectly black.

The Indians who accompanied the sick chief are so anxious for his safety that they remained with us all night, and in the morning,

Monday 26, when we gave him some cream of tartar, and portable soup, with directions how to treat him, they still lingered about us in hopes we might do something effectual, though we desired them to take him home.

The hunters sent out yesterday returned with Hohastilpilp, and a number of inferior chiefs and warriors. They had passed Commearp creek at the distance of one and a half miles, and a larger creek three miles beyond; they then went on till they were stopped by a large creek ten miles above our camp, and finding it too deep and rapid to pass, they returned home. On their way, they stopped at a village four miles up the second creek, which we have never visited, and where they purchased bread and roots on very moderate terms; an article of intelligence very pleasing at the present moment, when our stock of meat is again exhausted. We have however still agreeable prospects, for the river is rising fast, as the snows visibly diminish, and we saw a salmon in the river to-day. We also completed our canoe.

Tuesday 27. The horse which the Indians gave us some time ago, had gone astray; but in our present dearth of provisions we searched for him and killed him. Observing that we were in want of food, Hohastilpilp informed us that most of the horses which we saw running at large belonged to him or his people, and requested that whenever we wished any meat we would make use of them without restraint. We have, indeed, on more than one occasion, had to admire the generosity of this Indian, whose conduct presents a model of what is due to strangers in distress. A party was sent to the village discovered yesterday, and returned with a large supply of bread and roots. Sergeant Ordway and two men were also despatched to Lewis's river, about half a day's ride to the south, where we expect to obtain salmon, which are said to be very abundant at that place. The three men who had attempted to go to the Quamah flats, returned with five deer; but although they had proceeded some distance up Collins's creek, it continued too deep for them to cross. The Indians who accompanied the chief, were so anxious to have the operation of sweating him performed under our inspection, that we determined to gratify them by making a second attempt. The hole was therefore enlarged, and the father of the chief, a very good looking old man, went in with him, and held him in a proper position. This strong evidence of feeling is directly opposite to the received opinions of the insensibility of savages, nor are we less struck by the kindness and attention paid to the sick man by those who are unconnected with him, which are the more surprising, as the long illness of three years might be supposed to exhaust their sympathy. We could not produce as complete a perspiration as we desired, and after he was taken out, he complained of suffering considerable pain, which we relieved with a few drops of laudanum, and he then rested well. The next morning,

Wednesday 28, he was able to use his arms, and feels better than he has done for many months, and set up during the greater part of the day.

We sent to the village of Tunnachemootolt for bread and roots, and a party of hunters set out to hunt up a creek, about eight miles above us. In the evening, another party, who had been so fortunate as to find a ford across Collins's creek, returned from the Quamah flats with eight deer, of which they saw great numbers, though there were but few bears. Having now a tolerable stock of meat, we were occupied during the following day,

Thursday 29, in various engagements in the camp. The Indian chief is still rapidly recovering, and for the first time during the last twelve months, had strength enough to wash his face. We had intended to repeat the sweating to-day, but as the weather was cloudy, with occasional rain, we declined it. This operation, though violent, seems highly efficacious; for our own man, on whom the experiment was first made, is recovering his strength very fast, and the restoration of the chief is wonderful. He continued to improve, and on the following day,

Friday 30, after a very violent sweating, was able to move one of his legs and thighs, and some of his toes; the fingers and arms being almost entirely restored to their former strength. Parties were sent out as usual to hunt and trade with the Indians. Among others, two of the men who had not yet exchanged their stock of merchandise for roots, crossed the river for that purpose, in our boat. But as they reached the opposite shore, the violence of the current drove the boat broadside against some trees, and she immediately filled and went to the bottom. With difficulty one of the men was saved, but the boat itself, with three blankets, a blanket-coat, and their small pittance of merchandise, were irrevocably lost.

Saturday, 31. Two men visited the Indian village, where they purchased a dressed bear skin, of a uniform pale reddish brown colour, which the Indians called yackah in contradistinction to hohhost, or the white bear. This remark induced us to inquire more particularly into their opinions as to the several species of bears; and we therefore produced all the skins of that animal which we had killed at this place, and also one very nearly white, which we had purchased. The natives immediately classed the white, the deep and the pale grizly red, the grizly dark brown, in short, all those with the extremities of the hair of a white or frosty colour, without regard to the colour of the ground of the foil, under the name of hohhost. They assured us, that they were all of the same species with the white bear; that they associated together, had longer nails than the others, and never climbed trees. On the other hand, the black skins, those which were black, with a number of entire white hairs intermixed, or with a white breast, the uniform bay, the brown, and light reddish brown, were ranged under the class yackkah, and were said to resemble each other in being smaller, and having shorter nails than the white bear, in climbing trees, and being so little vicious that they could be pursued with safety. This distinction of the Indians seems to be well founded, and we are inclined to believe,

First, That the white or grizly bear of this neighbourhood form a distinct species, which moreover is the same with those of the same colour on the upper part of the Missouri, where the other species are not found.

Second, That the black and reddish brown, &c. is a second species, equally distinct from the white bear of this country, as from the black bear of the Atlantic and Pacific oceans, which two last seem to form only one species. The common black bear are indeed unknown in this country; for the bear of which we are speaking, though in most respects similar, differs from it in having much finer, thicker, and longer hair, with a great proportion of fur mixed with it, and also in having a variety of colours, while the common black bear has no intermixture or change of colour, but is of a uniform black.

In the course of the day the natives brought us another of our original stock of horses, of which we have now recovered all except two, and those, we are informed, were taken back by our Shoshonee guide, when he returned home. They amount to sixty-five, and most of them fine strong active horses, in excellent order.

Sunday, June 1. Two of our men who had been up the river to trade with the Indians, returned quite unsuccessful. Nearly opposite to the village, their horse fell with his load, down a steep cliff, into the river, across which he swam. An Indian on the opposite side, drove him back to them, but in crossing most of the articles were lost, and the paint melted. Understanding their intentions, the Indians attempted to come over to them, but having no canoe, were obliged to use a raft, which struck on a rock, upset, and the whole store of roots and bread were destroyed. This failure completely exhausted our stock of merchandise; but the remembrance of what we suffered from cold and hunger during the passage of the Rocky mountains, makes us anxious to increase our means of subsistence and comfort when we again encounter the same inconvenience. We therefore created a new fund, by cutting off the buttons from our clothes, preparing some eye-water, and basilicon, to which were added some phials, and small tin boxes, in which we had once kept phosphorus. With this cargo two men set out in the morning,

Monday 2, to trade, and brought home three bushels of roots and some bread, which, in our situation, was as important as the return of an East India ship. In the meantime, several hunters went across Collins's creek to hunt on the Quamash grounds, and the Indians informed us that there were great quantities of moose to the southeast of the east branch of Lewis's river, which they call the Tommanamah. We had lately heard that some Indians who reside at some distance, on the south side of the Kooskooskee, are in possession of two tomahawks, one of which was left at our camp at Musquitoe creek, the other had been stolen while we were encamped at the Chopunnish last autumn. This last we were anxious to obtain, in order to give to the relations of our unfortunate companion, sergeant Floyd, to whom it once belonged. We therefore sent Drewyer yesterday with Neeshnepahkeeook and Hohastilpilp, the two chiefs, to demand it. On their arrival, it seemed that the present owner, who had purchased it from the thief, was himself at the point of death; so that his relations were unwilling to give it up, as they meant to bury it in the grave with the deceased. But the influence of Neeshnepahkeeook at length succeeded; and they consented to surrender the tomahawk on receiving two strands of beads and a handkerchief, from Drewyer, and from each of the chiefs a horse, to be killed at the funeral of the deceased, according to the custom of the country.

Soon after their return, serjeant Ordway and his party, for whose safety we had now become extremely anxious, came home from Lewis's river, with some roots of cows and seventeen salmon. The distance, however, from which they were brought, was so great, that most of them were nearly spoiled; but such as continued sound, were extremely delicious, the flesh being of a fine rose colour, with a small mixture of yellow, and so fat that they were cooked very well without the addition of any oil or grease.

When they set out on the 27th, they had hoped to reach the salmon fishery in the course of that day, but the route by which the guides led them was so circuitous, that they rode seventy miles before they reached their place of destination, in the evening of the twenty ninth. After going for twenty miles up the Commearp creek, through an open plain, broken only by the hills and timber along the creek, they then entered a high, irregular, mountainous country, the soil of which was fertile, and well supplied with pine. Without stopping to hunt, although they saw great quantities of deer, and some of the bighorn, they hastened for thirty miles across this district to the Tommanamah, or east branch of Lewis's river; and not finding any salmon, descended that stream for twenty miles, to the fishery at a short distance below its junction with the south branch. Both these forks appear to come from or enter a mountainous country. The Tommanamah itself, they said, was about one hundred and fifty yards wide; its banks, for the most part, formed of solid perpendicular rocks, rising to a great height, and as they passed along some of its hills, they found that the snow had not yet disappeared, and the grass was just springing up. During its whole course it presented one continued rapid, till at the fishery itself, where the river widens to the space of two hundred yards, the rapid is nearly as considerable as at the great rapids of the Columbia. Here the Indians have erected a large house of split timber, one hundred and fifty feet long, and thirty-five wide, with a flat roof; and at this season is much resorted to by the men, while the women are employed in collecting roots. After remaining a day, and purchasing some fish, they returned home.

Tuesday, 3. Finding that the salmon has not yet appeared along the shores, as the Indians assured us they would in a few days, and that all the salmon which they themselves use, are obtained from Lewis's river, we begin to lose our hopes of subsisting on them. We are too poor, and at too great a distance from Lewis's river, to purchase fish at that place, and it is not probable that the river will fall sufficiently to take them before we leave this place. Our Indian friends sent an express to-day over the mountains to Traveller's-rest, in order to procure intelligence from the Ootlashoots, a band of Flatheads who have wintered on the east side of the mountains, and the same band which we first met on that river. As the route was deemed practicable for this express, we also proposed setting out, but the Indians dissuaded us from attempting it, as many of the creeks, they said, were still too deep to be forded; the roads very deep and slippery, and no grass as yet for our horses; but in twelve or fourteen days we shall no longer meet with the same obstacles: we therefore determined to set out in a few days for the Quamash flats, in order to lay in a store of provisions, so as to cross the mountains about the middle of the month.

For the two following days we continued hunting in our own neighbourhood, and by means of our own exertions, and trading with the Indians for trifling articles, succeeded in procuring as much bread and roots, besides other food as will enable us to subsist during the passage of the mountains. The old chief in the meantime gradually recovered the use of his limbs, and our own man was nearly restored to his former health. The Indians who had been with us, now returned, and invited us to their village on the following day,

Friday, June 6, to give us their final answer to a number of proposals which we had made to them. Neeshnepahkeeook then informed us, that they could not accompany us, as we wished, to the Missouri; but that in the latter end of the summer they meant to cross the mountain and spend the winter to the eastward. We had also requested some of their young men to go with us, so as to effect a reconciliation between them and the Pahkees, in case we should meet these last. He answered, that some of their young men would go with us, but they were not selected for that purpose, nor could they be until a general meeting of the whole nation, who were to meet in the plain on Lewis's river, at the head of Commearp. This meeting would take place in ten or twelve days, and if we set out before that time, the young men should follow us. We therefore depend but little on their assistance as guides, but hope to engage for that purpose, some of the Ootlashoots near Traveller's-rest creek. Soon after this communication, which was followed by a present of dried quamash, we were visited by Hohastilpilp and several others, among whom were the two young chiefs who had given us horses some time ago.

CHAPTER XXX.

The party mingle in the diversions of the Willetpos Indians, a tribe hitherto unnoticed—their joy on the prospect of a return—description of the vegetables growing on the Rocky mountains—various preparations made to resume their journey—the party set out, and arrive at Hungry creek—the serious and desponding difficulties that obstructed their progress—they are compelled to return, and to wait for a guide across the mountains—their distress for want of provisions—they resolve to return to the Quamash flats they are at last so fortunate as to procure Indian guides, with whom they resume their journey to the falls of the Missouri—the danger of the route described—their scarcity of provisions, and the danger of their journey, their course lying along the ridges of the mountains—description of the warm springs, where the party encamp—the fondness of the Indians for bathing in them.

SATURDAY, June 7, 1806. The two young chiefs returned after breakfast to their village on Commearp creek, accompanied by several of our men, who were sent to purchase ropes and bags for packing, in exchange for some parts of an old seine, bullets, old files, and pieces of iron. In the evening they returned with a few strings but no bags. Hohastilpilp crossed the river in the course of the day, and brought with him a horse, which he gave one of our men who had previously made him a present of a pair of Canadian shoes or shoepacks. We were all occupied in preparing packs and saddles for our journey; and as we intend to visit the Quamash flats on the tenth, in order to lay in a store of provisions for the journey over the mountains, we do not suffer the men to disturb the game in that neighbourhood.

Sunday, 8. The Cutnose visited us this morning with ten or twelve warriors: among these were two belonging to a band of Chopunnish, which we had not yet seen, who call themselves Willetpos, and reside on the south side of Lewis's river. One of them gave a good horse, which he rode, in exchange for one of ours, which was unable to cross the mountain, on receiving a tomahawk in addition. We were also fortunate in exchanging two other horses of inferior value for others much better, without giving any thing else to the purchaser. After these important purchases, several foot races were run between our men and the Indians: the latter, who are very active, and fond of these races, proved themselves very expert, and one of them was as fleet as our swiftest runners. After the races were over, the men divided themselves into two parties and played prison bass, an exercise which we are desirous of encouraging, before we begin the passage over the mountains, as several of them are becoming lazy from inaction. At night these games were concluded by a dance. One of the Indians informed us that we could not pass the mountains before the next full moon, or about the first of July; because, if we attempted it before that time, the horses would be forced to travel without food three days on the top of the mountains. This intelligence was disagreeable, as it excited a doubt as to the most proper time for passing the mountains; but having no time to lose, we are determined to risk the hazards, and start as soon as the Indians generally consider it practicable, which is about the middle of this month.

Monday, 9. Our success yesterday encouraged us to attempt to exchange some more of our horses, whose backs were unsound, but we could dispose of one only. Hohastilpilp, who visited us yesterday, left us with several Indians, for the plains near Lewis's river, where the whole nation are about to assemble. The Brokenarm too, with all his people, stopped on their way to the general rendezvous, at the same place. The Cutnose, or Neeshnepahkeeook, borrowed a horse, and rode down a few miles after some young eagles. He soon returned with two of the gray kind, nearly grown, which he meant to raise for the sake of the feathers. The young chief, who some time since made us a present of two horses, came with a party of his people and passed the night with us. The river, which is about one hundred and fifty yards wide, has been discharging vast bodies of water, but notwithstanding its depth, the water has been nearly transparent, and its temperature quite as cold as our best springs. For several days, however, the river has been falling, and is now six feet lower than it has been, a strong proof that the great body of snow has left the mountains. It is, indeed, nearly at the same height as when we arrived here; a circumstance which the Indians consider as indicating the time when the mountains may be crossed. We shall wait, however, a few days, because the roads must still be wet and slippery, and the grass on the mountains will be improved in a short time. The men are in high spirits at the prospect of setting out, and amused themselves during the afternoon with different games.

Tuesday, 10. After collecting our horses, which took much time, we set out at eleven o'clock for the Quamash flats. Our stock is now very abundant, each man being well mounted, with a small load on a second horse, and several supernumerary ones, in case of accident or want of food. We ascended the river hills, which are very high, and three miles in extent; our course being north 22° east, and then turned to north 15° west, for two miles till we reached Collins's creek. It is deep and difficult to cross, but we passed without any injury, except wetting some of our provisions, and then proceeded due north for five miles to the eastern edge of the Quamash flats near where we first met the Chopunnish in the autumn. We encamped on the bank of a small stream, in a point of woods, bordering the extensive level and beautiful prairie which is intersected by several rivulets, and as the quamash is now in blossom, presents a perfect resemblance of lakes of clear water.

A party of Chopunnish, who had overtaken us a few miles above, halted for the night with us, and mentioned that they too had come down to hunt in the flats, though we fear they expect that we will provide for them during their stay.

The country through which we passed is generally free from stone, extremely fertile, and supplied with timber, consisting of several species of fir, long-leafed pine and larch. The undergrowth is chokecherry, near the water courses, and scattered through the country, black alder, a large species of red root now in bloom, a plant resembling the pawpaw in its leaf, and bearing a berry with five valves of a deep purple colour. There were also two species of sumach, the purple haw, seven bark, serviceberry, gooseberry, the honeysuckle, bearing a white berry, and a species of dwarf pine, ten or twelve feet high, which might be confounded with the young pine of the long-leafed species, except that the former bears a cone of a globular form, with small scales, and that its leaves are in fascicles of two resembling in length and appearance the common pitch pine. We also observed two species of wild rose, both quinquepetalous, both of a damask red colour, and similar in the stem; but one of them is as large as the common red rose of our gardens; its leaf too is somewhat larger than that of the other species of wild rose, and the apex, as we saw them last year, were more than three times the size of the common wild rose.

We saw many sandhill cranes, and some ducks in the marshes near our camp, and a greater number of burrowing squirrels, some of which we killed, and found them as tender and well flavoured as our gray squirrels.

Wednesday, 11. All our hunters set out by daylight; but on their return to dinner, had killed nothing except a black bear and two deer. Five of the Indians also began to hunt, but they were quite unsuccessful, and in the afternoon returned to their village. Finding that the game had become shy and scarce, the hunters set out after dinner with orders to stay out during the night, and hunt at a greater distance from the camp, in ground less frequented. But the next day they returned with nothing except two deer. They were therefore again sent out, and about noon the following day, seven of them came in with eight deer out of a number, as well as a bear, which they had wounded, but could not take. In the meantime we had sent two men forward about eight miles to a prairie on this side of Collins's creek, with orders to hunt till our arrival. Two other hunters returned towards night, but they had killed only one deer, which they had hung up in the morning, and it had been devoured by the buzzards. An Indian who had spent the last evening with us, exchanged a horse for one of ours, which being sick, we gave a small axe and a knife in addition. He seemed very much pleased, and set out immediately to his village, lest we should change our minds and give up the bargain, which is perfectly allowable in Indian traffic. The hunters resumed the chase in the morning, but the game is now so scarce that they killed only one deer. We therefore cut up and dried all the meat we had collected, packed up all our baggage, and hobbled our horses to be in readiness to set out. But in the morning,

Sunday, 15, they had straggled to such a distance, that we could not collect them without great difficulty, and as it rained very hard, we waited till it should abate. It soon, however, showed every appearance of a settled rain, and we therefore set out at ten o'clock. We crossed the prairie at the distance of eight miles, where we had sent our hunters, and found two deer which they had hung up for us. Two and a half miles farther, we overtook the two men at Collins's creek. They had killed a third deer, and had seen one large and another white bear. After dining we proceeded up the creek about half a mile, then crossing through a high broken country for about ten miles, reached an eastern branch of the same creek, near which we encamped in the bottom, after a ride of twenty-two miles. The rains during the day made the roads very slippery, and joined to the quantity of fallen timber, rendered our progress slow and laborious to the horses, many of which fell through without suffering any injury. The country through which we passed has a thick growth of long-leafed pine, with some pitch pine, larch, white-pine, white cedar or arborvitæ of large size, and a variety of firs. The undergrowth consists chiefly of reed root, from six to ten feet in height, with the other species already enumerated. The soil is in general good, and has somewhat of a red cast, like those near the southwest mountain in Virginia. We saw in the course of our ride the speckled woodpecker, the logcock or large woodpecker, the bee-martin, and found the nest of a humming bird, which had just began to lay its eggs.

Monday, 16. We readily collected our horses, and having taken breakfast, proceeded at six o'clock up the creek, through handsome meadows of fine grass, and a great abundance of quamash. At the distance of two miles we crossed the creek, and ascended a ridge in a direction towards the northeast. Fallen timber still obstructed our way so much, that it was eleven o'clock before we had made seven miles, to a small branch of Hungry creek. In the hollows and on the north side of the hills large quantities of snow still remain, in some places to the depth of two or three feet. Vegetation too is proportionally retarded, the dog-tooth violet being just in bloom, and the honeysuckle, huckleberry, and a small species of white maple, beginning to put forth their leaves. These appearances in a part of the country comparatively low, are ill omens of the practicability of passing the mountains. But being determined to proceed, we halted merely to take a hasty meal, while the horses were grazing, and then resumed our march. The route was through thick woods and over high hills, intersected by deep ravines and obstructed by fallen timber. We found much difficulty also in following the road, the greater part of it being now covered with snow, which lies in great masses eight or ten feet deep, and would be impassable were it not so firm as to bear our horses. Early in the evening we reached Hungry creek, at the place where captain Clarke had left a horse for us as we passed in September, and finding a small glade with some grass, though not enough for our horses, we thought it better to halt for the night, lest by going further we should find nothing for the horses to eat. Hungry creek is small at this place, but is deep, and discharges a torrent of water, perfectly transparent, and cold as ice. During the fifteen miles of our route to-day, the principal timber was the pitch pine, white-pine, larch, and fir. The long-leafed pine extends but a small distance on this side of Collins's creek, and the white-cedar does not reach beyond the branch of Hungry creek on which we dined. In the early part of the day we saw the columbine, the blue-bell, and the yellow flowering pea in bloom. There is also in these mountains a great quantity of angelica, stronger to the taste, and more highly scented than that common in the United States. The smell is very pleasant, and the natives, after drying and cutting them into small pieces, wear them in strings around their necks.

Friday 17. We find lately that the air is pleasant in the course of the day, but notwithstanding the shortness of the night, becomes very cold before morning. At an early hour we collected our horses, and proceeded down the creek, which we crossed twice with much difficulty and danger, in consequence of its depth and rapidity. We avoided two other crossings of the same kind, by crossing over a steep and rocky hill. At the distance of seven miles, the road begins the ascent of the main ridges which divide the waters of the Chopunnish and Kooskooskee rivers. We followed it up a mountain for about three miles, when we found ourselves enveloped in snow, from twelve to fifteen feet in depth, even on the south side of the mountain, with the fullest exposure to the sun. The winter now presented itself in all its rigours, the air was keen and cold, no vestige of vegetation was to be seen, and our hands and feet were benumbed. We halted at the sight of this new difficulty. We already knew, that to wait till the snows of the mountains had dissolved, so as to enable us to distinguish the road, would defeat our design of returning to the United States this season. We now found also that as the snow bore our horses very well, travelling was infinitely easier than it was last fall, when the rocks and fallen timber had so much obstructed our march. But it would require five days to reach the fish-weirs at the mouth of Colt creek, even if we were able to follow the proper ridges of the mountains; and the danger of missing our direction is exceedingly great, while every track is covered with snow. During these five days too we have no chance of finding either grass or underwood for our horses, the snow being so deep. To proceed, therefore, under such circumstances, would be to hazard our being bewildered in the mountains, to insure the loss of our horses, and should we even be so fortunate as to escape with our lives, we might be obliged to abandon all our papers and collections. It was therefore decided not to venture any further; to deposit here all the baggage and provisions, for which we had no immediate use, and reserving only subsistence for a few days, return while our horses were yet strong, to some spot where we might live by hunting, till a guide could be procured to conduct us across the mountains. Our baggage was placed on scaffolds and carefully covered, as were also the instruments and papers, which we thought it safer to leave than to risk them over the roads and creeks by which we came. Having completed this operation, we set out at one o'clock, and treading back our steps, reached Hungry creek, which we ascended for two miles, and finding some scanty grass, we encamped. The rain fell during the greater part of the evening, and as this was the first time that we have ever been compelled to make any retrograde movement, we feared that it might depress the spirits of the men; but though somewhat dejected at the circumstance, the obvious necessity precluded all repining. During the night our horses straggled in search of food to a considerable distance among the thick timber on the hill sides, nor could we collect them till nine o'clock the next morning,

Wednesday, 18. Two of them were however still missing, and we therefore directed two of the party to remain and hunt for them. At the same time, we despatched Drewyer and Shannon to the Chopunnish, in the plains beyond the Kooskooskee, in order to hasten the arrival of the Indians who had promised to accompany us; or at any rate, to procure a guide to conduct us to Traveller's-rest. For this purpose they took a rifle, as a reward to any one who would engage to conduct us, with directions to increase the reward, if necessary, by an offer of two other guns, to be given immediately, and ten horses, at the falls of the Missouri; we then resumed our route. In crossing Hungry creek, one of the horses fell, and rolling over with the rider, was driven for a considerable distance among the rocks; but he fortunately escaped without losing his gun or suffering any injury. Another of the men was cut very badly, in a vein in the inner side of the leg, and we had great difficulty in stopping the blood. About one o'clock we halted for dinner at the glade, on a branch of Hungry creek, where we had dined on the 16th. Observing much track of deer, we left two men at this place to hunt, and then proceeded to Collins's creek, where we encamped in a pleasant situation, at the upper end of the meadows two miles above our encampment of the 15th inst. The hunters were immediately sent out, but they returned without having killed any thing, though they saw some few tracks of deer, very great appearance of bear, and what is of more importance, a number of what they thought were salmon-trout, in the creek. We therefore hope, by means of these fish and other game to subsist at this place without returning to the Quamash flats, which we are unwilling to do, since there are in these meadows great abundance of good food for our horses.

Thursday, 19. The hunters renewed the chase at a very early hour, but they brought only a single fish at noon. The fishermen were more unsuccessful, for they caught no fish, and broke their two Indian gigs. We, however, mended them with a sharp piece of iron, and towards evening they took a single fish, but instead of finding it the salmon of this spring's arrival, which would of course have been fine, it proved to be a salmon trout of the red kind, which remain all winter in the upper parts of the rivers and creeks, and are generally poor at this season. In the afternoon, the two men who were left behind, in search of the horses, returned without being able to find them, and the other two hunters arrived from Hungry creek with a couple of deer. Several large morels were brought in to-day, and eaten, as we were now obliged to use them without either salt, pepper or grease, and seemed a very tasteless insipid food. Our stock of salt is now wholly exhausted, except two quarts, which we left on the mountain. The musquitoes have become very troublesome since we arrived here, particularly in the evening.

Friday, 20. The scantiness of our subsistence was now such that we were determined to make one effort to ascertain if it be possible to remain here. The hunters therefore set out very early. On their return in the evening, they brought one deer, and a brown bear of the species called by the Chopunnish yahhar, the talons of which were remarkably short, broad at the base, and sharply pointed. It was in bad order, and the flesh of bear in this situation is much inferior to lean venison or elk. We also caught seven trout. But the hunters now reported that game was so scarce, and so difficult to be approached, in consequence of thick underbrush and fallen timber, that with their utmost exertions, they could not procure us subsistence for more than one or two days longer. We determined, therefore, to set out in the morning for the Quamash flats, where we should hear sooner from the Chopunnish on the subject of our guide, and also renew our stock of food, which is now nearly exhausted. Determined, as we now are, to reach the United States, if possible, this winter, it would be destructive to wait till the snows have melted from the road. The snows have formed a hard coarse bed without crust, on which the horses walk safely without slipping; the chief difficulty, therefore, is to find the road. In this we may be assisted by the circumstance, that, although, generally ten feet in depth, the snow has been thrown off by the thick and spreading branches of the trees, and from round the trunk: the warmth of the trunk itself, acquired by the reflexion of the sun, or communicated by natural heat of the earth, which is never frozen under these masses, has dissolved the snow so much, that immediately at the roots, its depth is not more than one or two feet. We therefore hope, that the marks of the baggage rubbing against the trees, may still be perceived, and we have decided, in case the guide cannot be procured, that one of us will take three or four of our most expert woodsmen, and with several of our best horses, and an ample supply of provisions, go on two days' journey in advance, and, endeavour to trace the route by the marks of the Indian baggage on the trees, which they would then mark more distinctly, with a tomahawk. When they should have reached two days' journey beyond Hungry creek, two of the men were to be sent back, to apprise the rest of their success, and if necessary, cause them to delay there, lest, by advancing too soon, they should be forced to halt where no food could be obtained for the horses. If the trace of the baggage is too indistinct, the whole party is to return to Hungry creek, and we will then attempt the passage by ascending the main southwest branch of Lewis's river through the country of the Shoshonees, over to Madison or Gallatin rivers. On that route, the Chopunnish inform us, there is a passage not obstructed by snow at this period of the year. That there is such a passage, we learnt from the Shoshonees, whom we first met on the east fork of Lewis's river; but they also represented it as much more difficult than that by which we came, being obstructed by high steep rugged mountains, followed by an extensive plain, without either wood or game. We are, indeed, inclined to prefer the account of the Shoshonees, because they would have certainly recommended that route had it been better than the one we have taken; and because there is a war between the Chopunnish and the Shoshonees, who live on that route, the former are less able to give accurate information of the state of the country. This route too, is so circuitous, that it would require a month to perform it, and we therefore consider it as the extreme resource. In hopes of soon procuring a guide to lead us over a more practicable route, we collected our horses at an early hour in the morning,

Saturday, 21, and proceeded towards the flats. The mortification of being obliged to tread back our steps, rendered still more tedious a route always so obstructed by brush and fallen timber, that it could not be passed without difficulty and even danger to our horses. One of these poor creatures wounded himself so badly in jumping over fallen logs that he was rendered unfit for use, and sickness has deprived us of the service of a second. At the pass of Collins's creek we met two Indians, who returned with us about half a mile, to the spot where we had formerly slept in September, and where we now halted to dine and let our horses graze. These Indians had four supernumerary horses, and were on their way to cross the mountains. They had seen Drewyer and Shannon, who they said would not return for two days. We pressed them to remain with us till that time, in order to conduct us over the mountains, to which they consented, and deposited their stores of roots and bread in the bushes at a little distance. After dinner we left three men to hunt till our return, and then proceeded; but we had not gone further than two miles when the Indians halted in a small prairie, where they promised to remain at least two nights, if we did not overtake them sooner. We left them, and about seven in the evening found ourselves at the old encampment on the flats; and were glad to find that four hunters whom we had sent ahead, had killed a deer for supper.

Sunday, 22. At daylight all the hunters set out, and having chased through the whole country, were much more successful than we even hoped, for they brought in eight deer and three bear. Hearing too that the salmon was now abundant in the Kooskooskee, we despatched a man to our old encampment above Collins's creek, for the purpose of purchasing some with a few beads, which were found accidentally in one of our waistcoat pockets. He did not return in the evening, nor had we heard from Drewyer and Shannon, who we begin to fear have had much difficulty in engaging a guide, and we were equally apprehensive that the two Indians might set out to-morrow for the mountains. Early in the morning,

Monday, 23, therefore, we despatched two hunters to prevail on them, if possible, to remain a day or two longer, and if they persisted in going on, they were to accompany them with the three men at Collins's creek, and mark the route, as far as Traveller's rest, where they were to remain till we joined them by pursuing the same road.

Our fears for the safety of Drewyer, Shannon, and Whitehouse, were fortunately relieved by their return in the afternoon. The former brought three Indians, who promised to go with us to the falls of the Missouri, for the compensation of two guns. One of them is the brother of the Cutnose, and the other two had each given us a horse, at the house of the Brokenarm, and as they are men of good character, and respected in the nation, we have the best prospect of being well served. We therefore secured our horses near the camp, and at an early hour next morning,

Tuesday 24, set out on a second attempt to cross the mountains. On reaching Collins's creek, we found only one of our men, who informed us that a short time before he arrived there yesterday, the two Indians, tired of waiting, had set out, and the other four of our men had accompanied them as they were directed. After halting, we went on to Fish creek, the branch of Hungry creek, where we had slept on the nineteenth instant. Here we overtook two of the party who had gone on with the Indians, and had now been fortunate enough to persuade them to wait for us. During their stay at Collins's creek, they had killed a single deer only, and of this they had been very liberal to the Indians, whom they were prevailing upon to remain, so that they were without provisions, and two of them had set out for another branch of Hungry creek, where we shall meet them to-morrow.

In the evening the Indians, in order as they said to bring

fair weather for our journey, set fire to the woods. As these consist chiefly of tall fir trees, with very numerous dried branches, the blaze was almost instantaneous, and as the flame mounted to the tops of the highest trees, resembled a splendid display of fire-works. In the morning,

Wednesday, 25, one of our guides complained of being sick, a symptom by no means pleasant, for sickness is generally with an Indian the pretext for abandoning an enterprise which he dislikes. He promised, however, to overtake us, and we therefore left him with his two companions, and set out at an early hour. At eleven o'clock we halted for dinner at the branch of Hungry creek, where we found our two men, who had killed nothing. Here too we were joined, rather unexpectedly by our guides, who now appeared disposed to be faithful to their engagements. The Indian was indeed really sick, and having no other covering except a pair of moccasins and an elk skin dressed without the hair, we supplied him with a buffaloe robe. In the evening we arrived at Hungry creek, and halted for the night about a mile and a half below our encampment of the sixteenth.

Thursday, 26. Having collected our horses, and taken breakfast, we set out at six o'clock, and pursuing our former route, at length began to ascend, for the second time, the ridge of mountains. Near the snowy region we killed two of the small black pheasants, and one of the speckled pheasant. These birds generally inhabit the higher parts of the mountains, where they feed on the leaves of pines and firs; but both of them seem solitary and silent birds, for we have never heard either of them make a noise in any situation, and the Indians inform us that they do not in flying drum or produce a whirring sound with their wings. On reaching the top of the mountain, we found our deposit perfectly untouched. The snow in the neighbourhood has melted nearly four feet since the seventeenth. By measuring it accurately, and comparing it by a mark which we then made, the general depth we discover to have been ten feet ten inches, though in some places still greater; but at this time it is about seven feet. It required two hours to arrange our baggage and to prepare a hasty meal, after which the guides urged us to set off, as we had a long ride to make before reaching a spot where there was grass for our horses. We mounted, and following their steps, sometimes crossed abruptly steep hills, and then wound along their sides, near tremendous precipices, where, had our horses slipped, we should have been lost irrecoverably. Our route lay on the ridgy mountains which separate the waters of the Kooskooskee and Chopunnish, and above the heads of all the streams, so that we met no running water. The whole country was completely covered with snow, except that occasionally we saw a few square feet of earth, at the roots of some trees, round which the snow had dissolved. We passed our camp of September 18, and late in the evening reached the deserted spot, and encamped near a good spring of water. It was on the steep side of a mountain, with no wood and a fair southern aspect, from which the snow seems to have melted for about ten days, and given place to an abundant growth of young grass, resembling the green sward. There is also another species of grass, not unlike a flag, with a broad succulent leaf which is confined to the upper parts of the highest mountains. It is a favourite food of the horses, but at present is either covered with snow, or just making its appearance. There is a third plant peculiar to the same regions, and is a species of whortleberry. There are also large quantities of a species of bear-grass, which, though it grows luxuriantly over all these mountains, and preserves its verdure during the whole winter, is never eaten by horses.

In the night there came to the camp a Chopunnish, who had pursued us with a view of accompanying us to the falls of the Missouri. We now learnt that the two young Indians whom we had met on the twenty-first, and detained several days, were going merely on a party of pleasure to the Ootlashoots, or as they call them, Shallees, a band of Tushepahs, who live on Clarke's river, near Traveller's-rest. Early the next morning,

Friday, 27, we resumed our route over the heights and steep hills of the same great ridge. At eight miles distance we reached an eminence where the Indians have raised a conic mound of stone, six or eight feet high, on which is fixed a pole made of pine, about fifteen feet. Here we halted and smoked for some time at the request of the Indians, who told us, that in passing the mountains with their families, some men are usually sent on foot from this place to fish at the entrance of Colt creek, whence they rejoin the main party at the Quamash glade on the head of the Kooskooskee. From this elevated spot we have a commanding view of the surrounding mountains, which so completely inclose us, that although we have once passed them, we almost despair of ever escaping from them without the assistance of the Indians. The marks on the trees, which had been our chief dependence, are much fewer and more difficult to be distinguished than we had supposed; but our guides traverse this trackless region with a kind of instinctive sagacity; they never hesitate, they are never embarrassed; yet so undeviating is their step, that wherever the snow has disappeared, for even a hundred paces, we find the summer road. With their aid the snow is scarcely a disadvantage, for although we are often obliged to slip down, yet the fallen timber and the rocks, which are now covered, were much more troublesome when we passed in the autumn. The travelling road is indeed comparatively pleasant, as well as more rapid, the snow being hard and coarse, without a crust, and perfectly hard enough to prevent the horses sinking more than two or three inches. After the sun has been on it for some hours it becomes softer than early in the morning, yet they are almost always able to get a sure foothold. After some time we resumed our route, and at the distance of three miles descended a steep mountain, then crossing two branches of the Chopunnish river, just above their forks, began to mount a second ridge. Along this we proceeded for some time, and then, at the distance of seven miles, reached our camp of the sixteenth of September. Near this place we crossed three small branches of the Chopunnish, and then ascended a second dividing ridge, along which we continued for nine miles, when the ridge became somewhat lower, and we halted for the night on a position similar to that of our encampment last evening. We had now travelled twenty-eight miles without taking the loads from our horses or giving them any thing to eat, and as the snow where we halted has not much dissolved, there was still but little grass. Among the vegetation we observed great quantities of the white lily, with reflected petals, which are now in bloom, and in the same forwardness as they were in the plains on the tenth of May. As for ourselves, the whole stock of meat being gone, we distributed to each mess a pint of bear's oil, which, with boiled roots, made an agreeable dish. We saw several black-tailed or mule-deer, but could not get a shot at them, and were informed that there is an abundance of elk in the valley, near the fishery, on the Kooskooskee. The Indians also assert that on the mountains to our right are large numbers of what they call white buffaloe or mountain sheep. Our horses strayed to some distance to look for food, and in the morning,

Saturday, 28, when they were brought up, exhibited rather a gaunt appearance. The Indians, however, promised that we should reach some good grass at noon, and we therefore set out after an early breakfast. Our route lay along the dividing ridge, and across a very deep hollow, till at the distance of six miles we passed our camp of the fifteenth of September. A mile and a half further we passed the road from the right, immediately on the dividing ridge, leading by the fishery. We went on as we had done during the former part of the route over deep snows, when having made thirteen miles we reached the side of a mountain, just above the fishery, which having no timber, and a southern exposure, the snow had disappeared, leaving an abundance of fine grass. Our horses were very hungry as well as fatigued, and as there was no other spot within our reach this evening, where we could find any food for them, we determined to encamp, though it was not yet midday. But as there was no water in the neighbourhood, we melted snow for cooking, and early in the morning,

Sunday, 29, continued along the ridge which we have been following for several days, till at the end of five miles it terminated; and now bidding adieu to the snows in which we have been imprisoned, we descended to the main branch of the Kooskooskee. On reaching the water side, we found a deer which had been left for us by two hunters who had been despatched at an early hour to the warm springs, and which proved a very seasonable addition to our food; for having neither meat nor oil, we were reduced to a diet of roots, without salt or any other addition. At this place, about a mile and a half from the spot where Quamash creek falls in from the northeast, the Kooskooskee is about thirty yards wide, and runs with great velocity over a bed, which, like those of all the mountain streams, is composed of pebbles. We forded the river, and ascended for two miles the steep acclivities of a mountain, and at its summit found coming in from the right the old road which we had passed on our route last autumn. It was now much plainer and more beaten, which the Indians told us was owing to the frequent visits of the Ootlashoots, from the valley of Clark's river to the fishery; though there was no appearance of their having been here this spring. Twelve miles from our camp we halted to graze our horses on the Quamash flats, on the creek of the same name. This is a handsome plain of fifty acres in extent, covered with an abundance of quamash, and seems to form a principal stage or encampment for the Indians in passing the mountains. We saw here several young pheasants, and killed one of the small black kind, which is the first we have observed below the region of snow. In the neighbourhood were also seen the tracks of two barefoot Indians, which our companions supposed to be Ootlashoots, who had fled in distress from the Pahkees. Here we discovered that two of the horses were missing. We therefore sent two men in quest of them, and then went on seven miles further to the warm springs, where we arrived early in the afternoon. The two hunters who had been sent forward in the morning had collected no game, nor were several others, who went out after our arrival, more successful. We therefore had a prospect of continuing our usual diet of roots, when late in the afternoon the men returned with the stray horses and a deer for supper.

These warm springs are situated at the foot of a hill, on the north side of Traveller's-rest creek, which is ten yards wide at this place. They issue from the bottoms, and through the interstices of a gray freestone rock, which rises in irregular masses round their lower side. The principal spring, which the Indians have formed into a bath by stopping the run with stone and pebbles, is about the same temperature as the warmest bath used at the hot springs in Virginia. On trying, captain Lewis could with difficulty remain in it nineteen minutes, and then was affected with a profuse perspiration. The two other springs are much hotter, the temperature being equal to that of the warmest of the hot springs in Virginia. Our men as well as the Indians amused themselves with going into the bath; the latter, according to their universal custom, going first into the hot bath, where they remain as long as they can bear the heat, then plunging into the creek, which is now of an icy coldness, and repeating this operation several times, but always ending with the warm bath.

CHAPTER XXXI.

The party proceed on their journey with their Indian guides, and at length agree to divide, to take several routes, and to meet again at the mouth of Yellowstown river—the route of captain Lewis is to pursue the most direct road to the falls of the Missouri, then to ascend Maria's river, explore the country, and then to descend that river to its mouth—captain Lewis, accordingly, with nine men proceed up the eastern branch of Clarke's river and take leave of their Indian guides—description of that branch and character of the surrounding country—description of the Cokalahishkit river—they arrive at the ridge dividing the Missouri from the Columbia rivers—meet once more with the buffaloe and brown bear—immense herds of buffalo discovered on the borders of Medicine river—the party encamp on White-bear islands—singular adventure that befel M'Neil—captain Lewis, with three of his party, proceed to explore the source of Maria's river—Tansy river described, he reaches the dividing line of these two streams—general character of the surrounding country.

MONDAY, 30. We despatched some hunters ahead, and were about setting out, when a deer came to lick at the springs; we killed it, and being now provided with meat for dinner, proceeded along the north side of the creek, sometimes in the bottoms, and over the steep sides of the ridge, till at the distance of thirteen miles, we halted at the entrance of a small stream where we had stopped on the 12th of September. Here we observed a road to the right, which the Indians inform us leads to a fine extensive valley on Clarke's river, where the Shalees or Ootlashoots occasionally reside. After permitting our horses to graze, we went on along a road much better than any we have seen since entering the mountains, so that before sunset we made nineteen miles, and reached our old encampment on the south side of the creek near its entrance into Clarke's river. In the course of the day we killed six deer, of which there are great numbers, as well as bighorn and elk, in this neighbourhood. We also obtained a small gray squirrel like that on the coast of the Pacific, except that its belly was white. Among the plants was a kind of lady's slipper, or moccasin flower, resembling that common in the United States, but with a white corolla, marked with longitudinal veins of a pale red colour on the inner side.

Tuesday, July 1. We had now made one hundred and fifty-six miles from the Quamash flats, to the mouth of Traveller's-rest creek. This being the point where we proposed to separate, it was resolved to remain a day or two in order to refresh ourselves, and the horses, which have bore the journey extremely well, and are still in fine order, but require some little rest. We had hoped to meet here some of the Ootlashoots, but no tracks of them can be discovered. Our Indian companions express much anxiety lest they should have been cut off by the Pahkees during the winter, and mention the tracks of the two barefooted persons as a proof how much the fugitives must have been distressed.

We now formed the following plan of operations. Captain Lewis with nine men, are to pursue the most direct route to the falls of the Missouri, where three of his party are to be left to prepare carriages for transporting the baggage and canoes across the portage. With the remaining six he will ascend Maria's river, to explore the country and ascertain whether any branch of it reaches as far north as the latitude of fifty degrees, after which he will descend that river to its mouth. The rest of the men will accompany captain Clarke to the head of Jefferson river, which serjeant Ordway and a party of nine men will descend with the canoes and other articles deposited there. Captain Clarke's party, which will then be reduced to ten, will proceed to the Yellowstone at its nearest approach to the three forks of the Missouri. There he will build canoes, and go down that river with seven of his party, and wait at its mouth till the rest of the party join him. Serjeant Pryor, with two others, will then take the horses by land to the Mandans. From that nation he is to go to the British posts on the Assiniboin with a letter to Mr. Henry, to procure his endeavours to prevail on some of the Sioux chiefs to accompany him to the city of Washington.

Having made these arrangements, this and the following day were employed in hunting and repairing our arms. We were successful in procuring a number of fine large deer, the flesh of which was exposed to dry. Among other animals in this neighbourhood, are the dove, black woodpecker, lark woodpecker, logcock, prairie lark; sandhill crane, prairie hen, with the short and pointed tail; the robin, a species of brown plover, a few curlews, small blackbirds, ravens, hawks, and a variety of sparrows, as well as the bee martin, and several species of corvus. The musquetoes too have been excessively troublesome since our arrival here. The Indians assert also, that there are great numbers of the white buffaloe or mountain sheep, on the snowy heights of the mountains, west of Clarke's river. They generally inhabit the rocky and most inaccessible parts of the mountains, but as they are not fleet, are easily killed by the hunters.

The plants which most abound in this valley are the wild rose, the honeysuckle, with a white berry, the sevenbark, serviceberry, the elder, aspen and alder, the chokecherry, and both the narrow and broad-leafed willow. The principal timber consists of long-leafed pine, which grows as well in the river bottoms as on the hills; the firs and larch are confined to the higher parts of the hills, while on the river itself, is a growth of cottonwood, with a wider leaf than that of the upper part of the Missouri, though narrower than that which grows lower down that river. There are also two species of clover in this valley; one with a very narrow small leaf, and a pale red flower; the other with a white flower, and nearly as luxuriant in its growth as our red clover.

The Indians who had accompanied us, intended leaving us in order to seek their friends, the Ootlashoots; but we prevailed on them to accompany captain Lewis a part of his route, so as to show him the shortest road to the Missouri, and in the meantime amused them with conversation and running races, both on foot and with horses, in both of which they proved themselves hardy, athletic and active. To the chief, captain Lewis gave a small medal and a gun, as a reward for having guided us across the mountains; in return, the customary civility of exchanging names passed between them, by which the former acquired the title of Yomekollick, or white bearskin unfolded. The Chopunnish who had overtaken us on the 26th, made us a present of an excellent horse, for the good advice we gave him, and as a proof of his attachment to the whites, as well as of his desire to be at peace with the Pahkees. The next morning,

Thursday July 3, all our preparations being completed, we saddled our horses, and the two parties who had been so long companions, now separated with an anxious hope of soon meeting, after each had accomplished the purpose of his destination.

The nine men and five Indians who accompanied captain Lewis, proceeded in a direction due north, down the west side of Clark's river. Half a mile from the camp we forded Traveller's-rest creek, and two and a half miles further, passed a western branch of the river; a mile beyond this, was a small creek on the eastern side, and a mile lower down, the entrance of the eastern branch of the river. This stream is from ninety to one hundred and twenty yards wide, and its water, which is discharged through two channels, is more turbid than that of the main river. The latter is one hundred and fifty yards in width, and waters an extensive level plain and prairie, which on its lower parts are ornamented with long-leafed pine, and cottonwood, while the tops of the hills are covered with pine, larch, and fir. We proceeded two miles further to a place where the Indians advised us to cross, but having no boats, and timber being scarce, four hours were spent in collecting timber to make three small rafts; on which, with some difficulty and danger, we passed the river. We then drove our horses into the water and they swam to the opposite shore, but the Indians crossed on horseback, drawing at the same time their baggage alongside of them in small basins of deer skins. The whole party being now reassembled, we continued for three miles, and encamped about sunset at a small creek. The Indians now showed us a road at no great distance, which they said would lead up the eastern branch of Clarke's river, and another river called Cokalahishkit, or the *river of the road to buffaloe,* thence to Medicine river and the falls of the Missouri. They added, that not far from the dividing ridge of the waters of Clarke's river and the Missouri, the roads forked, and though both led to the falls, the left hand route was the best. The route was so well beaten that we could no longer mistake it, and having now shown us the way, they were anxious to go on in quest of their friends, the Shahlees, besides which, they feared, by venturing further with us, to encounter the Pahkees, for we had this afternoon seen a fresh track of a horse, which they supposed to be a Shahlee scout. We could not insist on their remaining longer with us; but as they had so kindly conducted us across the mountains, we were desirous of giving them a supply of provisions, and therefore distributed to them half of three deer, and the hunters were ordered to go out early in the morning, in hopes of adding to the stock.

The horses suffer so dreadfully from the musquetoes, that we are obliged to kindle large fires and place the poor animals in the midst of the smoke. Fortunately, however, it became cold after dark, and the musquetoes disappeared.

Friday, July 4. The hunters accordingly set out, but returned unsuccessful about eleven o'clock. In the meantime we were joined by a young man of the Palloatpallah tribe, who had set out a few days after us, and had followed us alone across the mountains, the same who had attempted to pass the mountains in June, while we were on the Kooskooskee, but was obliged to return. We now smoked a farwell pipe with our estimable companions, who expressed every emotion of regret at parting with us, which they felt the more, because they did not conceal their fears of our being cut off by the Pahkees. We also gave them a shirt, a handkerchief, and a small quantity of ammunition. The meat which they received from us was dried and left at this place as a store during the homeward journey. This circumstance confirms our belief, that there is no route along Clarke's river to the Columbian plains, so near or so good as that by which we came; for, although these people mean to go for several days' journey down that river, to look for the Shalees, yet they intend returning home by the same pass of the mountain through which they conducted us. This route is also used by all the nations whom we know west of the mountains who are in the habit of visiting the plains of the Missouri; while on the other side all the war paths of the Pahkees, which fall into this valley of Clarke's river, concentre at Travellers'-rest, beyond which these people have never ventured to the west.

Having taken leave of the Indians, we mounted our horses, and proceeded up the eastern branch of Clarke's river through the level plain in which we were encamped. At the distance of five miles we had crossed a small creek fifteen yards wide, and now entered the mountains. The river is here closely confined within the hills for two miles, when the bottom widens into an extensive prairie, and the river is one hundred and ten yards in width. We went three miles further, over a high plain succeeded by a low and level prairie, to the entrance of the Cokalahishkit. This river empties itself from the northeast, is deep, rapid, and about sixty yards wide, with banks, which though not high, are sufficiently bold to prevent the water from overflowing. The eastern branch of Clarke's river is ninety yards wide above the junction, but below it spreads to one hundred. The waters of both are turbid, though the Cokalahishkit is the clearer of the two; the beds of both are composed of sand and gravel, but neither of them is navigable on account of the rapids and shoals which obstruct their currents. Before the junction of these streams, the country had been bare of trees, but as we turned up the north branch of the Cokalahishkit, we found a woody country, though the hills were high and the low grounds narrow and poor. At the distance of eight miles in a due east course, we encamped in a bottom, where there was an abundance of excellent grass. The evening proved fine and pleasant, and we were no longer annoyed by musquitoes. Our only game were two squirrels, one of the kind common to the Rocky mountains, the second a ground squirrel of a species we had not seen before. Near the place where we crossed Clarke's river, we saw at a distance, some wild horses, which are said, indeed, to be very numerous on this river as well as on the heads of the Yellowstone.

Saturday, July 5. Early in the morning we proceeded on for three and a half miles, in a direction north 75° east, then inclining to the south, crossed an extensive, beautiful, and well watered valley, nearly twelve miles in length, at the extremity of which we halted for dinner. Here we obtained a great quantity of quamash, and shot an antelope from a gang of females, who at this season herd together, apart from the bucks. After dinner we followed the course of the river eastwardly for six miles, to the mouth of a creek thirty-five yards wide, which we called Werner's creek. It comes in from the north, and waters a high extensive prairie, the hills near which are low, and supplied with the long-leafed pine, larch, and some fir. The road then led north 22° west, for four miles, soon after which it again turned north 73° east, for two and a half miles, over a handsome plain, watered by Werner's creek, to the river, which we followed on its eastern direction, through a high prairie, rendered very unequal by a vast number of little hillocks and sinkholes, and at three miles distance encamped near the entrance of a large creek, twenty yards wide, to which we gave the name of Seaman's creek. We had seen no Indians, although near the camp were the concealed fires of a war party, who had passed about two months ago.

Sunday, 6. At sunrise we continued our course eastward along the river. At seven miles distance we passed the north fork of the Cokalahishkit, a deep and rapid stream, forty-five yards in width, and like the main branch itself somewhat turbid, though the other streams of this country are clear. Seven miles further the river enters the mountains, and here end those extensive prairies on this side, though they widen in their course towards the southeast, and form an Indian route to Dearborn's river, and thence to the Missouri. From the multitude of knobs irregularly scattered through them, captain Lewis called this country the Prairie of the Knobs. They abound in game, as we saw goats, deer, great numbers of the burrowing squirrels, some curlews, bee martins, woodpeckers, plover, robins, doves, ravens, hawks, ducks, a variety of sparrows, and yesterday observed swans on Werner's creek. Among the plants we observed the southern wood, and two other species of shrubs, of which we preserved specimens.

On entering the high grounds we followed the course of the river through the narrow bottoms, thickly timbered with pine and cottonwood intermixed, and variegated with the boisrouge, which is now in bloom, the common small blue flag and pepper-grass; and at the distance of three and a half miles, reached the two forks of the river mentioned by the Indians. They are nearly equal in width, and the road itself here forks and follows each of them. We followed that which led us in a direction north 75° east, over a steep high hill, thence along a wide bottom to a thickly wooded side of a hill, where the low grounds are narrow, till we reached a large creek, eight miles from the forks and twenty-five from our last encampment. Here we halted for the night. In the course of the day the track of the Indians, whom we supposed to be the Pahkees, continued to grow fresher, and we passed a number of old lodges and encampments. At seven o'clock the next morning,

Monday, 7, we proceeded through a beautiful plain on the north side of the river, which seems here to abound in beaver. The low grounds possess much timber, and the hills are covered chiefly with pitch pine, that of the long-leafed kind having disappeared since we left the Prairie of the Knobs. At the distance of twelve miles we left the river or rather the creek, and having for four miles crossed, in a direction north 15° east, two ridges, again struck to the right, which we followed through a narrow bottom, covered with low willows and grass, and abundantly supplied with both deer and beaver. After seven miles we reached the foot of a ridge, which we ascended in a direction north 45° east, through a low gap of easy ascent from the westward, and on descending it were delighted at discovering that this was the dividing ridge between the waters of the Columbia and those of the Missouri. From this gap the Fort mountain is about twenty miles in a northeastern direction. We now wound through the hills and hollows of the mountains, passing several rivulets, which run to the right, and at the distance of nine miles from the gap encamped, after making thirty-two miles. We procured some beaver, and this morning saw some signs and tracks of buffaloe, from which it seems those animals do sometimes penetrate to a short distance within the mountains.

Tuesday, 8. At three miles from our camp we reached a stream, issuing from the mountains to the southwest, though it only contains water for a width of thirty feet, yet its bed is more than three times that width, and from the appearance of the roots and trees in the neighbouring bottom, must sometimes run with great violence; we called it Dearborn's river. Half a mile further we observed from a height the Shishequaw mountain, a high insulated mountain of a conic form, standing several miles in advance of the eastern range of the Rocky mountains, and now about eight miles from us, and immediately on our road, which was in a northwest direction. But as our object was to strike Medicine river, and hunt down to its mouth in order to procure skins for the food and gear necessary for the three men who were to be left at the falls, none of whom are hunters, we determined to leave the road, and therefore proceeded due north, through an open plain, till we reached Shishequaw creek, a stream about twenty yards wide, with a considerable quantity of timber in its low grounds. Here we halted and dined, and now felt, by the luxury of our food, that we were approaching once more the plains of the Missouri, so rich in game. We saw a great number of deer, goats, wolves, and some barking squirrels, and for the first time caught a distant prospect of two buffaloe. After dinner we followed the Shishequaw for six and a half miles, to its entrance into Medicine river, and along the banks of this river for eight miles, when we encamped on a large island. The bottoms continued low, level, and extensive; the plains too are level; but the soil of neither is fertile, as it consists of a light coloured earth, intermixed with a large proportion of gravel; the grass in both is generally about nine inches high. Captain Lewis here shot a large and remarkably white wolf. We had now made twenty-eight miles; and set out early the next morning,

Wednesday, 9; but the air soon became very cold, and it began to rain. We halted for a few minutes in some old Indian lodges, but finding that the rain continued we proceeded on, though we were all wet to the skin, and halted for dinner at the distance of eight miles. The rain, however, continued, and we determined to go no further. The river is about eighty yards wide, with banks which, though low, are seldom overflowed; the bed is composed of loose gravel and pebbles, the water clear and rapid, but not so much as to impede the navigation. The bottoms are handsome, wide, and level, and supplied with a considerable quantity of narrow-leafed cottonwood. During our short ride we killed two deer and a buffaloe, and saw a number of wolves and antelopes. The next morning early,

Thursday, 10, we set out, and continued through a country similar to that of yesterday, with bottoms of wide-leafed cottonwood occasionally along the borders, though for the most part the low grounds are without timber. In the plains are great quantities of two species of prickly pear, now in bloom. Gooseberries of the common red kind are in abundance and just beginning to ripen, but there are no currants. The river has now widened to an hundred yards; is deep, crowded with islands, and in many parts rapid. At the distance of seventeen miles, the timber disappears totally from the river bottoms. About this part of the river, the wind, which had blown on our backs, and constantly put the elk on their guard, shifted round, and we then shot three of them, and a brown bear. Captain Lewis halted to skin them, while two of the men took the pack-horses forward to seek for an encampment. It was nine o'clock before he overtook them, at the distance of seven miles in the first grove of cottonwood. They had been pursued as they came along by a very large bear, on which they were afraid to fire, lest their horses being unaccustomed to the gun, might take fright and throw them. This circumstance reminds us of the ferocity of these animals, when we were last near this place, and admonishes us to be very cautious. We saw vast numbers of buffaloe below us, which kept a dreadful bellowing during the night. With all our exertions we were unable to advance more than twenty-four miles, owing to the mire, through which we are obliged to travel, in consequence of the rain. The next morning, however,

Friday, 11, was fair, and enlivened by great numbers of birds, who sang delightfully in the clusters of cottonwood. The hunters were sent down Medicine river to hunt elk, while captain Lewis crossed the high plain, in a direction 75° east, to the Whitebear island, a distance of eight miles, where the hunters joined him. They had seen elk; but in this neighbourhood the buffaloe are in such numbers, that on a moderate computation, there could not have been fewer than ten thousand within a circuit of two miles. At this season, they are bellowing in every direction, so as to form an almost continued roar, which at first alarmed our horses, who being from the west of the mountains, are unused to the noise and appearance of these animals. Among the smaller game are the brown thrush, pidgeons, doves, and a beautiful bird called a buffaloe-pecker.

Immediately on our arrival we began to hunt, and by three in the afternoon had collected a stock of food and hides enough for our purpose. We then made two canoes, one in the form of a basin, like those used by the Mandans, the other consisting of two skins, in a form of our own invention. They were completed the next morning,

Saturday, 12; but the wind continued so high that it was not till towards night that we could cross the river in them, and make our horses swim. In the meantime, nearly the whole day was consumed in search after our horses, which had disappeared last night, and seven of which were not recovered at dark, while Drewyer was still in quest of them. The river is somewhat higher than it was last summer, the present season being much more moist than the preceding one, as may be seen in the greater luxuriance of the grass.

Sunday, 13. We formed our camp this morning at our old station, near the head of the Whitebear islands, and immediately went to work in making gear. On opening the cache, we found the bear skins entirely destroyed by the water, which, in a flood of the river, had penetrated to them. All the specimens of plants were unfortunately lost; the chart of the Missouri, however, still remained unhurt, and several articles contained in trunks and boxes had suffered but little injury; but a phial of laudanum had lost its stopper, and ran into a drawer of medicines, which it spoiled beyond recovery. The musquetoes have been so troublesome that it was impossible even to write without the assistance of a musquetoe bier. The buffaloe are leaving us fast on their way to the southeast.

Monday, 14. We continued making preparations for transporting our articles, and as the old deposit was too damp, we secured the trunks on a high scaffold, covered with skins, among the thick brush on a large island: a precaution against any visit from the Indians, should they arrive before the main party arrives here. The carriage wheels were in good order, and the iron frame of the boat had not suffered materially. The buffaloe have now nearly disappeared, leaving behind them a number of large wolves who are now prowling about us.

Tuesday, 15. To our great joy Drewyer returned to-day from a long search after the horses; for we had concluded, from his long stay, that he had probably met with a bear, and with his usual intrepidity attacked the animal, in which case, if by any accident he should be separated from his horse, his death would be almost inevitable. Under this impression, we resolved to set out to-morrow in quest of him, when his return relieved us from our apprehensions. He had searched for two days before he discovered that the horses had crossed Dearborn's river, near a spot where was an Indian encampment, which seemed to have been abandoned about the time the horses were stolen, and which was so closely concealed that no trace of a horse could be seen within the distance of a quarter of a mile. He crossed the river and pursued the track of these Indians westward, till his horse became so much fatigued that he despaired of overtaking them, and then returned. These Indians we suppose to be a party of Tushepaws, who have ventured out of the mountains to hunt buffaloe. During the day we were engaged in drying meat and dressing skins. At night M'Neal, who had been sent in the morning to examine the cache at the lower end of the portage, returned; but had been prevented from reaching that place by a singular adventure. Just as he arrived near Willow run, he approached a thicket of brush, in which was a white bear, which he did not discover till he was within ten feet of him: his horse started, and wheeling suddenly round, threw M'Neal almost immediately under the bear, who started up instantly, and finding the bear raising himself on his hind feet to attack him, struck him on the head with the butt end of his musket; the blow was so violent that it broke the breech of the musket and knocked the bear to the ground, and before he recovered, M'Neal seeing a willow tree close by, sprang up, and there remained while the bear closely guarded the foot of the tree until late in the afternoon. He then went off, and M'Neal being released came down, and having found his horse, which had strayed off to the distance of two miles, returned to camp. These animals are, indeed, of a most extraordinary ferocity, and it is matter of wonder, that in all our encounters we have had the good fortune to escape. We are now troubled with another enemy, not quite so dangerous, though even more disagreeable: these are the musquetoes, who now infest us in such myriads, that we frequently get them into our throats when breathing, and the dog even howls with the torture they occasion. Having now accomplished the object of our stay, captain Lewis determined to leave serjeant Gass with two men and four horses to assist the party who are expected to carry our effects over the portage, whilst he, with Drewyer, and the two Fields, with six horses, proceeded to the sources of Maria's river. Accordingly, early in the morning,

Wednesday 16, captain Lewis descended in a skin canoe to the lower side of Medicine river, where the horses had previously been sent, and then rode with his party to the fall of forty-seven feet, where he halted for two hours to dine, and took a sketch of the fall. In the afternoon they proceeded to the great falls, near which they slept under a shelving rock, with a happy exemption from musquetoes. These falls have lost much of their grandeur since we saw them, the river being much lower now than at that time, though they still form a most sublime spectacle. As we came along, we met several white bear, but they did not venture to attack us. There were but few buffaloe, however, the large having principally passed the river, directed their course downwards. There are, as usual, great numbers of goats and antelopes dispersed through the plains, and large flocks of geese, which raise their young about the entrance of Medicine river. We observe here also the cuckoo, or as it is sometimes called, the raincraw, a bird which is not known either within or west of the Rocky mountains.

Thursday, 17. After taking a second draught of the falls, captain Lewis directed his course N. 10° W. with an intention of striking Maria's river at the point to which he had ascended it in 1804. The country is here spread into wide and level plains, swelling like the ocean, in which the view is uninterrupted by a single tree or shrub, and is diversified only by the moving herds of buffaloe. The soil consists of a light-coloured earth, intermixed with a large proportion of coarse gravel without sand, and is by no means so fertile as either the plains of the Columbia, or those lower down the Missouri. When dry it cracks, and is hard and thirsty while in its wet state: it is as soft and slimy as soap. The grass is naturally short, and at this time is still more so from the recent passage of the buffaloe.

Among the birds which we met was the party-coloured plover, with the head and neck of a brick red, a bird which frequents the little ponds scattered over the plains. After travelling twenty miles we reached Tansy river, and as we could not go as far as Maria's river this evening, and perhaps not find either wood or water before we arrived there, we determined to encamp. As we approached the river, we saw the fresh track of a bleeding buffaloe, a circumstance by no means pleasant, as it indicated the Indians had been hunting, and were not far from us. The tribes who principally frequent this country, are the Minnetarees of Fort de Prairie, and the Blackfoot Indians, both of whom are vicious and profligate rovers, and we have therefore every thing to fear, not only from their stealing our horses, but even our arms and baggage, if they are sufficiently strong. In order therefore to avoid, if possible, an interview with them, we hurried across the river to a thick wood, and having turned out the horses to graze, Drewyer went in quest of the buffaloe to kill it, and ascertain whether the wound was given by the

Indians, while the rest reconnoitred the whole country. In about three hours they all returned without having seen the buffaloe or any Indians in the plains. We then dined, and two of the party resumed their search, but could see no signs of Indians, and we therefore slept in safety. Tansy river is here about fifty yards wide, though its water occupies only thirty-five feet, and is not more than three in depth. It most probably rises within the first range of the Rocky mountains, and its general course is from east to west, and as far as we are able to trace it through wide bottoms, well supplied with both the long and broad-leafed cottonwood. The hills on its banks, are from one hundred to one hundred and fifty feet in height, and possess bluffs of earth, like the lower part of the Missouri: the bed is formed of small gravel and mud; the water turbid, and of a whitish tint; the banks low, but never overflowed; in short, except in depth and velocity, it is a perfect miniature of the Missouri.

Friday, 18. A little before sunrise we continued on a course N. 25° W. for six miles, when we reached the top of a high plain, which divides the waters of Maria and Tansy rivers, and a mile further reached a creek of the former, about twenty-five yards wide, though with no water except in occasional pools in the bed. Down this creek we proceeded for twelve miles through thick groves of timber on its banks, passing such immense quantities of buffaloe, that the whole seemed to be a single herd. Accompanying them were great numbers of wolves, besides which we saw some antelopes and hares. After dinner we left the creek which we called Buffaloe creek, and crossing the plain for six miles, came to Maria's river and encamped in a grove of cottonwood, on its western side, keeping watch through the night lest we should be surprised by the Indians. Captain Lewis was now convinced that he was above the point to which he had formerly ascended, and fearing that some branch might come in on the north, between that point and our present position, he early in the morning,

Saturday, 19, despatched two hunters, who descended the river in a direction north 80° east, till they came to our former position, at the distance of six miles, without seeing any stream except Buffaloe creek. Having completed an observation of the sun's meridian altitude, captain Lewis proceeded along the north side of Maria's river. The bottoms are in general about half a mile wide, and possess considerable quantities of cottonwood timber, and an underbrush, consisting of honeysuckle, rose bushes, narrow-leafed willow, and the plant called by the engagees, buffaloe grease. The plains are level and beautiful, but the soil is thin and overrun with prickly pears. It consists of a sort of white or whitish-blue clay, which after being trodden, when wet, by the buffaloe, stands up in sharp hard points, which are as painful to the horses as the great quantity of small gravel, which is every where scattered over the ground, is in other parts of the plains. The bluffs of the river are high, steep, and irregular, and composed of a sort of earth which easily dissolves and slips into the water, though with occasional strata of freestone near the tops. The bluffs of the Missouri above Maria's river, differ from these, in consisting of a firm red or yellow clay, which does not yield to water, and a large proportion of rock. The buffaloe are not so abundant as they were yesterday; but there are still antelopes, wolves, geese, pidgeons, doves, hawks, ravens, crows, larks, and sparrows, though the curlew has disappeared. At the distance of eight miles a large creek falls in on the south side, and seven miles beyond it, another thirty yards wide, which seem to issue from three mountains, stretching from east to west, in a direction north 10° west from its mouth, and which, from their loose, irregular, and rugged appearance, we called the Broken mountains. That in the centre terminates in a conic spire, for which reason we called it the Tower mountain. After making twenty miles we halted for the night, and the next morning,

Sunday, 20, continued our route up the river, through a country resembling that which we passed yesterday, except that the plains are more broken, and the appearances of mineral salts, common to the Missouri plains, are more abundant than usual; these are discerned in all the pools, which indeed at present contain the only water to be found throughout the plains, and are so strongly impregnated as to be unfit for any use, except that of the buffaloe, who seem to prefer it to even the water of the river. The low grounds are well timbered, and contain also silk-grass, sand-rush, wild liquorice, and sunflowers, the barb of which are now in bloom. Besides the geese, ducks, and other birds common to the country, we have seen fewer buffaloe to-day than yesterday, though elk, wolves, and antelopes continue in equal numbers. There is also much appearance of beaver, though none of otter. At the distance of six miles we passed a creek from the south; eighteen miles further one from the north; four miles beyond which we encamped. The river is here one hundred and twenty yards wide, and its water is but little diminished as we ascend. Its general course is very straight. From the apparent descent of the country to the north and above the Broken mountains, it seems probable that the south branch of the Saskashawan receives some of its waters from these plains, and that one of its streams must, in descending from the Rocky mountains, pass not far from Maria's river, to the northeast of the Broken mountains. We slept in peace, without being annoyed by the musquetoes, whom we have not seen since we left the Whitebear islands.

CHAPTER XXXII.

Captain Lewis and his party still proceed on the route mentioned in the last chapter, and arrive at the forks of Maria's river; of which river a particular description is given—alarmed by the evidence that they are in the neighbourhood of unfriendly Indians, and much distressed for want of provisions, the weather proving unfavourable, they are compelled to return—the face of the country described—interview with the unfriendly Indians, called Minnetarees of Fort de Prairie—mutual consternation—resolution of captain Lewis—they encamp together for the night, apparently with amicable dispositions—the conversation that ensued between these new visitants—the conflict occasioned by the Indians attempting to seize the rifles and horses of the party, in which one is mortally wounded—captain Lewis kills another Indian, and his narrow escape—having taken four horses belonging to the Indians, they hastened with all expedition to join the party attached to captain Clarke—arriving near the Missouri they are alarmed by the sound of rifles, which proves fortunately to be from the party of their friends, under the command of serjeant Ordway—the two detachments thus fortunately united, leave their horses, and descend the Missouri in canoes—they continue their route down the river to form a junction with captain Clarke—vast quantities of game found in their passage down the river—captain Lewis accidentally wounded by one of his own party—they proceed down the Missouri, and at length join captain Clarke.

MONDAY, 21. At sunrise we proceeded along the northern side of the river for a short distance, when finding the ravines too steep, we crossed to the south; but after continuing for three miles, returned to the north and took our course through the plains, at some distance from the river. After making fifteen miles, we came to the forks of the river, the largest branch of which bears south 75° west to the mountains, while the course of the other is north 40° west. We halted for dinner, and believing, on examination, that the northern branch came from the mountains, and would probably lead us to the most northern extent of Maria's river, we proceeded along, though at a distance over the plains, till we struck it eight miles from the junction. The river is about thirty yards wide, the water clear, but shallow, rapid, and unfit for navigation. It is closely confined between cliffs of freestone, and the adjacent country broken and poor. We crossed to the south side, and proceeded for five miles, till we encamped under a cliff, where not seeing any timber, we made a fire of buffaloe dung, and passed the night. The next day,

Tuesday, 22, we went on; but as the ground was now steep and unequal, and the horses' feet very sore, we were obliged to proceed slowly. The river is still confined by freestone cliffs, till at the distance of seven miles the country opens, is less covered with gravel, and has some bottoms, though destitute of timber or underbrush. The river here makes a considerable bend to the northwest, so that we crossed the plains for eleven miles when we again crossed the river. Here we halted for dinner, and having no wood, made a fire of the dung of buffaloe, with which we cooked the last of our meat, except a piece of spoiled buffaloe. Our course then lay across a level beautiful plain, with wide bottoms near the bank of the river. The banks are about three or four feet high, but are not overflowed. After crossing for ten miles a bend of the river towards the south, we saw, for the first time during the day, a clump of cottonwood trees in an extensive bottom, and halted there for the night. This place is about ten miles below the foot of the Rocky mountains; and being now able to trace distinctly that the point at which the river issued from those mountains, was to the south of west, we concluded that we had reached its most northern point, and as we have ceased to hope that any branches of Maria's river extend as far north as the fiftieth degree of latitude, we deem it useless to proceed further, and rely chiefly on Milk and Whiteearth rivers for the desired boundary. We therefore determined to remain here two days, for the purpose of making the necessary observations, and resting our horses. The next morning,

Wednesday, 23, Drewyer was sent to examine the bearings of

the river, till its entrance into the mountains, which he found to be at the distance of ten miles, and in a direction south 50° west; he had seen also the remains of a camp of eleven leathern lodges, recently abandoned, which induced us to suppose that the Minnetarees of Fort de Prairie are somewhere in this neighbourhood; a suspicion which was confirmed by the return of the hunters, who had seen no game of any kind. As these Indians have probably followed the buffaloe towards the main branch of Maria's river, we shall not strike it above the north branch. The course of the mountains still continues from southeast to northwest; in which last direction from us, the front range appears to terminate abruptly at the distance of thirty-five miles. Those which are to the southwest, and more distinctly in view, are of an irregular form, composed chiefly of clay, with a very small mixture of rock, without timber, and although low are yet partially covered with snow to their bases. The river itself has nearly double the volume of water which it possessed when we first saw it below, a circumstance to be ascribed, no doubt, to the great evaporation and absorption of the water in its passage through these open plains. The rock in this neighbourhood is of a white colour, and a fine grit, and lies in horizontal strata in the bluffs of the river. We attempted to take some fish, but could procure only a single trout. We had, therefore, nothing to eat, except the grease which we pressed from our tainted meat, and formed a mush of cows, reserving one meal more of the same kind for to-morrow. We have seen near this place a number of the whistling squirrel, common in the country watered by the Columbia, but which we observed here for the first time in the plains of the Missouri. The cottonwood too, of this place, is similar to that of the Columbia. Our observations this evening were prevented by clouds. The weather was clear for a short time in the morning,

Thursday, 24, but the sky soon clouded over, and it rained during the rest of the day. We were therefore obliged to remain one day longer for the purpose of completing our observations. Our situation now became unpleasant from the rain, the coldness of the air, and the total absence of all game; for the hunters could find nothing of a large kind, and we were obliged to subsist on a few pigeons and a kettle of mush made of the remainder of our bread of cows. This supplied us with one more meal in the morning,

Friday, 25, when finding that the cold and rainy weather would still detain us here, two of the men were despatched to hunt. They returned in the evening with a fine buck, on which we fared sumptuously. In their excursion they had gone as far as the main branch of Maria's river, at the distance of ten miles, through an open extensive valley, in which were scattered a great number of lodges lately evacuated. The next morning,

Saturday, 26, the weather was still cloudy, so that no observation could be made, and what added to our disappointment, captain Lewis's chronometer stopped yesterday from some unknown cause, though when set in motion again it went as usual. We now despaired of taking the longitude of this place; and as our staying any longer might endanger our return to the United States during the present season, we, therefore, waited till nine o'clock, in hopes of a change of weather; but seeing no prospect of that kind, we mounted our horses, and leaving with reluctance our position, which we now named Camp Disappointment, directed our course across the open plains, in a direction nearly southeast. At twelve miles distance we reached a branch of Maria's river, about sixty-five yards wide, which we crossed, and continued along its southern side for two miles, where it is joined by another branch, nearly equal in size from the southwest, and far more clear than the north branch, which is turbid, though the beds of both are composed of pebbles. We now decided on pursuing this river to its junction with the fork of Maria's river, which we had ascended, and then cross the country obliquely to Tansy river, and descend that stream to its confluence with Maria's river. We, therefore, crossed and descended the river, and at one mile below the junction, halted to let the horses graze in a fertile bottom, in which were some Indian lodges, that appear to have been inhabited during the last winter. We here discern more timber than the country in general possesses;

for besides an undergrowth of rose, honeysuckle, and redberry bushes, and a small quantity of willow timber, the three species of cottonwood, the narrow-leafed, the broad-leafed, and the species known to the Columbia, though here seen for the first time on the Missouri, are all united at this place. Game too, appears in greater abundance. We saw a few antelopes and wolves, and killed a buck, besides which we saw also two of the small burrowing foxes of the plains, about the size of the common domestic cat, and of a reddish brown colour, except the tail, which is black.

At the distance of three miles, we ascended the hills close to the river side, while Drewyer pursued the valley of the river on the opposite side. But scarcely had captain Lewis reached the high plain, when he saw about a mile on his left, a collection of about thirty horses. He immediately halted, and by the aid of his spy-glass discovered that one half of the horses were saddled, and that on the eminence above the horses, several Indians were looking down towards the river, probably at Drewyer. This was a most unwelcome sight. Their probable numbers rendered any contest with them of doubtful issue; to attempt to escape would only invite pursuit, and our horses were so bad that we must certainly be overtaken; besides which, Drewyer could not yet be aware that the Indians were near, and if we ran he would most probably be sacrificed. We therefore determined to make the best of our situation, and advance towards them in a friendly manner. The flag which we had brought in case of any such accident was therefore displayed, and we continued slowly our march towards them. Their whole attention was so engaged by Drewyer, that they did not immediately discover us. As soon as they did see us, they appeared to be much alarmed and ran about in confusion, and some of them came down the hill and drove their horses within gunshot of the eminence, to which they then returned, as if to wait our arrival. When we came within a quarter of a mile, one of the Indians mounted and rode at full speed to receive us; but when within a hundred paces of us, he halted, and captain Lewis who had alighted to receive him, held out his hand, and beckoned to him to approach, he only looked at us for some time, and then, without saying a word, returned to his companions with as much haste as he had advanced. The whole party now descended the hill and rode towards us. As yet we saw only eight, but presumed that there must be more behind us, as there were several horses saddled. We however advanced, and captain Lewis now told his two men that he believed these were the Minnetarees of Fort de Prairie, who, from their infamous character, would in all probability attempt to rob them; but being determined to die, rather than lose his papers and instruments, he intended to resist to the last extremity, and advised them to do the same, and to be on the alert should there be any disposition to attack us. When the two parties came within a hundred yards of each other, all the Indians, except one, halted; captain Lewis therefore ordered his two men to halt while he advanced, and after shaking hands with the Indian, went on and did the same with the others in the rear, while the Indian himself shook hands with the two men. They all now came up, and after alighting, the Indians asked to smoke with us. Captain Lewis, who was very anxious for Drewyer's safety, told them that the man who had gone down the river had the pipe, and requested that as they had seen him, one of them would accompany R. Fields to bring him back. To this they assented, and Fields went with a young man in search of Drewyer. Captain Lewis now asked them by signs if they were the Minnetarees of the north, and was sorry to learn by their answer that his suspicion was too true. He then inquired if there was any chief among them. They pointed out three; but though he did not believe them, yet it was thought best to please them, and he therefore gave to one a flag, to another a medal, and to a third a handkerchief. They appeared to be well satisfied with these presents, and now recovered from the agitation into which our first interview had thrown them, for they were really more alarmed than ourselves at the meeting. In our turn, however, we became equally satisfied on finding that they were not joined by any more of their companions, for we consider ourselves quite a match for eight Indians, particularly as these have but two guns, the rest being armed with only eye-dogs and bows and arrows.

As it was growing late captain Lewis proposed that they should encamp together near the river; for he was glad to see them and had a great deal to say to them. They assented; and being soon joined by Drewyer, we proceeded towards the river, and after descending a very steep bluff, two hundred and fifty feet high, encamped in a small bottom. Here the Indians formed a large semicircular tent of dressed buffaloe skins, in which the two parties assembled, and by the means of Drewyer, the evening was spent in conversation with the Indians. They informed us that they were a part of a large band which at present lay encamped on the main branch of Maria's river, near the foot of the Rocky mountains, and at the distance of a day and a half's journey from this place. Another large band were hunting buffaloe near the Broken mountains, from which they would proceed in a few days to the north of Maria's river. With the first of these there was a white man. They added, that from this place to the establishment on the Saskashawan, at which they trade, is only six days' easy march; that is, such a day's journey as can be made with their women and children, so that we computed the distance at one hundred and fifty miles. There they carry the skins of wolves and some beavers, and exchange them for guns, ammunition, blankets, spirituous liquors, and the other articles of Indian traffic. Captain Lewis in turn informed them that he had come from a great distance up the large river which runs towards the rising sun; that he had been as far as the great lake where the sun sets; that he had seen many nations, the greater part of whom were at war with each other, but by his mediation were restored to peace; and all had been invited to come and trade with him west of the mountains: he was now on his way home, but had left his companions at the falls, and come in search of the Minnetarees, in hopes of inducing them to live at peace with their neighbours, and to visit the trading houses which would be formed at the entrance of Maria's river. They said that they were anxious of being at peace with the Tushepaws, but those people had lately killed a number of their relations, as they proved by showing several of the party who had their hair cut as a sign of mourning. They were equally willing, they added, to come down and trade with us, Captain Lewis therefore proposed that they should send some of their young men to invite all their band to meet us at the mouth of Maria's river, and the rest of the party to go with us to that place, where he hoped to find his men, offering them ten horses and some tobacco in case they would accompany us. To this they made no reply. Finding them very fond of the pipe, captain Lewis, who was desirous of keeping a constant watch during the night, smoked with them until a late hour, and as soon as they were all asleep, he woke R. Fields, and ordering him to rouse us all in case any Indian left the camp, as they would probably attempt to steal our horses, he lay down by the side of Drewyer in the tent with all the Indians, while the Fields were stretched near the fire at the mouth of it. At sunrise,

Sunday 27, the Indians got up and crowded round the fire near which J. Fields, who was then on watch, had carelessly left his rifle, near the head of his brother, who was still asleep. One of the Indians slipped behind him, and unperceived, took his brother's and his own rifle, while at the same time, two others seized those of Drewyer and captain Lewis. As soon as Fields turned round, he saw the Indian running off with the rifles, and instantly calling his brother, they pursued him for fifty or sixty yards, and just as they overtook him, in the scuffle for the rifles, R. Fields stabbed him through the heart with his knife; the Indian ran about fifteen steps and fell dead. They now ran back with their rifles to the camp. The moment the fellow touched his gun, Drewyer, who was awake, jumped up and wrested her from him. The noise awoke captain Lewis, who instantly started from the ground and reached to seize his gun, but finding her gone, drew a pistol from his belt and turning about saw the Indian running off with her. He followed him and ordered him to lay her down, which he was doing just as the Fields came up, and were taking aim to shoot him, when captain Lewis ordered them not to fire, as the Indian did not appear to intend any mischief. He dropped the gun and was going slowly off as Drewyer came out and asked permission to kill him, but this captain Lewis forbid as he had not yet attempted to shoot us. But finding that the Indians were now endeavouring to drive off all the horses, he ordered three of them to follow the main party who were chasing the horses up the river, and fire instantly upon the thieves; while he, without taking time to run for his shot-pouch, pursued the fellow who had stolen his gun and another Indian, who were driving away the horses on the left of the camp. He pressed them so closely that they left twelve of their horses, but continued to drive off one of our own. At the distance of three hundred paces they entered a steep niche in the river bluffs, when captain Lewis, being too much out of breath to pursue them any further, called out, as he did several times before, that unless they gave up the horse he would shoot them. As he raised his gun one of the Indians jumped behind a rock and spoke to the other, who stopped at the distance of thirty paces, as captain Lewis shot him in the belly. He fell on his knees and right elbow, but raising himself a little, fired, and then crawled behind a rock. The shot had nearly been fatal, for captain Lewis, who was bareheaded, felt the wind of the ball very distinctly. Not having his shot-pouch, he could not reload his rifle, and having only a single load also for his pistol, he thought it most prudent not to attack the Indians, and therefore retired slowly to the camp. He was met by Drewyer, who hearing the report of the guns, had come to his assistance, leaving the Fields to pursue the Indians. Captain Lewis ordered him to call out to them to desist from the pursuit, as we could take the horses of the Indians in place of our own, but they were at too great a distance to hear him. He therefore returned to the camp, and whilst he was saddling the horses, the Fields returned with four of our own, having followed the Indians until two of them swam the river, two others ascended the hills, so that the horses became dispersed. We, however, were rather gainers by this contest, for we took four of the Indian horses, and lost only one of our own. Besides which, we found in the camp four shields, two bows with quivers, and one of the guns which we took with us, and also the flag which we had presented to them, but left the medal round the neck of the dead man, in order that they might be informed who we were. The rest of their baggage, except some buffaloe meat, we left; and as there was no time to be lost, we mounted our horses, and after ascending the river hills, took our course through the beautiful level plains, in a direction a little to the south of east. We had no doubt but that we should be immediately pursued by a much larger party, and that as soon as intelligence was given to the band near the Broken mountains, they would hasten to the mouth of Maria's river to intercept us. We hope, however, to be there before them, so as to form a junction with our friends. We therefore pushed our horses as fast as we possibly could; and fortunately for us, the Indian horses were very good, the plains perfectly level, and without many stones or prickly pears, and in fine order for travelling after the late rains. At eight miles from our camp we passed a stream forty yards wide, to which, from the occurrence of the morning, we gave the name of Battle river. At three o'clock we reached Rose river, five miles above where we had formerly passed it, and having now came by estimate sixty-three miles, halted for an hour and a half to refresh our horses; then pursued our journey seventeen miles further, when, as the night came on, we killed a buffaloe, and again stopped for two hours. The sky was now overclouded, but as the moon gave light enough to show us the route, we continued along through immense herds of buffaloe for twenty miles, and then almost exhausted with fatigue, halted at two in the morning,

Monday, 28, to rest ourselves and the horses. At daylight we awoke sore and scarcely able to stand; but as our own lives as well as those of our companions depended on our pressing forward, we mounted our horses and set out. The men were desirous of crossing the Missouri, at the Grog spring, where Rose river approaches so near the river, and passing down the southwest side of it, and thus avoid the country at the junction of the two rivers, through which the enemy would most probably pursue us. But as this circuitous route would consume the whole day, and the Indians might in the meantime attack the canoes at the point, captain Lewis told his party it was now their duty to risk their lives for their friends and companions; that he would proceed immediately to the point, to give the alarm to the canoes, and if they had not yet arrived, he would raft the Missouri, and after hiding the baggage, ascend the river on foot through the woods till he met them. He told them also that it was his determination, in case they were attacked in crossing the plains, to tie the bridles of the horses and stand together till they had either routed their enemies, or sold their lives as dearly as possible. To this they all assented, and we therefore continued our route to the eastward, till at the distance of twelve miles we came near the Missouri, when we heard a noise which seemed like the report of a gun. We therefore quickened our pace for eight miles further, and about five miles from the Grog spring, now heard distinctly the noise of several rifles, from the river. We hurried to the bank, and saw with exquisite satisfaction our friends coming down the river. They landed to greet us, and after turning our horses loose, we embarked with our baggage, and went down to the spot where we had made a deposit. This, after reconnoitering the adjacent country, we opened; but unfortunately the cache had caved in, and most of the articles were injured. We took whatever was still worth preserving, and immediately proceeded to the point, where we found our deposits in good order. By a singular good fortune we were here joined by serjeant Gass and Willard from the falls, who had been ordered to bring the horses here to assist in collecting meat for the voyage, as it had been calculated that the canoes would reach this place much sooner than captain Lewis's party. After a very heavy shower of rain and hail, attended with violent thunder and lightning, we left the point, and giving a final discharge to our horses, went over to the island where we had left our red periogue, which however we found so much decayed that we had no means of repairing her: we, therefore, took all the iron work out of her, and proceeded down the river fifteen miles, and encamped near some cottonwood trees, one of which was of the narrow-leafed species, and the first of that species we had remarked as we ascended the river.

Serjeant Ordway's party, which had left the mouth of Madison river on the 13th, had descended in safety to the Whitebear islands, where he arrived on the 19th, and after collecting the baggage, left the falls on the 27th in the white periogue, and five canoes, while serjeant Gass and Willard set out at the same time by land with the horses, and thus fortunately met together.

Tuesday, 29. A violent storm of rain and hail came on last night, and as we had no means of making a shelter, we lay in the rain, and during the whole day continued so exposed. The two small canoes were sent ahead in order to hunt elk and buffaloe, which are in immense quantities, so as to provide shelter as well as food for the party. We then proceeded very rapidly with the aid of a strong current, and after passing at one o'clock the Natural walls, encamped late in the evening at our former encampment of the 29th of May, 1805. The river is now as high as it has been during the present season, and every little rivulet discharges torrents of water, which bring down such quantities of mud and sand, that we can scarcely drink the water of the Missouri. The buffaloe continue to be very numerous, but the elk are few. The bighorns, however, are in great numbers along the steep cliffs of the river, and being now in fine order, their flesh is extremely tender, delicate, and well flavoured, and resembles in colour and flavour our mutton, though it is not so strong. The brown curlew has disappeared, and has probably gone to some other climate after rearing its young in these plains.

Wednesday, 30. The rain still prevented us from stopping to dry our baggage, and we therefore proceeded with a strong current, which joined to our oars, enabled us to advance at the rate of seven miles an hour. We went on shore several times for the purpose of hunting, and procured several bighorns, two buffaloe, a beaver, an elk, and a female brown bear, whose talons were six and a quarter inches in length. In the evening we encamped on an island two miles above Goodrich's island, and early in the morning,

Thursday, 31, continued our route in the rain, passing, during the greater part of the day, through high pine hills, succeeded by low grounds abounding in timber and game. The buffaloe are scarce; but we procured fifteen elk, fourteen deer, two bighorns, and a beaver. The elk are in fine order, particularly the males, who now herd together in small parties. Their horns have reached their full growth, but ill retain the velvet or skin which covers them. Through the bottoms are scattered a number of lodges, some of which seem to have been built last winter, and were probably occupied by the Minnetarees of Fort de Prairie. The river is still rising, and more muddy than we have ever seen it. Late last night we took shelter from the rain in some old Indian lodges, about eight miles below the entrance of Northmountain creek, and then set out,

Friday, August 1, at an early hour. We passed the Muscleshell river at eleven o'clock, and fifteen miles further landed at some Indian lodges, where we determined to pass the night, for the rain still continued, and we feared that the skins of the bighorn would spoil by being constantly wet. Having made fires, therefore, and exposed them to dry, we proceeded to hunt. The next day,

Saturday, 2, was fair and warm, and we availed ourselves of this occasion to dry all our baggage in the sun. Such is the immediate effect of fair weather, that since last evening the river has fallen eighteen inches. Two men were sent forward in a canoe to hunt; and now, having reloaded our canoes, we resolved to go on as fast as possible, and accordingly set out,

Sunday, 3, at an early hour, and without stopping as usual to cook a dinner, encamped in the evening two miles above our camp of May 12, 1805. We were here joined by the two hunters, who had killed twenty-nine deer since they left us. These animals are in great abundance in the river bottoms, and very gentle. We passed also a great number of elk, wolves, some bear, beaver, geese, a few ducks, the party-coloured corvus, a calumet eagle, some bald eagles, and red-headed woodpeckers, but very few buffaloe. By four o'clock next morning,

Monday, 4, we were again in motion. At eleven we passed the Bigdry river, which has now a bold, even, but shallow current, sixty yards in width, and halted for a few minutes at the mouth of Milk river. This stream is at present full of water, resembling in colour that of the Missouri, and as it possesses quite as much water as Maria's river, we have no doubt that it extends to a considerable distance towards the north. We here killed a very large rattlesnake. Soon after we passed several herds of buffaloe and elk, and encamped at night, two miles below the gulf, on the northeast side of the river. For the first time this season we were saluted with the cry of the whippoorwill, or goatsucker of the Missouri.

Tuesday, 5. We waited until noon in hopes of being overtaken by two of the men, who had gone ahead in a canoe, to hunt two days ago, but who were at a distance from the river, as we passed them. As they did not arrive by that time, we concluded that they had passed us in the night, and therefore proceeded until late, when we encamped about ten miles below Littledry river. We again saw great numbers of buffaloe, elk, deer, antelope, and wolves; also eagles, and other birds, among which were geese and a solitary pelican, neither of whom can fly at present, as they are now shedding the feathers of their wings. We also saw several bear, one of them the largest, except one, we had ever seen, for he measured nine feet from the nose to the extremity of the tail.

During the night a violent storm came on from the northeast with such torrents of rain that we had scarcely time to unload the canoes before they filled with water. Having no shelter, we ourselves were completely wet to the skin, and the wind and cold air made our situation very unpleasant. We left it early,

Wednesday, 6; but after we had passed Porcupine river, were, by the high wind, obliged to lie by until four o'clock, when the wind abating we continued, and at night encamped five miles below our camp of the 1st of May, 1805. Here we were again drenched by the rain, which lasted all the next morning,

Thursday, 7; but being resolved, if possible, to reach the Yellowstone, a distance of eighty-three miles, in the course of the day, we set out early, and being favoured by the rapid current and good oarsmen, proceeded with great speed. In passing Martha's river, we observed that its mouth is at present a quarter of a mile lower than it was last year. Here we find for the first time the appearance of coal-burnt hills and pumicestone, which seem always to accompany each other. At this place also are the first elms and dwarf cedars in the bluffs of the river. The ash first makes its appearance in one solitary tree at the Ash rapid, but is seen occasionally scattered through the low grounds at the Elk rapid, and thence downwards, though it is generally small. The whole country on the northeast side, between Martha and Milk rivers, is a beautiful level plain, with a soil much more fertile than that higher up the river. The buffaloe, elk, and other animals still continue numerous; as are also the bear, who lie in wait at the crossing places, where they seize elk and the weaker cattle, and then stay by the carcase in order to keep off the wolves, till the whole is devoured. At four o'clock we reached the mouth of Yellowstone, where we found a note from captain Clarke, informing us of his intention of waiting for us a few miles below. We therefore left a memorandum for our two huntsmen, whom we now supposed must be behind us, and then pursued our course till night came on, and not being able to overtake captain Clarke, we encamped. In the morning,

Friday, 8, we set out in hopes of overtaking captain Clarke; but after descending to nearly the entrance of White-earth river without being able to see him, we were at a loss what to conjecture. In this situation we landed, and began to caulk and repair the canoes, as well as prepare some skins for clothing, for since we left the Rocky mountains we have had no leisure to make clothes, so that the greater part of the men are almost naked. In these occupations we passed this and the following day, without any interruption except from the musquetoes, which are very troublesome, and then having completed the repairs of the canoes, we embarked,

Sunday, 10, at five in the afternoon; but the wind and rain prevented us going further than near the entrance of White-earth river. The next day,

Monday 11, being anxious to reach the Burnt hills by noon, in order to ascertain the latitude, we went forward with great rapidity; but by the time we reached that place, it was twenty minutes too late to take the meridian altitude. Having lost the observation, captain Lewis observed on the opposite side of the river, a herd of elk on a thick sandbar of willows, and landed with Cruzatte to hunt them. Each of them fired and shot an elk. They then reloaded and took different routes in pursuit of the game, when just as captain Lewis was taking aim at an elk, a ball struck him in the left thigh, about an inch below the joint of the hip, and missing the bone, went through the left thigh and grazed the right to the depth of the ball. It instantly occurred to him that Cruzatte must have shot him by mistake for an elk, as he was dressed in brown leather, and Cruzatte had not a very good eye-sight. He therefore called out that he was shot, and looked towards the place from which the ball came; but seeing nothing, he called on Cruzatte by name several times, but received no answer. He now thought that as Cruzatte was out of hearing, and the shot did not seem to come from more than forty paces distance, it must have been fired by an Indian; and not knowing how many might be concealed in the bushes, he made towards the periogue, calling out to Cruzatte to retreat as there were Indians in the willows. As soon as he reached the periogue, he ordered the men to arms, and mentioning that he was wounded, though he hoped not mortally by the Indians, bade them follow him to relieve Cruzatte. They instantly followed for an hundred paces, when his wound became so painful, and his thigh stiffened in such a manner, that he could go no further. He therefore ordered the men to proceed, and if overpowered by numbers, retreat towards the boats, keeping up a fire; then limping back to the periogue, he prepared himself with his rifle, a pistol, and the air-gun, to sell his life dearly in case the men should be overcome. In this state of anxiety and suspence he remained for about twenty minutes, when the party returned with Cruzatte, and reported that no Indians could be seen in the neighbourhood. Cruzatte was now much alarmed, and declared that he had shot an elk after captain Lewis left him, but disclaimed every idea of having intentionally wounded his officer. There was no doubt but that he was the person who gave the wound, yet as it seemed to be perfectly accidental, and Cruzatte had always conducted himself with propriety, no further notice was taken of it. The wound was now dressed, and patent lint put into the holes; but though it bled considerably, yet as the ball had touched neither a bone nor an artery, we hope that it may not prove fatal. As it was, however, impossible for him to make the observation of the latitude of the Burnt hills, which is chiefly desirable, as being the most northern parts of the Missouri, he declined remaining till to-morrow, and proceeded on till evening. Captain Lewis could not now be removed without great pain, as he had a high fever. He therefore remained on board during the night, and early the next morning,

Tuesday, 12, proceeded with as much expedition as possible, and soon afterwards we put ashore to visit a camp, which we found to be that of Dickson and Hancock, the two Illinois traders, who told us that they had seen captain Clarke yesterday. As we stopped with them, we were overtaken by our two hunters, Colter and Collins, who had been missing since the third, and whose absence excited much uneasiness. They informed us, that after following us the first day, they concluded that we must be behind, and waited for us during several days, when they were convinced of their mistake, and had then come on as rapidly as they could. We made some presents to the two traders, and then proceeded till at one o'clock we joined our friends and companions under captain Clarke

CHAPTER XXXIII.

The party commanded by captain Clarke, previous to his being joined by captain Lewis, proceed along Clarke's river, in pursuance of the route mentioned in a preceding chapter—their sorry commemoration of our national anniversary—an instance of Sacajawea's strength of memory—description of the river and of the surrounding country as the party proceed—several of the horses belonging to the party supposed to be stolen by their Indian neighbours—they reach Wisdom river—extraordinary heat of a spring—the strong attachment of the party for tobacco, which they find on opening a cache—serjeant Ordway recovers the horses—captain Clarke divides his party, one detachment of which was to descend the river—they reach Gallatin and Jefferson rivers, of which a description is given—arrive at the Yellowstone river—some account of Otter and Beaver rivers—an example of Indian fortification—one of the party seriously and accidentally wounded—engaged in the construction of canoes—twenty-four horses stolen, probably by the Indians, in one night.

THURSDAY, July 3, 1806. On taking leave of captain Lewis and the Indians, the other division, consisting of captain Clarke with fifteen men and fifty horses, set out through the valley of Clarke's river, along the western side of which they rode in a southern direction. The valley is from ten to fifteen miles in width, tolerably level, and partially covered with the long-leafed and the pitch pine, with some cottonwood, birch, and sweet willow on the borders of the streams. Among the herbage are two species of clover, one the white clover common to the western parts of the United States, the other much smaller both in its leaf and blossom than either the red or white clover, and particularly relished by the horses. After crossing eight different streams of water, four of which were small, we halted at the distance of eighteen miles on the upper side of a large creek, where we let our horses graze, and after dinner resumed our journey in the same direction we had pursued during the morning, till at the distance of eighteen miles further, we encamped on the north side of a large creek. The valley became more beautiful as we proceeded, and was diversified by a number of small open plains, abounding with grass, and a variety of sweet-scented plants, and watered by ten streams which rush from the western mountains with considerable velocity. The mountains themselves are covered with snow about one fifth from the top, and some snow is still to be seen on the high points and in the hollows of the mountains to the eastward. In the course of our ride we saw a great number of deer, a single bear, and some of the burrowing squirrels common about the Quamash flats. The musquetoes too were very troublesome.

Friday, July 4. Early in the morning three hunters were sent out, and the rest of the party having collected the horses and breakfasted, we proceeded at seven o'clock up the valley, which is now contracted to the width of from eight to ten miles, with a good proportion of pitch pine, though its low lands, as well as the bottoms of the creeks, are strewed with large stones. We crossed five creeks of different sizes, but of great depth, and so rapid, that in passing the last, several of the horses were driven down the stream, and some of our baggage wet. Near this river we saw the tracks of two Indians, whom we supposed to be Shoshonees. Having made sixteen miles, we halted at an early hour for the purpose of doing honour to the birth-day of our country's independence. The festival was not very splendid, for it consisted of a mush made of cows and a saddle of venison, nor had we any thing to tempt us to prolong it. We therefore went on till at the distance of a mile we came to a very large creek, which, like all those in the valley, had an immense rapidity of descent; and we therefore proceeded up for some distance, in order to select the most convenient spot for fording. Even there, however, such was the violence of the current, that although the water was not higher than the bellies of the horses, the resistance they made in passing, caused the stream to rise over their backs and loads. After passing the creek we inclined to the left, and soon after struck the road which we had descended last year, near the spot where we dined on the 7th of September. Along this road we continued on the west side of Clarke's river, till at the distance of thirteen miles, during which we passed three more deep large creeks, we reached its western branch, where we encamped, and having sent out two hunters, despatched some men to examine the best ford across the river. The game of to-day consisted of four deer; though wc also saw a herd of ibex, or bighorn. By daylight the next morning,

Saturday, July 5, we again examined the fords, and having discovered what we conceived to be the best, began the passage at a place where the river is divided by small islands into six different channels. We, however, crossed them all without any damage, except wetting some of our provisions and merchandise; and at the distance of a mile came to the eastern branch, up which we proceeded about a mile, till we came into the old road we had descended in the autumn. It soon led us across the river, which we found had fallen to the same depth at which we found it last autumn, and along its eastern bank to the foot of the mountain nearly opposite Flower creek. Here we halted to let our horses graze, near a spot where there was still a fire burning and the tracks of two horses, which we presumed to be Shoshonees; and having dried all our provisions, proceeded at about four o'clock, across the mountain into the valley where we had first seen the Flatheads. We then crossed the river, which we now perceived took its rise from a high peaked mountain at about twenty miles to the northeast of the valley, and then passed up it for two miles, and encamped after a ride of twenty miles during the day. As soon as we halted several men were despatched in different directions to examine the road, and from their report, concluded that the best path would be one about three miles up the creek. This is the road travelled by the Ootlashoots, and will certainly shorten our route two days at least, besides being much better, as we had been informed by the Indians, than by that we came last fall.

Sunday, 6. The night was very cold, succeeded by frost in the morning; and as the horses were much scattered, we were not able to set out before nine o'clock. We then went along the creek for three miles, and leaving to the right the path by which we came last fall, pursued the road taken by the Ootlashoots, up a gentle ascent to the dividing mountain which separates the waters of the middle fork of Clarke's river, from those of Wisdom and Lewis's rivers. On reaching the other side, we came to Glade creek, down which we proceeded, crossing it frequently into the glades on each side, where the timber is small, and in many places destroyed by fire; where are great quantities of quamash now in bloom. Throughout the glades are great numbers of holes made by the whistling or burrowing squirrel; and we killed a hare of the large mountain species. Along these roads there are also appearances of old buffaloe paths, and some old heads of buffaloes; and as these animals have wonderful sagacity in the choice of their routes, the coincidence of a buffaloe with an Indian road, was the strongest assurance that it was the best. In the afternoon we passed along the hillside, north of the creek, till, in the course of six miles, we entered an extensive level plain. Here the tracks of the Indians scattered so much that we could no longer pursue it, but Sacajaweah recognised the plain immediately. She had travelled it often during her childhood, and informed us that it was the great resort of the Shoshonees, who came for the purpose of gathering quamash and cows, and of taking beaver, with which the plain abounded, and that Glade creek was a branch of Wisdom river, and that on reaching the higher part of the plain, we should see a gap in the mountains, on the course to our canoes, and from that gap a high point of mountain covered with snow. At the distance of a mile we crossed a large creek from the right, rising, as well as Fish creek, in a snowy mountain, over which there is a gap. Soon after, on ascending a rising ground, the country spreads itself into a beautiful plain, extending north and south about fifteen miles wide and thirty in length, and surrounded on all sides by high points of mountains covered with snow, among which was the gap pointed out by the squaw, bearing S. 56° E. We had not gone two miles from the last creek when we were overtaken by a violent storm of wind, accompanied with hard rain, which lasted an hour and a half. Having no shelter, we formed a solid column to protect ourselves from the gust, and then went on five miles to a small creek, where finding some small timber, we encamped for the night, and dried ourselves. We here observed some fresh signs of Indians, who had been gathering quamash. Our distance was twenty-six miles. In the morning,

Monday, 7, our horses were so much scattered, that although we sent out hunters in every direction, to range the country for six or eight miles, nine of them could not be recovered. They were the most valuable of all our horses, and so much attached to some of their companions, that it was difficult to separate them in the day-time. We therefore presumed that they must have been stolen by some roving Indians, and accordingly left a party of five men to continue the pursuit, while the rest went on to the spot where the canoes had been deposited. Accordingly we set out at ten o'clock, and pursued a course S. 56° E. across the valley, which we found to be watered by four large creeks, with extensive low and miry bottoms; and then reached Wisdom river, along the northeast side of which we continued, till at the distance of sixteen miles we came to the three branches. Near that place we stopped for dinner at a hot spring situated in the open plain. The bed of the spring is about fifteen yards in circumference, and composed of loose, hard, gritty stones, through which the water boils in great quantities. It is slightly impregnated with sulphur, and so hot that a piece of meat about the size of three fingers, was completely done in twenty-five minutes. After dinner we proceeded across the eastern branch, and along the north side of the middle branch for nine miles, when we reached the gap in the mountains, and took our last leave of this extensive valley, which we called the Hotspring valley. It is indeed a beautiful country; though enclosed by mountains covered with snow, the soil is exceedingly fertile and well supplied with esculent plants; while its numerous creeks furnish immense quantities of beaver. Another valley less extensive and more rugged opened itself to our view as we passed through the gap; but as we had made twenty-five miles, and the night was advancing, we halted near some handsome springs, which fall into Willard's creek. After a cold night, during which our horses separated and could not be collected till eight o'clock in the morning,

Tuesday 8, we crossed the valley along the southwest side of Willard's creek for twelve miles, when it entered the mountains, and then turning S. 20° E. came to the Shoshonee cove, after riding seven miles; whence we proceeded down the west branch of Jefferson river, and at the distance of nine miles, reached its forks, where we had deposited our merchandise in the month of August. Most of the men were in the habit of chewing tobacco; and such was their eagerness to procure it after so long a privation, that they scarcely took the saddles from their horses before they ran to the cave, and were delighted at being able to resume this fascinating indulgence. This was one of the severest privations which we have encountered. Some of the men, whose tomahawks were so constructed as to answer the purposes of pipes, broke the handles of these instruments, and after cutting them into small fragments, chewed them; the wood having, by frequent smoking, become strongly impregnated with the taste of that plant. We found every thing safe, though some of the goods were a little damp, and one of the canoes had a hole. The ride of this day was twenty-seven miles in length, and through a country diversified by low marshy grounds, and high, open, and stony plains, terminated by high mountains, on the tops and along the northern sides of which the snow still remained. Over the whole were scattered great quantities of hysop and the different species of shrubs, common to the plains of the Missouri.

We had now crossed the whole distance from Travellers'-rest creek to the head of Jefferson's river, which seems to form the best and shortest route over the mountains, during almost the whole distance of one hundred and sixty-four miles. It is, in fact, a very excellent road, and by cutting a few trees, might be rendered a good route for wagons, with the exception of about four miles over one of the mountains, which would require some levelling.

Wednesday, 9. We were all occupied in raising and repairing the canoes, and making the necessary preparations for resuming our journey to-morrow. The day proved cold and windy, so that the canoes were soon dried. We were here overtaken by serjeant Ordway and his party, who had discovered our horses near the head of the creek on which we encamped, and although they were very much scattered, and endeavoured to escape as fast as they could, he brought them back. The squaw found to-day a plant which grows in the moist lands, the root of which is eaten by the Indians. The stem and leaf, as well as the root of this plant, resemble the common carrot, in form, size and taste, though the colour is of somewhat a paler yellow. The night continued very cold, and in the morning,

Thursday 10, a white frost covered the ground; the grass was frozen, and the ice three quarters of an inch thick in a basin of water. The boats were now loaded, and captain Clarke divided his men into two bands, one to descend the river with the baggage, while he, with the other, proceeded on horseback to the Rochejaune. After breakfast the two parties set out, those on shore skirting the eastern side of Jefferson river, through Service valley, and over the Rattlesnake mountain, into a beautiful and extensive country, known among the Indians by the name of Hahnahappapchah, or Beaverhead valley, from the number of those animals to be found in it, and also from a point of land resembling the head of a beaver. It extends from the Rattlesnake mountain as low as Frazier's creek, and is about fifty miles in length, in a direct line, while its width varies from ten to fifteen miles, being watered in its whole course by the Jefferson and six different creeks. The valley is open and fertile, and besides the innumerable quantities of beaver and otter, with which its creeks are supplied, the bushes of the low grounds are a favourite resort for deer, while on the higher parts of the valley are seen scattered groups of antelopes, and still further, on the steep sides of the mountains, we observed many of the bighorn, which take refuge there from the wolves and bears. At the distance of fifteen miles the two parties stopped to dine, when captain Clarke finding that the river became wider and deeper, and that the canoes could advance more rapidly than the horses, determined to go himself by water, leaving serjeant Pryor with six men, to bring on the horses. In this way they resumed their journey after dinner, and encamped on the eastern side of the river, opposite the head of the Three-thousand-mile island. The beaver were basking in great numbers along the shore; they saw also some young wild geese and ducks. The musquetoes were very troublesome during the day, but after sunset the weather became cool and they disappeared. The next morning,

Friday, 11, captain Clarke sent four men ahead to hunt, and after an early breakfast proceeded down a very narrow channel, which was rendered more difficult by a high southwest wind, which blew from the high snowy mountains in that quarter, and met them in the face at every bend of the river, which was now become very crooked. At noon they passed the high point of land on the left, to which Beaverhead valley owes its name, and at six o'clock reached Philanthropy river, which was at present very low. The wind now shifted to the northeast, and though high, was much warmer than before. At seven o'clock they reached their encampment at the entrance of Wisdom river on the sixth of August. They found the river very high, but falling. Here too, they overtook the hunters, who had killed a buck and some young geese. Besides these they had seen a great number of geese and sandhill cranes, and some deer. The beaver too were in great quantities along the banks of the rivers, and through the night were flapping their tails in the water round the boats. Having found the canoe which had been left here as they ascended, they employed themselves,

Saturday, 12, till eight o'clock in drawing out the nails and making paddles of the sides of it. Then leaving one of their canoes here, they set out after breakfast. Immediately below the forks the current became stronger than above, and the course of the river straighter, as far as Panther creek, after which it became much more crooked. A high wind now arose from the snowy mountains to the northwest, so that it was with much difficulty and some danger they reached, at three o'clock, the entrance of Field's creek. After dining at that place, they pursued their course and stopped for the night below their encampment of the 31st of July last. Beaver, young geese, and deer continued to be their game, and they saw some old signs of buffaloe. The musquetoes also were still very troublesome.

Sunday, 13. Early in the morning they set out, and at noon reached the entrance of Madison river, where serjeant Pryor had arrived with the horses about an hour before. The horses were then driven across Madison and Gallatin rivers, and the whole party halted to dine and unload the canoes below the mouth of the latter. Here the two parties separated; serjeant Ordway with nine men set out in six canoes to descend the river, while captain Clarke with the remaining ten, and the wife and child of Chaboneau, were to proceed by land, with fifty horses, to Yellowstone river. They set out at five in the afternoon from the forks of the Missouri, in a direction nearly eastward; but as many of the horses had sore feet, they were obliged to move slowly, and after going four miles, halted for the night on the bank of Gallatin's river. This is a beautiful stream, and though the current is rapid and obstructed by islands near its mouth, is navigable for canoes. On its lower side the land rises gradually to the foot bf a mountain, running almost parallel to it; but the country below it and Madison's river is a level plain, covered at present with low grass, the soil being poor, and injured by stones and strata of hard white rock along the hill sides. Throughout the whole, game was very abundant. They procured deer in the low grounds; beaver and otter were seen in Gallatin's river, and elk, wolves, eagles, hawks, crows, and geese, were seen at different parts of the route. The plain was intersected by several great roads, leading to a gap in the mountain, about twenty miles distant, in a direction E. N. E. but the Indian woman, who was acquainted with the country, recommended a gap more to the southward. This course captain Clarke determined to pursue; and therefore at an early hour in the morning,

Monday, 14, crossed Gallatin's river in a direction south 78° east, and passing over a level plain, reached the Jefferson at the distance of six miles. That river is here divided into many channels, which spread themselves for several miles through the low grounds, and are dammed up by the beaver in such a manner, that after attempting in vain to reach the opposite side, they were obliged to turn short about to the right, till with some difficulty they reached a low but firm island, extending nearly in the course they desired to follow. The squaw now assured captain Clarke that the large road from Medicine river to the gap we were seeking, crossed the upper part of this plain. He therefore proceeded four miles up the plain and reached the main channel of the river, which is still navigable for canoes, though much divided and dammed up by multitudes of beaver. Having forded the river, they passed through a little skirt of cottonwood timber to a low open plain, where they dined. They saw elk, deer, and antelopes, and in every direction the roads made by the buffaloe, as well as some old signs of them. The squaw informed them, that but a few years ago these animals were numerous, not only here but even to the sources of Jefferson's river; but of late they have disappeared, for the Shoshonees being fearful of going west of the mountains, have hunted this country with more activity, and of course driven the buffaloe from their usual haunts. After dinner they continued inclining to the south of east, through an open level plain, till at the distance of twelve miles they reached the three forks of Gallatin's river. On crossing the southerly branch, they fell into the buffaloe road, described by the squaw, which led them up the middle branch for two miles; this branch is provided with immense quantities of beaver, but is sufficiently navigable for small canoes, by unlading at the worst dams. After crossing, they went on a mile further, and encamped at the beginning of the gap in the mountain, which here forms a kind of semicircle, through which the three branches of the river pass. Several roads come in from the right and left, all tending to the gap. A little snow still remains on a naked mountain to the eastward, but in every other direction the mountains are covered with great quantities.

Tuesday, 15. After an early breakfast they pursued the buffaloe road over a low gap in the mountain to the heads of the eastern fork of Gallatin's river, near which they had encamped last evening, and at the distance of six miles reached the top of the dividing ridge, which separates the waters of the Missouri and the Yellowstone; and on descending the ridge, they struck one of the streams of the latter river. They followed its course through an open country, with high mountains on each side, partially covered with pine, and watered by several streams, crowded as usual with beaver dams. Nine miles from the top of the ridge they reached the Yellowstone itself, about a mile and a half below where it issues from the Rocky mountains. It now appeared that the communication between the two rivers was short and easy. From the head of the Missouri at its three forks to this place is a distance of forty-eight miles, the greater part of which is through a level plain; indeed, from the forks of the eastern branch of Gallatin's river, which is there navigable for small canoes, to this part of the Yellowstone, the distance is no more than eighteen miles, with an excellent road over a high, dry country, with hills of inconsiderable height and no difficulty in passing. They halted three hours to rest their horses, and then pursued the buffaloe road along the bank of the river. Although just leaving a high snowy mountain, the Yellowstone is already a bold, rapid, and deep stream, one hundred and twenty yards in width. The bottoms of the river are narrow within the mountains, but widen to the extent of nearly two miles in the valley below, where they are occasionally overflowed, and the soil gives nourishment to cottonwood, rose-bushes, honeysuckle, rushes, common coarse grass, a species of rye, and such productions of moist lands. On each side these low grounds are bounded by dry plains of coarse gravel and sand, stretching back to the foot of the mountains, and supplied with a very short grass. The mountains on the east side of the river are rough and rocky, and still retain great quantities of snow, and two other high snowy mountains may be distinguished, one bearing north fifteen or twenty miles, the other nearly east. They have no covering except a few scattered pine, nor indeed was any timber fit for even a small canoe to be seen. At the distance of nine miles from the mountain, a river discharges itself into the Yellowstone, from the northwest, under a high rocky cliff. It rises from the snowy mountains in that direction; is about thirty-five yards wide; has a bold, deep current; is skirted by some cottonwood and willow trees, and like the Yellowstone itself, seems to abound in beaver. They gave it the name of Shields's river, after one of the party. Immediately below is a very good buffaloe road, which obviously leads from its head through a gap in the mountain, over to the waters of the Missouri. They passed Shields's river, and at three miles further, after crossing a high rocky hill, encamped in a low bottom, near the entrance of a small creek. As they came through the mountains they had seen two black bear and a number of antelopes, as well as several herds of elk, of between two and three hundred in number, but they were able to kill only a single elk. The next morning,

Wednesday, 16, therefore, a hunter was despatched ahead, while the party collected the straggling horses. They then proceeded down the river, which is very straight, and has several islands covered with cottonwood and willow; but they could not procure a single tree large enough for a canoe, and being unwilling to trust altogether to skin canoes, captain Clarke preferred going on until they found some timber. The feet of the horses were now nearly worn to the quick, particularly the hind feet, so that they were obliged to make a sort of moccasin of green buffaloe skin, which relieved them very much in crossing the plains. After passing a bold creek from the south, of twenty yards in width, they halted for dinner on an island, then went on till at night they encamped near the entrance of another small stream, having made twenty-six miles during the day. They saw some bear and great numbers of antelopes and elks; but the soreness of their horses' feet rendered it difficult to chase them. One of the men caught a fish which they had not seen before; it was eight inches long, and resembled a trout in form, but its mouth was like that of the sturgeon, and it had a red streak passing on each side from the gills to the tail. In the plains were but few plants except the silk-grass, the wild indigo, and the sunflower, which are now all in bloom. The high grounds on the river are faced with a deep freestone rock, of a hard, sharp grit, which may also be seen in perpendicular strata throughout the plain.

Thursday, 17. It rained during the night, and as the party had no covering but a buffaloe skin, they rose drenched with water; and pursuing their journey at an early hour, over the point of a ridge, and through an open low bottom, reached at the distance of six and a half miles, a part of the river, where two large creeks enter immediately opposite to each other; one from the northwest, the other from the south of southwest. These captain Clarke called Rivers-across. Ten miles and a half further they halted for dinner below the entrance of a large creek on the northeast side, about thirty yards in width, which they named Otter river. Nearly opposite to this is another, to which they gave the name of Beaver river. The waters of both are of a milky colour, and the banks well supplied with small timber. The river is now becoming more divided by islands, and a number of small creeks fall in on both sides. The largest of these is about seven miles from the Beaver river, and enters on the right: they called it Bratton's river, from one of the men. The highlands too approach the river more nearly than before, but although their sides are partially supplied with pine and cedar, the growth is still too small for canoes. The buffaloe is beginning to be more abundant, and to-day, for the first time on this river, they saw a pelican; but deer and elk are now more scarce than before. In one of the low bottoms of the river was an Indian fort, which seems to have been built during the last summer. It was built in the form of a circle, about fifty feet in diameter, five feet high, and formed of logs, lapping over each other, and covered on the outside with bark set up an end. The entrance also was guarded by a work on each side of it, facing the river. These intrenchments, the squaw informs us, are frequently made by the Minnetarees and other Indians at war with the Shoshonees, when pursued by their enemies on horseback. After making thirty-three miles, they encamped near a point of woods in the narrow bottom of the river.

Friday, 18. Before setting out they killed two buffaloe, which ventured near the camp, and then pursued their route over the ridges of the highlands, so as to avoid the bends of the river, which now washes the feet of the hills. The face of the country is rough and stony, and covered with immense quantities of the prickly pear. The river is nearly two hundred yards wide, rapid as usual, and with a bed of coarse gravel and round stones. The same materials are the basis of the soil in the high bottoms, with a mixture of dark brown earth. The river hills are about two hundred feet high, and still faced with a dark freestone rock; and the country back of them broken into open waving plains. Pine is the only growth of importance; but among the smaller plants were distinguished the purple, yellow, and black currants, which are now ripe, and of an excellent flavour. About eleven o'clock a smoke was descried to the S. S. E. towards the termination of the Rocky mountains, intended most probably, as a signal by the Crow Indians, who have mistaken us for their enemies, or as friends to trade with them. They could not however stop to ascertain the truth of this conjecture, but rode on, and after passing another old Indian fort, similar to that seen yesterday, halted for the night on a small island, twenty-six miles from their camp of last evening. One of the hunters in attempting to mount his horse, after shooting a deer, fell on a small piece of timber, which ran nearly two inches into the muscular part of his thigh. The wound was very painful; and were it not for their great anxiety to reach the United States this season, the party would have remained till he was cured: but the time was too precious to wait. The gentlest and strongest horse was therefore selected, and a sort of litter formed in such a manner as to enable the sick man to lie nearly at full length. They then proceeded gently, and at the distance of two miles passed a river entering from the southeast side, about forty yards wide, and called by the Indians Itchkeppearja, or Rose river, a name which it deserves, as well from its beauty as from the roses which we saw budding on its borders. Soon after they passed another Indian fort on an island, and after making nine miles, halted to let the horses graze, and sent out a hunter to look for timber to make a canoe, and procure, if possible, some wild ginger to make a poultice for Gibson's thigh, which was now exceedingly painful, in consequence of his constrained position. He returned, however, without being able to find either; but brought back two bucks, and had had a contest with two white bears who had chased him; but being on horseback he escaped, after wounding both of them. There are great quantities of currants in the plains, but almost every blade of grass for many miles have been destroyed by immense swarms of grasshoppers, who appear to be ascending the river. After taking some refreshment they proceeded, and found that the hills became lower on both sides; those on the right overhanging the river in cliffs of a darkish yellow earth, and the bottoms widening to several miles in extent. The timber too, although chiefly cottonwood, is coming large.

They had not gone far when Gibson's wound became so violently painful that he could no longer remain on horseback. He was therefore left with two men under the shade of a tree, while captain Clarke went on to seek for timber. At the distance of eighteen miles from his camp of last night he halted near a thick grove of trees, some of which were large enough for small canoes, and then searched all the adjacent country till evening, when Gibson was brought on to the camp. The game of to-day consisted of six deer, seven elk, and an antelope. The smoke which had been seen on the 17th, was again distinguished this afternoon, and one of the party reported that he had observed an Indian on the highlands on the opposite side of the river. The next morning at daylight,

Sunday, 20, two good judges of timber were sent down the river in quest of lumber, but returned without being able to find any trees larger than those near the camp, nor could they procure any for axe-handles except chokecherry. Captain Clarke determined therefore to make two canoes, which being lashed together, might be sufficient to convey the party down the river, while a few men might lead the horses to the Mandan nation. Three axes were now sharpened with a file, and some of the men proceeded to cut down two of the largest trees, on which they worked till night. The rest of the party were occupied in dressing skins for clothes, or in hunting, in which they were so fortunate as to procure a deer, two buffaloe and an elk. The horses being much fatigued, they were turned out to rest for a few days; but in the morning,

Monday, 21, twenty-four of them were missing. Three hunters were sent in different directions to look for them; but all returned unsuccessful, and it now seemed probable that the Indians who had made the smoke a few days since, had stolen the horses. In the meantime the men worked so diligently on the canoes that one of them was nearly completed. Late in the evening, a very black cloud accompanied with thunder and lightning rose from the southeast, and rendered the weather extremely warm and disagreeable. The wind too was very high, but shifted towards morning,

Tuesday, 22, to the northeast, and became moderately cool. Three men were now despatched in quest of the horses, but they came back without being able to discover even a track, the plains being so hard and dry that the foot makes no impression. This confirms the suspicion of their being stolen by the Indians, who would probably take them across the plains, to avoid being pursued by their traces; besides, the improbability of their voluntarily leaving rushes and grass of the river bottoms to go on the plains, where they could find nothing but a short dry grass. Four men were again sent out with orders to encircle the camp for a great distance round, but they too returned with no better success than those who had preceded them. The search was resumed in the morning,

Wednesday, 23, and a piece of a robe, and a moccasin, were discovered not far from the camp. The moccasin was worn out in the sole, and yet wet, and had every appearance of having been left but a few hours before. This sign was conclusive that the Indians had taken our horses, and were still prowling about for the remainder, who fortunately escaped last night, by being in a small prairie, surrounded by thick timber. At length Labiche, who is one of the best trackers, returned from a very wide circuit, and informed captain Clarke that he had traced the tracks of the horses, which were bending their course rather down the river towards the open plains, and from the track, going very rapidly. All hopes of recovering them were now abandoned. The Indians are not the only plunderers who surround the camp, for last night the wolves or dogs stole the greater part of the dried meat from the scaffold. The wolves, which constantly attend the buffaloe, are here in great numbers, for this seems to be the commencement of the buffaloe country. Besides them, are seen antelopes, pidgeons, doves, hawks, ravens, crows, larks, sparrows, eagles, bank-martins, &c. &c. great numbers of geese too, which raise their young on this river, have passed the camp. The country itself consists of beautiful level plains, but the soil is thin and stony, and both plains and low grounds are covered with great quantities of prickly pear.

At noon the two canoes were finished. They are twenty-eight feet long, sixteen or eighteen inches deep, and from sixteen to twenty-four inches wide, and being lashed together, every thing was prepared for setting out to-morrow; Gibson having now recovered. Serjeant Pryor was now directed with Shannon and Windsor, to take our horses to the Mandans, and if he found that Mr. Henry was on the Assiniboin river, to go thither and deliver him a letter, the object of which was to prevail on the most distinguished chiefs of the Sioux to accompany him to Washington.

CHAPTER XXXIV.

Captain Clarke proceeds with his party down the river—description of an Indian lodge—serjeant Pryor arrives with the horses left by the party when they embarked in their canoes—his difficulty in bringing them on—remarkable rock discovered by captain Clarke, and the beauty of the prospect from the summit—they continue their route down the river, of which a particular description is given, as well as of the surrounding country—Yellowstone and Bighorn river compared—great quantities of game found on the banks of the rivers—immense herds of buffaloe—fierceness of the white bear—encamp at the junction of the Yellowstone and Missouri—a general outline given of Yellowstone river, comprehending the shoals—its entrance recommended for the formation of a trading establishment—the sufferings of the party from the musquetoes—serjeant Pryor, who with a detachment of the party was to have brought on the horses, arrives, and reports that they were all stolen by the Indians—deprived of these animals, they form for themselves Indian canoes of the skins of beasts, and of curious structure, with which they descend the river over the most difficult shoals and dangerous rapids—meet with two white men unexpectedly, from whom they procure intelligence of the Indians formerly visited by the party.

THURSDAY, July 24. The canoes were loaded, and serjeant Pryor and his party set out with orders to proceed down to the entrance of the Bighorn river, which was supposed to be at no great distance, and where they should be taken in the boats across the Yellowstone. At eight o'clock captain Clarke embarked in the little flotilla, and proceeded on very steadily down the river, which continues to be about two hundred yards wide, and contains a number of islands, some of which are supplied with a small growth of timber. At the distance of a mile from the camp, the river passes under a high bluff for about twenty-three miles, when the bottoms widen on both sides. At the distance of twenty-nine miles, a river falls in from the south. This was the river supposed to be the Bighorn; but afterwards, when the Bighorn was found, the name of Clarke's fork was given to this stream. It is a bold river, one hundred and fifty yards wide at the entrance, but a short distance above, is contracted to a hundred yards. The water is of a light muddy colour, and much colder than that of the Yellowstone, and its general course is south and east of the Rocky mountains. There is a small island situated immediately at the entrance; and this or the adjoining main land would form a very good position for a fort. The country most frequented by the beaver begins here, and that which lies between this river and the Yellowstone is, perhaps, the best district for the hunters of that animal. About a mile before reaching this river, there is a ripple in the Yellowstone, on passing which the canoes took in some water. The party therefore landed to bail the boats, and then proceeded six miles further to a large island, where they halted for the purpose of waiting for serjeant Pryor. It is a beautiful spot with a rich soil, covered with wild rye, and a species of grass like the blue-grass, and some of another kind, which the Indians wear in plaits round the neck, on account of a strong scent resembling that of the vanilla. There is also a thin growth of cottonwood scattered over the island. In the centre is a large Indian lodge which seems to have been built during the last summer. It is in the form of a cone, sixty feet in diameter at the base, composed of twenty poles, each forty-five feet long, and two and a half in circumference, and the whole structure covered with bushes. The interior was curiously ornamented. On the tops of the poles were feathers of eagles, and circular pieces of wood, with sticks across them in the form of a girdle: from the centre was suspended a stuffed buffaloe skin: on the side fronting the door was hung a cedar bush: on one side of the lodge a buffaloe's head; on the other several pieces of wood stuck in the ground. From its whole appearance, it was more like a lodge for holding councils, than an ordinary dwelling house. Serjeant Pryor not having yet arrived, they went on about fifteen and a half miles further to a small creek on the right, to which they gave the name of Horse creek, and just below it overtook serjeant Pryor with the horses. He had found it almost impossible, with two men, to drive on the remaining horses, for as soon as they discovered a herd of buffaloe the loose horses, having been trained by the Indians to hunt, immediately set off in pursuit of them, and surrounded the buffaloe herd with almost as much skill as their riders could have done. At last he was obliged to send one horseman forward, and drive all the buffaloe from the route. The horses were here driven across, and sergeant Pryor again proceeded with an additional man to his party. The river is now much more deep and navigable, and the current more regular than above Clarke's fork, and although much divided by well-wooded islands, when collected, the stream is between two and three hundred feet in width. Along its banks are some beaver, and an immense number of deer, elk, and buffaloe. Towards night they passed a creek from the southeast, thirty-five yards wide, which they called Pryor's creek; half a mile below which they encamped, after making sixty-nine and a half miles during the day. At sunrise the next morning,

Friday, 25, they resumed their voyage, and passed a number of islands and small streams, and occasionally high bluffs, composed of a yellow gritty stone. A storm of rain and high southwest wind soon overtook them, and obliged them to land and form a sort of log hut, covered with deer skins. As soon as it ceased they proceeded, and about four o'clock, after having made forty-nine miles, captain Clarke landed to examine a very remarkable rock situated in an extensive bottom on the right, about two hundred and fifty paces from the shore. It is nearly four hundred paces in circumference, two hundred feet high, and accessible only from the northeast, the other sides being a perpendicular cliff of a light coloured gritty rock. The soil of the top is five or six feet deep, of a good quality, and covered with short grass. The Indians have carved the figures of animals and other objects on the sides of the rock, and on the top are raised two piles of stones. From this height the eye ranged over a large extent of variegated country:—On the southwest the Rocky mountains covered with snow; a low mountain, about forty miles distant, bearing south 15° east, and in a direction north 55° west; and at the distance of thirty-five miles, the southern extremity of what are called the Littlewolf mountains. The low grounds of the river extend nearly six miles to the southward, when they rise into plains reaching to the mountains, and watered with a large creek, while at some distance below a range of highland, covered with pine, stretches on both sides of the river, in a direction north and south. The north side of the river, for some distance, is surrounded by jutting romantic cliffs; these are succeeded by rugged hills, beyond which the plains are again open and extensive; and the whole country is enlivened by herds of buffaloe, elk and wolves. After enjoying the prospect from this rock, to which captain Clarke gave the name of Pompey's pillar, he descended, and continued his course. At the distance of six or seven miles, he stopped to get two bighorns, which were shot from the boat; and while on shore, saw in the face of the cliff on the left, about twenty feet above the water, the fragment of a rib of a fish, three feet long, and nearly three inches round, incrusted in the rock itself, and though neither decayed nor petrified is very rotten. After making fifty-eight miles they reached the entrance of a stream on the right, about twenty-two yards wide, and which discharges a great quantity of muddy water. Here they encamped rather earlier than usual, on account of a heavy squall, accompanied with some rain. Early next morning,

Saturday, 26, they proceeded. The river is now much divided by stony islands and bars; but the current, though swift, is regular, and there are many very handsome islands covered with cottonwood. On the left shore the bottoms are very extensive; the right bank is formed of high cliffs of a whitish gritty stone; and beyond these, the country on both sides is diversified with waving plains, covered with pine. At the distance of ten miles is a large creek on the right, about forty yards in width, but containing very little water; and in the course of the day, two smaller streams on the left, and a fourth on the right. At length, after coming sixty-two miles, they landed at the entrance of the Bighorn river; but finding the point between the two composed of soft mud and sand, and liable to be overflowed, they ascended the Bighorn for half a mile, then crossed and formed a camp on its lower side. Captain Clarke then walked up the river. At the distance of seven miles, a creek, twenty yards wide, which from the colour of the water he called Muddy creek, falls in on the northeast, and a few miles further, the river bends to the east of south. The bottoms of the river are extensive, and supplied chiefly with cottonwood trees, variegated with great quantities of rosebushes. The current is regular and rapid; and like the Missouri, constantly changes so as to wash away the banks on one side, leaving sandbars on the other. Its bed contains much less of the large gravel than that of the Yellowstone, and its water is more muddy, and of a brownish colour, while the Yellowstone has a lighter tint. At the junction, the two rivers are nearly equal in breadth, extending from two hundred to two hundred and twenty yards, but the Yellowstone contains much more water, being ten or twelve feet deep, while the depth of the Bighorn varies from five to seven feet. This is the river which had been described by the Indians as rising in the Rocky mountains, near the Yellowstone, and the sources of the river Platte, and then finds its way through the Cote Noir, and the eastern range of the Rocky mountains. In its long course it receives two large rivers, one from the north and the other from the south, and being unobstructed by falls, is navigable in canoes for a great distance, through a fine rich open country, supplied with a great quantity of timber, and inhabited by beaver, and by numerous species of animals, among which are those from which it derives the name of Bighorn. There are no permanent settlements near it; but the whole country which it waters, is occasionally visited by roving bands of hunters from the Crow tribe, the Paunch, a band of Crows, and the Castahana, a small band of Snake Indians.

Sunday, 27. They again set out very early, and on leaving the Bighorn, took a last look at the Rocky mountains, which had been constantly in view from the first of May. The river now widens to the extent of from four to six hundred yards; is much divided by islands and sandbars; its banks generally low and falling in, and resembles the Missouri in many particulars; but its islands are more numerous, its waters less muddy, and the current more rapid. The water too is of a yellowish-white, and the round stones, which form the bars above the Bighorn, have given place to gravel. On the left side the river runs under cliffs of light, soft, gritty stone, varying in height from seventy to an hundred feet, behind which are level and extensive plains. On the right side of the river are low extensive bottoms, bordered with cottonwood, various species of willow, rosebushes, grape-vines, the redberry or buffaloe-grease bushes, and a species of sumach; to these succeed high grounds, supplied with pine, and still further on are level plains. Throughout the country are vast quantities of buffaloe, which, as this is the running season, keep a continued bellowing. Large herds of elk also are lying in every point, and are so gentle that they may be approached within twenty paces without being alarmed. Several beaver were seen in the course of the day; indeed, there is a greater appearance of those animals than there was above the Bighorn. Deer, however, are by no means abundant, and the antelopes, as well as the bighorns, are scarce.

Fifteen miles from the Bighorn river they passed a large dry creek on the left, to which they gave the name of Elk creek, and halted for breakfast about three miles further, at the entrance of Windsor's river, a stream from the left, which though fifty yards wide, contains scarcely any water. Forty-eight miles from the Bighorn is a large bed of a stream sixty yards wide, but with very little water. They called it Labiche's river. Several other smaller streams, or rather beds of creeks, were passed in the course of the day, and after coming eighty and a half miles, they encamped on a large island. At daylight the next morning,

Monday, 28, they proceeded down the smooth gentle current, passing by a number of islands and several creeks, which are now dry. These are, indeed, more like torrents, and like the dry brooks of the Missouri, merely serve to carry off the vast quantities of water which fall in the plains, and bring them also a great deal of mud, which contributes to the muddiness of the Yellowstone. The most distinguished of these are at the distance of six miles, a creek of eighty yards in width, from the northwest, and called by the Indians, Little-wolf river: twenty-nine miles lower another on the left, seventy yards in width, which they call Table creek, from several mounds in the plains to the northwest, the tops of which resemble a table. Four miles further a stream of more importance enters behind an island from the south. It is about one hundred yards in width, with a bold current of muddy water, and is probably the river called by the Indians the Little Bighorn; and another stream on the right, twenty-five yards wide, the Indian name of which is Mashaskap. Nearly opposite to this creek they encamped after making seventy-three miles. The river during part of the route is confined by cliffs, which on the right are of a soft, yellowish, gritty rock, while those on the left are harder, and of a lighter colour. In some of these cliffs were several stratas of coal of different thickness and heights above the water; but like that of the Missouri, is of an inferior quality.

Tuesday, 29. During the night there was a storm of thunder and lightning, with some rain, a high northeast wind, which continued during the morning, and prevented the party from making more than forty-one miles. The country resembles that passed yesterday; the dry beds of rivers continue, and large quantities of coal are seen in the sides of the cliffs. The river itself is now between five hundred yards and half a mile in width, and has more sand and bars of gravel than above. The beaver are in great numbers; and in the course of the day some catfish and a soft-shelled turtle were procured. In the evening they encamped on the left, opposite to the entrance of a stream, called by the Indians Lazeka, or Tongue river. This stream rises in the Cote Noir, and is formed of two branches, one having its sources with the heads of the Chayenne, the other with one of the branches of the Bighorn. It has a very wide bed, and a channel of water a hundred and fifty yards wide, but the water is of a light brown colour, very muddy, and nearly milkwarm. It is shallow, and its rapid current throws out great quantities of mud and some coarse gravel. Near the mouth is a large proportion of timber, but the warmth of the water would seem to indicate that the country through which it passed was open and without shade.

Wednesday, 30. They set out at an early hour, and after passing, at the distance of twelve miles, the bed of a river one hundred yards wide, but nearly dry at present, reached two miles below it a succession of bad shoals, interspersed with a hard, dark brown, gritty rock, extending for six miles, the last of which stretches nearly across the river, and has a descent of about three feet. At this place they were obliged to let the canoes down with the hand, for fear of their splitting on a concealed rock; though when the shoals are known a large canoe could with safety pass through the worst of them. This is the most difficult part of the whole Yellowstone river, and was called the Buffaloe shoal, from the circumstance of one of those animals being found in them. The neighbouring cliffs on the right are about one hundred feet high; on the left the country is low, but gradually rises, and at some distance from the shore present the first appearance of burnt hills which have been seen on the Yellowstone. Below the Buffaloe shoals the river is contracted to the width of three or four hundred yards, the islands less numerous, and a few scattering trees only are seen either on its banks or on the highlands: twenty miles from those shoals is a rapid, caused by a number of rocks strewed over the river; but though the waves are high, there is a very good channel on the left, which renders the passage secure. There was a bear standing on one of these rocks, which occasioned the name of the Bear rapid. As they were descending this rapid a violent storm from the northwest obliged them to take refuge in an old Indian lodge near the mouth of a river on the left, which has lately been very high, has widened to the distance of a quarter of a mile, but though its present channel is eighty-eight yards wide, there is not more water in it than would easily pass through a hole of an inch in diameter. It was called York's dry river. As soon as the rain and wind had abated, they resumed their journey, and at seven miles encamped under a spreading cottonwood tree on the left side, after making forty-eight miles. A mile and a half above on the opposite side is a river containing one hundred yards width of water, though the bed itself is much wider. The water is very muddy, and like its banks of a dark brown colour. Its current throws out great quantities of red stones; and this circumstance, with the appearance of the distant hills, induced captain Clarke to call it the Redstone, which he afterwards found to be the meaning of its Indian name, Wahasah.

Saturday, 31. During the whole night the buffaloe were prowling about the camp, and excited much alarm, lest in crossing the river they should tread on the boats and split them to pieces. They set out as usual, and at the distance of two miles passed a rapid of no great danger, which they called Wolf rapid, from seeing a wolf in them. At this place commences a range of highlands. These highlands have no timber, and are composed of earth of different colours, without much rock, but supplied throughout with great quantities of coal, or carbonated wood. After passing these hills the country again opens into extensive plains, like those passed yesterday, and the river is diversified with islands, and partially supplied with water by a great number of wide, but nearly dry brooks. Thus eighteen miles below the camp is a shallow, muddy stream on the left, one hundred yards wide, and supposed to be that known among the Indians by the name of Saasha, or Littlewolf river: five miles below on the right side is another river, forty yards wide, and four feet in depth, which, from the steep coal banks on each side, they called Oaktaroup, or Coal river; and at eighteen miles further a third stream of sixty yards in width, to which they gave the name of Gibson's river. Having made sixty-six miles, they halted for the night, and just as they landed, saw the largest white bear that any of the party had ever before seen, devouring a dead buffaloe on a sandbar. They fired two balls into him, and he then swam to the main land and walked along the shore. Captain Clarke pursued him, and lodged two more balls in his body; but though he bled profusely he made his escape, as night prevented them from following him. The next day,

Sunday, August 1, a high wind from ahead made the water rough, and retarded their progress, and as it rained during the whole day, their situation in the open boats was very disagreeable. The country bears in every respect the same appearance as that of yesterday, though there is some ash timber in the bottom, and low pine and cedar on the sides of the hills. The current of the river is less rapid, has more soft mud, and is more obstructed by sandbars, and the rain has given an unusual quantity of water to the brooks. The buffaloe now appear in vast numbers. A herd happened to be on their way across the river. Such was the multitude of these animals, that although the river, including an island, over which they passed was a mile in length, the herd stretched as thick as they could swim, completely from one side to the other, and the party was obliged to stop for an hour. They consoled themselves for the delay by killing four of the herd, and then proceeded till at the distance of forty-five miles on an island, below which two other herds of buffaloe, as numerous as the first, soon after crossed the river.

Monday, 2. The river is now about a mile wide, less rapid, and more divided by islands and bars of sand and mud than hitherto: the low grounds too are more extensive, and contain a greater quantity of cottonwood, ash, and willow trees. On the northwest is a low, level plain; on the southeast some rugged hills, on which we saw, without being able to approach, some of the bighorns. The buffaloe and elk, as well as the pursuers of both, the wolves, are in great numbers. On each side of the river are several dry brooks; but the only stream of any size is that they called Ibex river, on the right, about thirty yards wide, and sixteen miles from the camp. The bear which gave so much trouble on the head of the Missouri, are equally fierce in this quarter. This morning one of them, which was on a sandbar as the boat passed, raised himself on his hind feet, and after looking at the party, plunged in and swam towards them. He was received with three balls in the body; he then turned round and made for the shore. Towards evening another entered the water to swim across. Captain Clarke ordered the boat towards the shore, and just as the bear landed, shot the animal in the head. It proved to be the largest female they had ever seen, and so old that its tusks were worn quite smooth. The boats escaped with difficulty between two herds of buffaloe, which were crossing the river, and would probably have again detained the party. Among the elk of this neighbourhood are an unusual number of males, while higher up the river the numerous herds consist of females chiefly. After making eighty-four miles, they encamped among some ash and elm trees on the right. They, however, rather passed the night than slept there, for the musquitoes were so troublesome, that scarcely any of the party could close their eyes during the greater part of the time. They therefore set out early in the morning,

Tuesday, 3, to avoid the persecution of those insects. At the distance of two miles they passed Fields's creek, a stream thirty-five yards wide, which enters on the right, immediately above a high bluff, which is rapidly sinking into the river. Here captain Clarke went ashore in pursuit of some bighorns, but the musquitoes were so numerous, that he was unable to shoot with certainty. He therefore returned to the canoes; and soon after observing a ram of the same animals, sent one of the hunters, who shot it, and it was preserved entire as a specimen. About two o'clock they reached, eight miles below Fields's creek, the junction of the Yellowstone with the Missouri, and formed a camp on the point where they had encamped on the 26th of April, 1805. The canoes were now unloaded, and the baggage exposed to dry, as many of the articles were wet, and some of them spoiled.

The Rochejaune, or Yellowstone river, according to Indian information, has its remote sources in the Rocky mountains, near the peaks of the Rio del Norde, on the confines of New Mexico, to which country there is a good road during the whole distance along the banks of the Yellowstone. Its western waters are probably connected with those of Lewis's river, while the eastern branches approach the heads of Clarke's river, the Bighorn, and the Platte; so that it waters the middle portion of the Rocky mountains for several hundred miles from northwest to southeast. During its whole course from the point at which captain Clarke reached it to the Missouri, a distance which he computed at eight hundred and thirty-seven miles, this river is large and navigable for periogues, and even batteaux, there being none of the moving sandbars which impede the navigation of the Missouri, and only a single ledge of rocks, which, however, is not difficult to pass. Even its tributary waters, the Bighorn, Clarke's fork, and Tongue river, may be ascended in boats for a considerable distance. The banks of the river are low, but bold, and no where subject to be overflowed, except for a short distance below the mountains. The predominating colour of the river is a yellowish-brown; that of the Missouri, which possesses more mud, is of a deep drab colour; the bed of the former being chiefly composed of loose pebble; which, however, diminish in size in descending the river, till after passing the Lazeka, the pebble cease as the river widens, and the mud and sand continue to form the greater part of the bottom. Over these the water flows with a velocity constantly and almost equally decreasing in proportion to its distance from the mountains. From the mountains to Clarke's fork, the current may be estimated at four and a half miles per hour; thence as low as the Bighorn, at three and a half miles between that and the Lazeka at three miles; and from that river to the Wolf rapid, at two and three quarter miles; from which to its entrance, the general rapidity is two miles per hour. The appearance and character of the country present nearly similar varieties of fertile, rich, open lands. Above Clarke's fork, it consists of high waving plains bordered by stony hills, partially supplied with pine; the middle portion, as low as the Buffaloe shoals, contains less timber, and the number diminishes still lower, where the river widens, and the country spreads itself into extensive plains. Like all the branches of the Missouri which penetrate the Rocky mountains, the Yellowstone and its streams, within that district of country beyond Clarke's fork, abound in beaver and otter; a circumstance which strongly recommends the entrance of the latter river as a judicious position for the purposes of trade. To an establishment at that place, the Shoshonees, both within and westward of the Rocky mountains, would willingly resort, as they would be farther from the reach of the Blackfoot Indians, and the Minnetarees of Fort de Prairie, than they could be in trading with any factories on the Missouri. The same motive of personal safety, would most probably induce many of the tribes on the Columbia and Lewis's river to prefer this place to the entrance of Maria's river, at least for some years; and as the Crow and Paunch

Indians, the Castahanahs, and the Indians residing south of Clarke's fork, would also be induced to visit it, the mouth of that river might be considered as one of the most important establishments for the western fur trade. This too may be the more easily effected, as the adjacent country possesses a sufficiency of timber for the purpose, an advantage which is not found on any spot between Clarke's fork and the Rocky mountains.

Wednesday, 4. The camp became absolutely uninhabitable, in consequence of the multitude of musquetoes; the men could not work in preparing skins for clothing, nor hunt in the timbered low grounds; in short, there was no mode of escape, except by going on the sand-bars in the river; where, if the wind should blow, the insects do not venture; but when there is no wind, and particularly at night, when the men have no covering except their worn-out blankets, the pain they suffer is scarcely to be endured. There was also a want of meat, for the buffaloe were not to be found; an dthough the elk are very abundant, yet their fat and flesh is more difficult to dry in the sun, and is also much more easily spoiled than the meat or fat of either deer or buffaloe. Captain Clarke therefore determined to go on to some spot which should be free from musquetoes, and furnish more game. After having written a note to captain Lewis, to inform him of his intention, and stuck it on a pole, at the confluence of the two rivers, he loaded the canoes at five in the afternoon, and proceeded down the river to the second point and encamped on a sand-bar; but here the musquetoes seemed to be even more numerous than above. The face of the Indian child is considerably puffed up and swollen with the bites of these animals, nor could the men procure scarcely any sleep during the night, and they continued to harrass them the next morning,

Thursday 5, as thep proceeded. On one occasion captain Clarke went on shore and ascended a hill after one of the bighorns; but the musquetoes were in such multitudes that he could not keep them from the barrel of his rifle long enough to take aim. About ten o'clock, however, a light breeze sprung up from the northwest, and dispersed them in some degree. Captain Clarke then landed on a sandbar, intending to wait for captain Lewis, and went out to hunt. But not finding any buffaloe, he again proceeded in the afternoon, and having killed a large white bear, encamped under a high bluff exposed to a light breeze from the southwest, which blew away the musquetoes. About eleven o'clock, however, the wind became very high and a storm of rain came on, which lasted for two hours, accompanied with sharp lightning and loud peals of thunder. The party therefore rose,

Friday, 6, very wet, and proceeded to a sandbar below the entrance of Whiteearth river. Just above this place, the Indians had, apparently within seven or eight days past, been digging a root which they employ in making a kind of soup. Having fixed their tents, the men were employed in dressing skins and hunting. They shot a number of deer; but only two of them were fat, owing probably to the great quantities of musquetoes who annoy them whilst feeding. The next day,

Saturday, 7, after some severe rain, they proceeded at eleven o'clock, through intervals of rain and high wind till six in the evening, when they encamped on a sandbar. Here they had a very violent wind, for two hours, which left the air clear and cold, so that the musquetoes completely disappeared. On the following morning,

Sunday, 8, serjeant Pryor, accompanied by Shannon, Hall, and Windsor, arrived, but without the horses. They reported that on the second day after they left captain Clarke, they halted to let the horses graze near the bed of a large creek, which contained no running water; but soon after a shower of rain fell, and the creek swelled so suddenly, that several horses which had straggled across the dry bed of the creek, where obliged to swim back. They now determined to form their camp; but the next morning were astonished at not being able to find a single one of their horses. They immediately examined the neighbourhood, and soon finding the track of the Indians who had stolen the horses, pursued them for five miles, where the fugitives divided into two parties. They now followed the largest party five miles further, till they lost all hopes of overtaking the Indians, and returned to the camp; and packing the baggage on their backs, pursued a northeast course towards the Yellowstone. On the following night a wolf bit serjeant Pryor through the hand as he lay asleep, and made an attempt to seize Windsor, when Shannon discovered and shot him. They passed over a broken open country, and having reached the Yellowstone near Pompey's pillar, they determined to descend the river, and for this purpose made two skin canoes, such as they had seen among the Mandans and Ricaras. They are made in the following manner:—Two sticks of an inch and a quarter in diameter are tied together so as to form a round hoop, which serves for the brim, while a second hoop, for the bottom of the boat, is made in the same way, and both secured by sticks of the same size from the sides of the hoops, fastened by thongs at the edges of the hoops and at the interstices of the sticks: over this frame the skin is drawn closely and tied with thongs, so as to form a perfect basin, seven feet and three inches in diameter, sixteen inches deep, and with sixteen ribs or cross-sticks, and capable of carrying six or eight men with their loads. Being unacquainted with the river, they thought it most prudent to divide their guns and ammunition, so that in case of accident all might not be lost, and therefore built two canoes. In these frail vessels they embarked, and were surprised at the perfect security in which they passed through the most difficult choals and rapids of the river, without ever taking in water, even during the highest winds.

In passing the confluence of the Yellowstone and Missouri, he took down the note from the pole, supposing that captain Lewis had passed; and now learning where the party was, pressed on in the skin canoes to join them. The day was spent in hunting, so as to procure a number of skins to trade with the Mandans; for having now neither horses nor merchandise, our only resort in order to obtain corn and beans, is a stock of skins, which those Indians very much admire.

Monday, 9. A heavy dew fell this morning. Captain Clarke now proceeded slowly down the river, hunting through the low grounds in the neighbourhood after the deer and elk, till late in the afternoon he encamped on the southeast side. Here they remained during the next day,

Tuesday, 10, attempting to dry the meat, while the hunters were all abroad; but they could obtain nothing except an antelope and one blacktailed deer; those animals being very scarce on this part of the river. In the low grounds of the river captain Clarke found today a species of cherry which he had never seen before, and which seems peculiar to this small district of country, though even there it is not very abundant.

The men also dug up quantities of a large and very insipid root, called by thc Indians hankee, and by the engagees, the white apple. It is used by them in a dry and pounded state, so as to mix with their soup; but our men boiled it and eat it with meat. In descending the river yesterday, the squaw brought in a large well-flavoured gooseberry, of a rich crimson colour; and a deep purple berry of a species of currant, common on this river as low as the Mandans, and called by the engagees, the Indian currant.

Wednesday, 11. The next morning captain Clarke set out early, and landed on a sandbar about ten o'clock for the purpose of taking breakfast and drying the meat. At noon they proceeded on about two miles, when they observed a canoe near the shore. They immediately landed, and were equally surprised and pleased at discovering two men by the names of Dickson and Hancock, who had come from the Illinois on a hunting excursion up the Yellowstone. They had left the Illinois in the summer of 1804, and had spent the last winter with the Tetons, in company with a Mr. Ceautoin, who had come there as a trader, but whom they had robbed, or rather they had taken all his merchandise and given him a few robes in exchange. These men had met the boat which we had despatched from fort Mandan, on board of which they were told there was a Ricara chief on his way to Washington; and also another party of Yankton chiefs, accompanying Mr. Durion on a visit of the same kind. We were sorry to learn that the Mandans and Minnetarees were at war with the Ricaras, and had killed two of them. The Assiniboins too, are at war with the Mandans. They have, in consequence, prohibited the Northwestern company from trading to the Missouri, and even killed two of their traders near the Mouse river, and are now lying in wait for Mr. M'Kenzie of the Northwestern company, who had been for a long time among the

Minnetarees. These appearances are rather unfavourable to the project of carrying some of the chiefs to the United States; but we still hope, that by effecting a peace between the Mandans, Minnetarees, and Ricaras, the views of our government may be accomplished.

After leaving these trappers, captain Clarke went on and encamped nearly opposite the entrance of Goatpen creek, where the party were again assailed by their old enemies, the musquetoes.

CHAPTER XXXV.

The party, while descending the river in their skin canoes, are overtaken by the detachment under captain Lewis, and the whole party now once more happily united, descend the Missouri together—they once more revisit the Minnetaree Indians, and hold a council with that nation, as well as the Mahahas—captain Clarke endeavours to persuade their chiefs to accompany him to the United States, which invitation they decline, on account of their fears of the Sioux in their passage down the river—Colter, one of the party, requests and obtains liberty to remain amongst the Indians, for the purpose of hunting beaver—friendly deportment of the Mandans—council held by captain Clarke with the chiefs of the different villages—the chief named the Bigwhite, with his wife and son, agree to accompany the party to the United States, who takes an affecting farewell of his nation—Chaboneau with his wife and child, decline visiting the United States, and are left among the Indians—the party at length proceed on their journey, and find that the course of the Missouri is in some places changed since their passage up that river—they arrive amongst the Ricaras—character of the Chayennes; their dress, habits, &c.—captain Clarke offers to the chief of this nation a medal, which he at first refuses, believing it to be medicine, but which he is afterwards prevailed on to accept—the Ricaras refuse to permit one of their party to accompany captain Clarke to the United States until the return of their chief, who had formerly gone—the party proceed rapidly down the river—prepare to defend themselves against the Tetons, but receive no injury from them—incredible numbers of buffaloe seen near White river—they meet at last with the Tetons, and refuse their invitations to land—intrepidity of captain Clarke.

THURSDAY, August 12. The party continued slowly to descend the river. One of the skin canoes was by accident pierced with a small hole, and they halted for the purpose of mending it with a piece of elk skin, and also to wait for two of the party who were behind. Whilst there, they were overjoyed at seeing captain Lewis's boats heave in sight about noon. But this feeling was changed into alarm on seeing the boats reach the shore without captain Lewis, who they then learnt had been wounded the day before, and was then lying in the periogue. After giving to his wound all the attention in our power, we remained here some time, during which we were overtaken by our two men, accompanied by Dickson and Hancock, who wished to go with us as far as the Mandans. The whole party being now happily reunited, we left the two skin canoes, and all embarked together, about 3 o'clock, in the boats. The wind was however very high from the southwest, accompanied with rain, so that we did not go far before we halted for the night on a sandbar. Captain Lewis's wound was now sore and somewhat painful. The next day,

Friday, 13, they set out by sunrise, and having a very strong breeze from the northwest, proceeded on rapidly. At eight o'clock we passed the mouth of the Little Missouri. Some Indians were seen at a distance below in a skin canoe, and were probably some of the Minnetarees on their return from a hunting excursion, as we passed one of their camps on the southwest side, where they had left a canoe. Two other Indians were seen far off on one of the hills, and we shall therefore soon meet with our old acquaintances, the Mandans. At sunset we arrived at the entrance of Miry river, and encamped on the northeast side, having come by the assistance of the wind and our oars, a distance of eighty six miles. The air was cool, and the musquetoes ceased to trouble us as they had done.

Saturday, 14. We again set out at sunrise, and at length approached the grand village of the Minnetarees, where the natives had collected to view us as we passed. We fired the blunderbuss several times by way of salute, and soon after landed at the bank near the village of the Mahahas, or Shoe Indians, and were received by a crowd of people, who came to welcome our return. Among these were the principal chief of the Mahahas, and the chief of the Little Minnetaree village, both of whom expressed great pleasure at seeing us again; but the latter wept most bitterly. On inquiry, it appeared that his tears were excited because the sight of us reminded him of his son, who had been lately killed by the Blackfoot Indians. After remaining there a few minutes, we crossed to the Mandan village of the Blackcat, where all the inhabitants seemed very much pleased at seeing us. We immediately sent Chaboneau with an invitation for the Minnetarees to visit us, and despatched Drewyer to the lower village of the Mandans to bring Jesseaume as an interpreter. Captain Clarke, in the meantime, walked up to the village of the Blackcat, and smoked and eat with the chief. This village has been rebuilt since our departure, and was now much smaller; a quarrel having arisen among the Indians, in consequence of which a number of families had removed to the opposite side of the river. On the arrival of Jesseaume, captain Clarke addressed the chiefs. We spoke to them now, he said, in the same language we had done before; and repeated his invitation to accompany him to the United States, to hear in person the councils of their great father, who can at all times protect those who open their ears to his councils, and punish his enemies. The Blackcat in reply, declared that he wished to visit the United States, and see his great father, but was afraid of the Sioux, who had killed several of the Mandans since our departure, and who were now on the river below, and would intercept him if he attempted to go. Captain Clarke endeavoured to quiet his apprehensions by assuring him that he would not suffer the Sioux to injure one of our red children who should accompany us, and that they should return loaded with presents, and protected at the expense of the United States. The council was then broken up, after which we crossed and formed our camp on the other side of the river, where we should be sheltered from the rain. Soon after the chief of the Mahahas informed us, that if we would send to his village, we should have some corn. Three men were therefore despatched, and soon after returned loaded with as much as they could carry; and were soon followed by the chief and his wife, to whom we presented a few needles and other articles fit for women. In a short time the Borgue (the great chief of all the Minnetarees) came down, attended by several other chiefs, to whom, after smoking a pipe, captain Clarke now made a harangue, renewing his assurances of friendship and the invitation to go with us to Washington. He was answered by the Borgne, who began by declaring that he much desired to visit his great father, but that the Sioux would certainly kill any of the Mandans who should attempt to go down the river. They were bad people, and would not listen to any advice. When he saw us last, we had told him that we had made peace with all the nations below, yet the Sioux had since killed eight of his tribe, and stolen a number of their horses. The Ricaras too had stolen their horses, and in the contest his people had killed two of the Ricaras. Yet in spite of these dispositions he had always had his ears open to our counsels, and had actually made a peace with the Chayennes and the Indians of the Rocky mountains. He concluded by saying, that however disposed they were to visit the United States, the fear of the Sioux would prevent them from going with us. The council was then finished, and soon afterwards, an invitation was received from the Blackcat, who, on captain Clarke's arrival at his village, presented him with a dozen bushels of corn, which he said was a large proportion of what his people owned; and after smoking a pipe, declared that his people were too apprehensive of the Sioux to venture with us. Captain Clarke then spoke to the chiefs and warriors of the village. He told them of his anxiety that some of them should see their great father, and hear his good words and receive his gifts, and requested them to fix on some confidential chief who might accompany us. To this they made the same objections as before, till at length a young man offered to go, and the warriors all assented to it. But the character of this man was known to be bad, and one of the party with captain Clarke informed him that at the moment he had in his possession a knife which he had stolen. Captain Clarke therefore told the chief of this theft, and ordered the knife to be given up. This was done with a poor apology for having it in his possession, and captain Clarke then reproached the chiefs for wishing to send such a fellow to see and hear so distinguished a person as their great father. They all hung down their heads for some time, till the Blackcat apologized by saying, that the danger was such that they were afraid of sending any of their chiefs, as they considered his loss almost inevitable. Captain Clarke remained some time with them, smoking and relating various particulars of his journey, and then left them to visit the second chief of the Mandans (or the Blackcrow) who had expressed some disposition to accompany us. He seemed well inclined to the journey, but was unwilling to decide till he had called a council of his people, which he intended to do in the afternoon. On returning to the camp, he found the chief of the Mahahas, and also the chief of the Little Minnetaree village, who brought a present of corn on their mules, of which they possess several, and which they procure from the Crow Indians, who either buy or steal them on the frontiers of the Spanish settlements. A great number of the Indians visited us for the purpose of renewing their acquaintance, or of exchanging robes or other articles for the skins brought by the men.

In the evening we were applied to by one of our men, Colter, who was desirous of joining the two trappers who had accompanied us, and who now proposed an expedition up the river, in which they were to find traps and give him a share of the profits. The offer was a very advantageous one, and as he had always performed his duty, and his services might be dispensed with, we agreed that he might go, provided none of the rest would ask or expect a similar indulgence. To this they cheerfully answered, that they wished Colter every success, and would not apply for liberty to separate before we reached St. Louis. We, therefore, supplied him, as did his comrades also, with powder and lead, and a variety of articles which might be useful to him, and he left us the next day. The example of this man shows how easily men may be weaned from the habits of a civilized life to the ruder, but scarcely less fascinating manners of the woods. This hunter has been now absent for many years from the frontiers, and might naturally be presumed to have some anxiety, or some curiosity at least to return to his friends and his country; yet just at the moment when he is approaching the frontiers, he is tempted by a hunting scheme, to give up those delightful prospects, and go back without the least reluctance to the solitude of the woods.

In the evening Chaboneau, who had been mingling with the Indians, and had learned what had taken place during our absence, informed us, that as soon as we had left the Minnetarees, they sent out a war party against the Shoshonees, whom they attacked and routed, though in the engagement they lost two men, one of whom was the son of the chief of the Little Minnetaree village. Another war party had gone against the Racaras, two of whom they killed. A misunderstanding too had taken place between the Mandans and Minnetarees, in consequence of a dispute about a woman, which had nearly occasioned a war; but at length a pipe was presented by the Minnetarees, and a reconciliation took place.

Friday 16. The Mandans had offered to give us some corn, and on sending this morning, we found a greater quantity collected for our use than all our canoes would contain. We therefore thanked the chief and took only six loads. At ten o'clock the chiefs of the different villages came down to smoke with us. We therefore took this opportunity of endeavouring to engage the Borgne in our interests by a present of the swivel, which is no longer serviceable, as it cannot be discharged from our largest periogue. It was now loaded, and the chiefs being formed into a circle round it, captain Clarke addressed them with great ceremony. He said that he had listened with much attention to what had yesterday been declared by the Borgne, whom he believed to be sincere, and then reproached them with their disregard of our counsels, and their wars on the Shoshonees and Ricaras. Littlecherry, the old Minnetaree chief, answered that they had long staid at home and listened to our advice, but at last went to war against the Sioux because their horses had been stolen, and their companions killed; and that in an expedition against those people, they had met the Ricaras, who were on their way to strike them, and a battle ensued. But in future he said they would attend to our words and live at peace. The Borgne added, that his ears too would always be open to the words of his good father, and shut against bad counsel. Captain Clarke then presented to the Borgne the swivel, which he told him had announced the words of his great father to all the nations we had seen, and which, whenever it was fired, should recall those which we had delivered to him. The gun was then discharged, and the Borgne had it conveyed in great pomp to his village. The council was then adjourned.

In the afternoon captain Clarke walked up to the village of the

Littlecrow, taking a flag, which he intended to present to him, but was surprised on being told by him, that he had given over all intention of accompanying us, and refused the flag. He found that this was occasioned by a jealousy between him and the principal chief, Bigwhite: on the interference, however, of Jesseaume, the two chiefs were reconciled, and it was agreed that the Bigwhite himself should accompany us with his wife and son.

Saturday, 17. The principal chiefs of the Minnetarees came down to bid us farewell, as none of them could be prevailed on to go with us. This circumstance induced our interpreter, Chaboneau, with his wife and child, to remain here, as he could be no longer useful; and notwithstanding our offers of taking him with us to the United States, he said that he had there no acquaintance, and no chance of making a livelihood, and preferred remaining among the Indians. This man has been very serviceable to us, and his wife particularly useful among the Shoshonees. Indeed, she has borne with a patience truly admirable, the fatigues of so long a route, incumbered with the charge of an infant, who is even now only nineteen months old. We therefore paid him his wages, amounting to five hundred dollars and thirty-three cents, including the price of a horse and a lodge purchased of him; and soon afterwards dropped down to the village of the Bigwhite, attended on shore by all the Indian chiefs who went to take leave of him. We found him surrounded by his friends, who sat in a circle smoking, while the women were crying. He immediately sent his wife and son, with their baggage, on board, accompanied by the interpreter and his wife, and two children; and then after distributing among his friends some powder and ball, which we had given to him, and smoking a pipe with us, went with us to the river side. The whole village crowded about us, and many of the people wept aloud at the departure of the chief. As captain Clarke was shaking hands with the principal chiefs of all the villages, they requested that he would sit with them one moment longer. Being willing to gratify them, he stopped and ordered a pipe, after smoking which, they informed him that when they first saw us, they did not believe all that we then told them; but having now seen that our words were all true, they would carefully remember them, and follow our advice; that he might tell their great father that the young men should remain at home and not make war on any people except in defence of themselves. They requested him to tell the Ricaras to come and visit them without fear, as they meant that nation no harm, but were desirous of peace with them. On the Sioux, however, they had no dependence, and must kill them whenever they made war parties against their country. Captain Clarke, in reply, informed them that we had never insisted on their not defending themselves, but requested only that they would not strike those whom we had taken by the hand; that we would apprise the Ricaras of their friendly intentions, and that, although we had not seen those of the Sioux with whom they were at war, we should relate their conduct to their great father, who would take measures for producing a general peace among all his red children.

The Borgne now requested that we would take good care of this chief, who would report whatever their great father should say; and the council being then broken up, we took leave with a salute from a gun, and then proceeded. On reaching fort Mandan, we found a few pickets standing on the river side, but all the houses except one, had been burnt by an accidental fire. At the distance of eighteen miles we reached the old Ricara village, where we encamped on the southwest side, the wind being too violent, and the waves too high to permit us to go any further. The same cause prevented us from setting out before eight o'clock the next day,

Monday, 18. Soon after we embarked, an Indian came running down to the beach, who appeared very anxious to speak to us. We went ashore, and found it was the brother of the Bigwhite, who was encamped at no great distance, and hearing of our departure, came to take leave of the chief. The Bigwhite gave him a pair of leggings, and they separated in a most affectionate manner; and we then continued though the wind and waves were still high. The Indian chief seems quite satisfied with his treatment, and during the whole of his time was employed in pointing out the ancient monuments of the Mandans, or in relating their traditions. At length, after making forty miles, we encamped on the northeast side, opposite an old Mandan village, and below the mouth of Chesshetah river.

Tuesday, 19. The wind was so violent that we were not able to proceed until four in the afternoon, during which time the hunters killed four elk and twelve deer. We then went on for ten miles, and came to a sandbar. The rain and wind continued through the night, and during the whole of the next day,

Wednesday, 20, the waves were so high, that one man was constantly occupied in bailing the boats. We passed at noon, Cannonball river; and at three in the afternoon, the entrance of the river Wardepon, the boundary of the country claimed by the Sioux; and after coming eighty-one miles, passed the night on a sandbar. The plains are beginning to change their appearance, the grass becoming of a yellow colour. We have seen great numbers of wolves to-day, and some buffaloe and elk, though these are by no means so abundant as on the Yellowstone.

Since we passed in 1804, a very obvious change has taken place in the current and appearance of the Missouri. In places where at that time there were sandbars, the current of the river now passes, and the former channel of the river is in turn a bank of sand. Sandbars then naked, are covered with willows several feet high: the entrance of some of the creeks and rivers changed in consequence of the quantity of mud thrown into them; and in some of the bottoms are layers of mud eight inches in depth.

Thursday, 21. We rose after a night of broken rest, owing to the musquetoes, and having put our arms in order, so as to be prepared for an attack, continued our course. We soon met three traders, two of whom had wintered with us among the Mandans in 1804, and who were now on their way there. They had exhausted all their powder and lead; we therefore supplied them with both. They informed us that seven hundred Sioux had passed the Ricara towns on their way to make war against the Mandans and Minnetarees, leaving their women and children encamped near the Big-bend of the Missouri, and that the Ricaras all remained at home, without taking any part in the war. They also told us that the Pawnee, or Ricara chief, who went to the United States in the spring of 1805, died on his return near Sioux river.

We then left them, and soon afterwards arrived opposite to the upper Ricara villages. We saluted them with the discharge of four guns, which they answered in the same manner; and on our landing we were met by the greater part of the inhabitants of each village, and also by a band of Chayennes, who were encamped on a hill in the neighbourhood.

As soon as captain Clarke stepped on shore, he was greeted by the two chiefs to whom we had given medals on our last visit, and as they, as well as the rest, appeared much rejoiced at our return, and desirous of hearing from the Mandans, he sat down on the bank, while the Ricaras and Chayennes formed a circle round him; and after smoking, he informed them, as he had already done the Minnetarees, of the various tribes we had visited, and our anxiety to promote peace among our red brethren. He then expressed his regret at their having attacked the Mandans, who had listened to our counsels, and had sent on a chief to smoke with them, and to assure them that they might now hunt in the plains, and visit the Mandan villages in safety, and concluded by inviting some of the chiefs to accompany us to Washington. The man whom we had acknowledged as the principal chief when we ascended, now presented another, who he said was a greater chief than himself, and to him, therefore, he had surrendered the flag and medal with which we had honoured him. This chief, who was absent at our last visit, is a man of thirty-five years of age, a stout, well-looking man, and called by the Indians, Grayeyes.

He now made a very animated reply. He declared that the Ricaras were willing to follow the counsels we had given them, but a few of their bad young men would not live in peace, but had joined the Sioux, and thus embroiled them with the Mandans. These young men had, however, been driven out of the villages, and as the Ricaras were now separated from the Sioux, who were a bad people, and the cause of all their misfortunes, they now desired to be at peace with the Mandans, and would receive them with kindness and friendship. Several of the chiefs he said were desirous of visiting their great father, but as the chief who went to the United States last summer had not returned, and they had some fears for his safety, on account of the Sioux, they did not wish to leave home until they heard of him. With regard to himself, he would continue with his nation, to see that they followed our advice.

The sun being now very hot, the chief of the Chayennes invited us to his lodge, which was at no great distance from the river. We followed him, and found a very large lodge, made of twenty buffaloe skins, surrounded by eighteen or twenty lodges, nearly equal in size. The rest of the nation are expected to-morrow, and will make the number of one hundred and thirty or fifty lodges, containing from three hundred and fifty to four hundred men, at which the men of the nation may be computed. These Chayennes are a fine looking people, of a large stature, straight limbs, high cheek-bones and noses, and of a complexion similar to that of the Ricaras. Their ears are cut at the lower part, but few wear ornaments in them: the hair is generally cut over the eyebrows and small ornaments fall down the cheeks, the remainder being either twisted with horse or buffaloe hair, and divided over each shoulder, or else flowing loosely behind. Their decorations consist chiefly of blue beads, shells, red paint, brass rings, bears' claws, and strips of otter skins, of which last they, as well as the Ricaras, are very fond. The women are coarse in their features, with wide mouths, and ugly. Their dress consists of a habit falling to the midleg, and made of two equal pieces of leather, sewed from the bottom with arm holes, with a flap hanging nearly half way down the body, both before and behind. These are burnt various figures, by means of a hot stick, and adorned with beads, shells, and elks' tusks, which all Indians admire. The other ornaments are blue beads in the ears, but the hair is plain and flows down the back. The summer dress of the men is a simple buffaloe robe, a cloth round the waist, moccasins, and occasionally leggings. Living remote from the whites, they are shy and cautious, but are peaceably disposed, and profess to make war against no people except the Sioux, with whom they have been engaged in contests immemorially. In their excursions they are accompanied by their dogs and horses, which they possess in great numbers, the former serving to carry almost all their light baggage. After smoking for some time, captain Clarke gave a small medal to the Chayenne chief, and explained at the same time the meaning of it. He seemed alarmed at this present, and sent for a robe and a quantity of buffaloe meat, which he gave to captain Clarke, and requested him to take back the medal, for he knew that all white people were medicine, and he was afraid of the medal, or of any thing else which the white people gave to the Indians. Captain Clarke then repeated his intention in giving the medal, which was the medicine his great father had directed him to deliver to all chiefs who listened to his word and followed his counsels; and that as he had done so, the medal was given as a proof that we believed him sincere. He now appeared satisfied and received the medal, in return for which he gave double the quantity of buffaloe meat he had offered before. He seemed now quite reconciled to the whites, and requested that some traders might be sent among the Chayennes, who lived, he said, in a country full of beaver, but did not understand well how to catch them, and were discouraged from it by having no sale for them when caught. Captain Clarke promised that they should be soon applied with goods, and taught the best mode of catching beaver.

The Bigwhite, chief of the Mandans, now addressed them at some length, explaining the pacific intentions of his nation; and the Chayenne observed that both the Ricaras and Mandans seemed to be in fault; but at the end of the council the Mandan chief was treated with great civility, and the greatest harmony prevailed among them. The great chief, however, informed us, that none of the Ricaras could be prevailed on to go with us till the return of the other chief, and that the Chayennes were a wild people, and afraid to go. He invited captain Clarke to his house, and gave him two carrots of tobacco, two beaver skins, and a trencher of boiled corn and beans. It is the custom of all the nations on the Missouri, to offer to every white man food and refreshment when he first enters their tents.

Captain Clarke returned to the boats, where he found the chief of the lower village, who had cut off part of his hair, and disfigured himself in such a manner that we did not recognise him at first, until he explained that he was in mourning for his nephew, who had been killed by the Sioux. He proceeded with us to the village on the island, where we were met by all the inhabitants. The second chief, on seeing the Mandan, began to speak to him in a loud and threatning tone, till captain Clarke declared that the Mandans had listened to our councils, and that if any injury was done to the chief, we should defend him against every nation. He then invited the Mandan to his lodge, and after a very ceremonious smoking, assured captain Clarke that the Mandan was as safe as at home, for the Ricaras had opened their ears to our councils, as well as the Mandans. This was repeated by the great chief, and the Mandan and Ricara chiefs now smoked and conversed in great apparent harmony; after which we returned to the boats. The whole distance today was twenty-nine miles.

Friday, 22. It rained all night, so that we all rose this morning quite wet, and were about proceeding, when captain Clarke was requested to visit the chiefs. They now made several speeches, in which they said that they were unwilling to go with us, until the return of their countryman; and that, although they disliked the Sioux as the origin of all their troubles, yet as they had more horses than they wanted, and were in want of guns and powder, they would be obliged to trade once more with them for those articles, after which they would break off all connexion with them. He now returned to the boats, and after taking leave of the people, who seemed to regret our departure, and firing a salute of two guns, proceeded seventeen miles, and encamped below Grouse island. We made only seventeen miles today, for we were obliged to land near Wetarhoo river to dry our baggage, besides which the sandbars are now unusually numerous as the river widens below the Ricara villages. Captain Lewis is now so far recovered that he was able to walk a little to-day for the first time. While here we had occasion to notice that the Mandans as well as the Minnetarees and Ricaras keep their horses in the same lodges with themselves.

Saturday, 23. We set out early, but the wind was so high, that soon after passing the Sahwacanah, we were obliged to go on shore, and remain till three o'clock, when a heavy shower of rain fell and the wind lulled. We then continued our route, and after a day's journey of forty miles encamped. Whilst on shore we killed three deer and as many elk. Along the river are great quantities of grapes and choke-cherries, and also a species of currant which we have never seen before: it is black, with a leaf much larger than that of the other currants, and inferior in flavour to all of them.

Sunday, 24. We set out at sunrise, and at eight o'clock passed Lahoocat's island, opposite to the lower point of which we landed to examine a stratum of stone, near the top of a bluff of remarkably black clay. It is soft, white, and contains a very fine grit; and on being dried in the sun will crumble to pieces. The wind soon after became so high that we were obliged to land for several hours, but proceeded at five o'clock. After making forty-three miles, we encamped at the gorge of the Lookout bend of the Missouri. The Sioux have lately passed in this quarter, and there is now very little game, and that so wild, that we were unable to shoot any thing. Five of the hunters were therefore sent ahead before daylight next morning,

Monday, 25, to hunt in the Pawnee island, and we followed them soon after. At eight o'clock we reached the entrance of the Chayenne, where we remained till noon, in order to take a meridian observation. At three o'clock we passed the old Pawnee village, near which we had met the Tetons in 1804, and encamped in a large bottom on the northeast side, a little below the mouth of Notimber creek. Just above our camp the Ricaras had formerly a large village on each side of the river, and there are still seen the remains of five villages on the southwest side, below the Chayenne, and one also on Lahoocat's island; but these have all been destroyed by the Sioux. The weather was clear and calm, but by means of our oars we made forty-eight miles. Our hunters procured nothing except a few deer.

The skirt of timber in the bend above the Chayenne is inconsiderable, and scattered from four to sixteen miles on the southwest side of the river, and the thickest part is from the distance of from ten to six miles of the Chayenne. A narrow bottom of small cottonwood trees is also on the northeast point, at the distance of four miles above the river. A few large trees, and a small undergrowth of willows on the lower side bottom on the Missouri half a mile, and extend a quarter of a mile up the Chayenne: there is a bottom of cotton timber in the part above the Chayenne. The Chayenne discharges but a little water at its mouth, which resembles that of the Missouri.

Tuesday, 26. After a heavy dew we set out, and at nine o'clock reached the entrance of Teton river, below which were a raft and a skin canoe, which induced us to suspect that the Tetons were in the neighbourhood. The arms were therefore put in perfect order, and every thing prepared to revenge the slightest insult from those people, to whom it is necessary to show an example of salutary rigour. We, however, went on without seeing any of them, although we were obliged to land near Smoke creek for two hours, to stop a leak in the periogue. Here we saw great quantities of plums and grapes, but not yet ripe. At five o'clock we passed Louisville's fort, on Cedar island, twelve miles below which we encamped, having been able to row sixty miles, with the wind ahead during the greater part of the day.

Wednesday, 27. Before sunrise we set out with a stiff eastern breeze in our faces, and at the distance of a few miles landed on a sandbar near Tylor's river, and sent out the hunters, as this was the most favourable spot to recruit our stock of meat, which was now completely exhausted. But after a hunt of three hours, they reported that no game was to be found in the bottoms, the grass having been laid flat by the immense number of buffaloes which had recently passed over it; and that they saw only a few buffaloe bulls, which they did not kill, as they were quite unfit for use. Near this place we observed, however, the first signs of the wild turkey; and not long after landed in the Bigbend, and killed a fine fat elk, on which we feasted. Towards night we heard the bellowing of the buffaloe bulls, on the lower island of the Bigbend. We pursued this agreeable sound, and after killing some of the cows, encamped on the island, forty-five miles from the camp of last night.

Thursday, 28. We proceeded at an early hour, having previously despatched some hunters ahead, with orders to join us at our old camp a little above Corvus creek, where we intended remaining one day, in order to procure the skins and skeletons of some animals, such as the mule-deer, the antelope, the barking squirrel, and the magpie, which we were desirous of carrying to the United States, and which we had seen in great abundance. After rowing thirty-two miles we landed at twelve, and formed a camp in a high bottom, thinly timbered and covered with grass, and not crowded with musquetoes. Soon after we arrived the squaws and several of the men went to the bushes near the river, and brought great quantities of large well flavoured plums of three different species.

The hunters returned in the afternoon, without being able to procure any of the game we wished, except the barking squirrel, though they killed four common deer, and had seen large herds of buffaloe, of which they brought in two. They resumed their hunt in the morning,

Friday, 29, and the rest of the party were employed in dressing skins, except two, who were sent to the village of the barking squirrels, but could not see one of them out of their holes. At ten o'clock the skins were dressed, and we proceeded; and soon passed the entrance of White river, the water of which is at this time nearly the colour of milk. The day was spent in hunting along the river, so that we did not advance more than twenty-miles; but with all our efforts we were unable to kill either a mule-deer or an antelope, though we procured the common deer, a porcupine, and some buffaloe. These last animals are now so numerous that from an eminence we discovered more than we had ever seen before, at one time; and if it be not impossible to calculate the moving multitude, which darkened the whole plains, we are convinced that twenty thousand would be no exaggerated number. With regard to game in general, we observe that the greatest quantity of wild animals are usually found in the country lying between two nations at war.

Saturday, 30. We set out at the usual hour, but after going some distance were obliged to stop for two hours, in order to wait for one of the hunters. During this time we made an excursion to a large orchard of delicious plums, where we were so fortunate as to kill two buck elks. We then proceeded down the river, and were about landing at a place where we had agreed to meet all the hunters, when several persons appeared on the high hills to the northeast, whom, by the help of the spy-glass, we distinguished to be Indians. We landed on the southwest side of the river, and immediately after saw, on a height opposite to us, about twenty persons, one of whom, from his blanket great-coat, and a handkerchief round his head, we supposed to be a Frenchman. At the same time, eighty or ninety more Indians, armed with guns and bows and arrows, came out of a wood some distance below them, and fired a salute, which we returned. From their hostile appearance, we were apprehensive that they might be Tetons; but as from the country through which they were roving, it was possible that they were Yanktons, Pawnees, or Mahas, and therefore less suspicious, we did not know in what way to receive them. In order, however, to ascertain who they were, without risk to the party, captain Clarke crossed, with three persons who could speak different Indian languages, to a sandbar near the opposite side, in hopes of conversing with them. Eight young men soon met him on the sandbar, but none of them could understand either the Pawnee or Maha interpreter. They were then addressed in the Sioux language, and answered that they were Tetons, of the band headed by the Black-buffaloe, Tahtackasabah. This was the same who had attempted to stop us in 1804; and being now less anxious about offending so mischievous a tribe, captain Clarke told them that they had been deaf to our councils, had ill treated us two years ago, and had abused all the whites who had since visited them. He believed them, he added, to be bad people and they must therefore return to their companions, for if they crossed over to our camp we would put them to death. They asked for some corn, which captain Clarke refused; they then requested permission to come and visit our camp, but he ordered them back to their own people. He then returned, and all the arms were prepared in case of an attack; but when the Indians reached their comrades, and had informed their chiefs of our intention, they all set out on their way to their own camp; but some of them halted on a rising ground, and abused us very copiously, threatening to kill us if we came across. We took no notice of this for some time, till the return of three of our hunters, whom we were afraid the Indians might have met; but as soon as they joined us, we embarked; and to see what the Indians would attempt, steered near the side of their river. At this the party on the hill seemed agitated, some set out for their camp, others walked about, and one man walked towards the boats and invited us to land. As he came near, we recognised him to be the same who had accompanied us for two days in 1804, and who is considered as the friend of the whites. Unwilling, however, to have any interview with these people, we declined his invitation; upon which he returned to the hill, and struck the earth three times with his gun, a great oath among the Indians, who consider swearing by the earth as one of the most sacred forms of imprecation. At the distance of six miles we stopped on a bleak sandbar; where, however, we thought ourselves safe from attack during the night, and also free from musquetoes. We had now made only twenty-two miles; but in the course of the day had procured a mule-deer, which we much desired. About eleven in the evening the wind shifted to the northwest and it began to rain, accompanied with hard claps of thunder and lightning; after which the wind changed to southwest, and blew with such violence that we were obliged to hold the canoes for fear of their being driven from the sandbar; the cables of two of them however broke, and two others were blown quite across the river, nor was it till two o'clock that the whole party was reassembled, waiting in the rain for daylight.

CHAPTER XXXVI.

The party return in safety to St. Louis.

SUNDAY, August 31. We examined our arms, and proceeded with the wind in our favour. For some time we saw several Indians on the hills, but soon lost sight of them. In passing the dome, and the first village of barking squirrels, we stopped and killed two fox squirrels, an animal which we have not seen on the river higher than this place. At night we encamped on the northeast side, after a journey of seventy miles. We had seen no game, as usual, on the river; but in the evening the musquetoes soon discovered us.

Monday, September 1. We set out early, but were shortly compelled to put to shore, for half an hour, till a thick fog disappeared. At nine o'clock we passed the entrance of the Quicurre, which presents the same appearance as when we ascended, the water rapid and of a milky-white colour. Two miles below several Indians ran down to the bank, and beckoned to us to land; but as they appeared to be Tetons, and of a war party, we paid no attention to them, except to inquire to what tribe they belonged; but as the Sioux interpreter did not understand much of the language, they probably mistook his question. As one of our canoes was behind, we were afraid of an attack on the men, and therefore landed on an open commanding situation, out of the view of the Indians, in order to wait for them. We had not been in this position fifteen minutes, when we heard several guns, which we immediately concluded were fired at the three hunters; and being now determined to protect them against any number of Indians, captain Clarke with fifteen men ran up the river, whilst captain Lewis hobbled up the bank, and formed the rest of the party in such a manner as would best enable them to protect the boats. On turning a point of the river, captain Clarke was agreeably surprised at seeing the Indians remaining in the place where we left them, and our canoe at the distance of a mile. He now went on a sandbar, and when the Indians crossed, gave them his hand, and was informed that they had been amusing themselves with shooting at an old keg, which we had thrown into the river, and was floating down. We now found them to be part of a band of eighty lodges of Yanktons, on Plum creek, and therefore invited them down to the camp, and after smoking several pipes, told them that we had mistaken them for Tetons, and had intended putting every one of them to death, if they had fired at our canoe; but finding them Yanktons, who were good men, we were glad to take them by the hand as faithful children, who had opened their ears to our counsels. They saluted the Mandan with great cordiality, and one of them declared that their ears had indeed been opened, and that they had followed our advice since we gave a medal to their great chief, and should continue to do so. We now tied a piece of riband to the hair of each Indian, and gave them some corn. We made a present of a pair of leggings to the principal chief, and then took our leave, being previously overtaken by our canoe. At two o'clock we landed to hunt on Bonhomme island, but obtained a single elk only. The bottom on the northeast side is very rich, and so thickly overgrown with pea-vines and grass, interwoven with grape-vines, that some of the party who attempted to hunt there, were obliged to leave it and ascend the plain, where they found the grass nearly as high as their heads. These plains are much richer below than above the Quicurre, and the whole country is now very beautiful. After making fifty-two miles against a head wind, we stopped for the night on a sandbar, opposite to the Calumet bluff, where we had encamped on the first of September, 1804, and where our flag-staff was still standing. We suffered very much from the musquetoes, till the wind became so high as to blow them all away.

Tuesday, 2. At eight o'clock we passed the river Jacques, but soon after were compelled to land, in consequence of the high wind from the northeast, and remain till sunset: after which we went on to a sandbar twenty-two miles from our camp of last evening. Whilst we were on shore we killed three buffaloes, and four prairie fowls, which are the first we have seen in descending. Two turkies were also killed, and were very much admired by the Indians, who had never seen that animal before. The plains continue level and fertile, and in the low grounds there is much white oak, and some white ash in the ravines and high bottoms, with lyn and slippery elm occasionally. During the night the wind shifted to the southwest and blew the sand over us in such a manner, that our situation was very unpleasant. It lulled, however, towards daylight, and we then,

Wednesday, 3, proceeded. At eleven o'clock we passed the Redstone. The river is now crowded with sandbars, which are very differently situated now from what they were when we ascended. But notwithstanding these and the head wind, we made sixty miles before night, when we saw two boats and several men on shore. We landed, and found a Mr. James Airs, a partner of a house at Prairie de Chien, who had come from Mackinau by the way of Prairie de Chien and St. Louis with a license to trade among the Sioux for one year. He had brought two canoes loaded with merchandise, but lost many of his most useful articles in a squall some time since. After so long an interval, the sight of any one who could give us information of our country, was peculiarly delightful, and much of the night was spent in making inquiries into what had occurred during our absence. We found Mr. Airs a very friendly and liberal gentleman, and when we proposed to him to purchase a small quantity of tobacco, to be paid for in St. Louis, he very readily furnished every man of the party with as much as he could use during the rest of the voyage, and insisted on our accepting a barrel of flour. This last we found very agreeable, although we have still a little flour which we had deposited at the mouth of Maria's river. We could give in return only about six bushels of corn, which was all that we could spare. The next morning,

Thursday, 4, we left Mr. Airs about eight o'clock, and after passing the Big Sioux river, stopped at noon near Floyd's bluff. On ascending the hill we found that the grave of Floyd had been opened, and was now half uncovered. We filled it up, and then continued down to our old camp near the Maha village, where all our baggage, which had been wet by the rain of last night, was exposed to dry. There is no game on the river except wild geese and pelicans. Near Floyd's grave are some flourishing black walnut trees, which are the first we have seen on our return. At night we heard the report of several guns in a direction towards the Maha village, and supposed it to be the signal of the arrival of some trader. But not meeting him when we set out, the next morning,

Friday, 5, we concluded that the firing was merely to announce the return of the Mahas to the village, this being the season at which they return home from buffaloe hunting, to take care of their corn, beans and pumpkins. The river is now more crooked, the current more rapid, and crowded with snags and sawyers, and the bottoms on both sides well supplied with timber. At three o'clock we passed the Bluestone bluff, where the river leaves the highlands and meanders through a low rich bottom, and at night encamped, after making seventy-three miles.

Saturday, 6. The wind continued ahead, but the musquetoes was so tormenting that to remain was more unpleasant than even to advance, however slowly, and we therefore proceeded. Near the Little Sioux river we met a trading boat belonging to Mr. Augustus Chateau, of St. Louis, with several men, on their way to trade with the Yanktons at the river Jacques. We obtained from them a gallon of whiskey, and gave each of the party a dram, which is the first spirituous liquor any of them have tasted since the fourth of July 1805. After remaining with them for some time we went on to a sandbar, thirty miles from our last encampment, where we passed the night in expectation of being joined by two of the hunters. But as they did not come on, we set out next morning,

Sunday, 7, leaving a canoe with five men, to wait for them, but had not gone more than eight miles, when we overtook them; we therefore fired a gun, which was a signal for the men behind, which, as the distance in a direct line was about a mile, they readily heard and soon joined us. A little above the Soldier's river we stopped to dine on elk, of which we killed three, and at night, after making forty-four miles, encamped on a sandbar, where we hoped in vain to escape from the musquetoes. We therefore set out early the next morning,

Monday, 8, and stopped for a short time at the Council bluffs, to examine the situation of the place, and were confirmed in our belief that it would be a very eligible spot for a trading establishment. Being anxious to reach the Platte, we plied our oars so well, that by night we had made seventy-eight miles, and landed at our old encampment at Whitecatfish camp, twelve miles above that river. We had here occasion to remark the wonderful evaporation from the Missouri, which does not appear to contain more water, nor is its channel wider than at the distance of one thousand miles nearer its source, although within that space it receives about twenty rivers, some of them of considerable width, and a great number of creeks. This evaporation seems, in fact, to be greater now than when we ascended the river, for we are obliged to replenish the inkstand every day with fresh ink, nine tenths of which must escape by evaporation.

Tuesday, 9. By eight o'clock we passed the river Platte, which is lower than it was, and its waters almost clear, though the channel is turbulent as usual. The sandbars which obstructed the Missouri are, however, washed away, and nothing is to be seen except a few remains of the bar. Below the Platte, the current of the Missouri becomes evidently more rapid, and the obstructions from fallen timber increased. The river bottoms are extensive, rich, and covered with tall, large timber, which is still more abundant in the hollows of the ravines, where may be seen, oak, ash, elm, interspersed with some walnut and hickory. The musquetoes also, though still numerous, seem to lose some of their vigour. As we advance so rapidly, the change of climate is very perceptible, the air is more sultry than we have experienced for a long time before, and the nights so warm that a thin blanket is now sufficient, although a few days ago two were not burdensome. Late in the afternoon we encamped opposite to the Baldpated prairie, after a journey of seventy-three miles.

Wednesday, 10. We again set out early and the wind being moderate, though still ahead, we came sixty-five miles to a sandbar, a short distance above the grand Nemaha. In the course of the day we met a trader, with three men, on his way to the Pawnee Loups or Wolf Pawnees, on the Platte. Soon after another boat passed us with seven men from St. Louis, bound to the Mahas. With both of these trading parties we had some conversation, but our anxiety to go on would not suffer us to remain long with them. The Indians, and particularly the squaws and children are weary of the long journey, and we are not less desirous of seeing our country and friends. We saw on the shore, deer, rackoons, and turkies.

Thursday, 11. A high wind from the northwest detained us till after sunrise, when we proceeded slowly; for as the river is rapid and narrow, as well as more crowded with sandbars and timber than above, much caution is necessary in avoiding these obstacles, particularly in the present low state of the water. The Nemaha seems less wide than when we saw it before, and Wolf river has scarcely any water. In the afternoon we halted above the Nadowa to hunt, and killed two deer; after which we went on to a small island, forty miles from our last night's encampment. Here we were no longer annoyed by musquetoes, which do not seem to frequent this part of the river; and after having been persecuted with these insects during the whole route from the falls, it is a most agreeable exemption. Their noise was very agreeably changed for that of the common wolves, which were howling in different directions, and the prairie wolves, whose barking resembles precisely that of the common cur dog.

Friday, 12. After a thick fog and a heavy dew we set out by sunrise, and at the distance of seven miles met two periogues, one of them bound to the Platte, for the purpose of trading with the Pawnees, the other on a trapping expedition to the neighbourhood of the Mahas. Soon after we met the trading party under Mr. M'Clellan; and with them was Mr. Gravelines, the interpreter, whom we had sent with a Ricara chief to the United States. The chief had unfortunately died at Washington, and Gravelines was now on his way to the Ricaras, with a speech from the president, and the presents which had been made to the chief. He had also directions to instruct the Ricaras in agriculture. He was accompanied on this mission by old Mr.

Durion, our former Sioux interpreter, whose object was to procure, by his influence, a safe passage for the Ricara presents through the bands of Sioux, and also to engage some of the Sioux chiefs, not evceeding six, to visit Washington. Both of them were instructed to inquire particularly after the fate of our party, no intelligence having been received from us during a long time. We authorised Mr. Durion to invite ten or twelve Sioux chiefs to accompany him, particularly the Yanktons, whom we had found well disposed towards our country. The afternoon being wet, we determined to remain with Mr. M'Clellan during the night; and therefore, after sending on five hunters ahead, spent the evening in inquiries after occurrences in the United States during our absence; and by eight o'clock next morning,

Saturday, 13, overtook the hunters; but they had killed nothing. The wind being now too high to proceed safely through timber stuck in every part of the channel, we landed, and sent the small canoes ahead to hunt. Towards evening we overtook them, and encamped, not being able to advance more than eighteen miles. The weather was very warm, and the rushes in the bottoms so high and thick that we could scarcely hunt, but were fortunate enough to obtain four deer and a turkey, which, with the hooting owl, the common buzzard, crow, and hawk, were the only game we saw. Among the timber is the cottonwood, sycamore, ash, mulberry, pappaw, walnut, hickory, prickly ash, several species of elm, intermixed with great quantities of grapevines, and three kinds of peas.

Sunday, 14. We resumed our journey, and this being a part of the river to which the Kanzas resort, in order to rob the boats of traders, we held ourselves in readiness to fire upon any Indians who should offer us the slightest indignity, as we no longer needed their friendship, and found that a tone of firmness and decision is the best possible method of making proper impression on these freebooters. We, however, did not encounter any of them; but just below the old Kanzas village met three trading boats from St. Louis, on their way to the Yanktons and Mahas. After leaving them we saw a number of deer, of which we killed five, and encamped on an island, fifty-three miles from our encampment of last evening.

Monday, 15. A strong breeze ahead prevented us from advancing more than forty-nine miles to the neighbourhood of Haycabin creek. The river Kansas is very low at this time. About a mile below it we landed to view the situation of a high hill, which has many advantages for a trading house or fort; while on the shore we gathered great quantities of pappaws, and shot an elk. The low grounds are now delightful, and the whole country exhibits a rich appearance; but the weather is oppressively warm, and descending as rapidly as we do from a cool open country, between the latitude of 46 and 49°, in which we have been for nearly two years, to the wooded plains in 38 and 39°, the heat would be almost insufferable were it not for the constant winds from the south and southeast.

Tuesday, 16. We set out at an early hour, but the weather soon became so warm that the men rowed but little. In the course of the day we met two trading parties, on their way to the Pawnees and Mahas, and after making fifty-two miles, remained on an island till next morning,

Wednesday, 17, when we passed in safety the island of the Little Osage village. This place is considered by the navigators of the Missouri, as the most dangerous part of it, the whole water being compressed, for two miles, within a narrow channel, crowded with timber, into which the violence of the current is constantly washing the banks. At the distance of thirty miles we met a captain M'Clellan, lately of the United States' army, with whom we encamped. He informed us that the general opinion in the United States was that we were lost; the last accounts which had been heard of us being from the Mandan villages. Captain M'Clellan is on his way to attempt a new trade with the Indians. His plan is to establish himself on the Platte, and after trading with the Pawnees and Ottoes, prevail on some of their chiefs to accompany him to Santa Fee, where he hopes to obtain permission to exchange his merchandise for gold and silver, which is there in abundance. If this be granted, he can transport his goods on mules and horses from the Platte to some part of Louisiana, convenient to the Spanish settlements, where he may be met by the traders from New Mexico.

Thursday, 18. We parted with captain M'Clellan, and within a few miles passed the Grand river, below which we overtook the hunters, who had been sent forward yesterday afternoon. They had not been able to kill any thing, nor did we see any game except one bear and three turkies, so that our whole stock of provisions is one biscuit for each person; but as there is an abundance of pappaws, the men are perfectly contented. The current of the river is more gentle than it was when we ascended, the water being lower though still rapid in places where it is confined. We continued to pass through a very fine country, for fifty-two miles, when we encamped nearly opposite to Mine river. The next morning,

Friday, 19, we worked our oars all day, without taking time to hunt, or even landing, except once to gather pappaws; and at eight o'clock reached the entrance of the Osage river, a distance of seventy-two miles. Several of the party have been for a day or two attacked with a soreness in the eyes; the eye-ball being very much swelled and the lid appearing as if burnt by the sun, and extremely painful, particularly when exposed to the light. Three of the men are so much affected by it, as to be unable to row. We therefore turned one of the boats adrift, and distributed the men among the other canoes, when we set out a little before daybreak,

Saturday, 20. The Osage is at this time low, and discharges but a very small quantity of water. Near the mouth of Gasconade, where we arrived at noon, we met five Frenchmen on their way to the Great Osage village. As we moved along rapidly, we saw on the banks some cows feeding, and the whole party almost involuntarily raised a shout of joy at seeing this image of civilization and domestic life.

Soon after we reached the little French village of Lacharette, which we saluted with a discharge of four guns, and three hearty cheers. We then landed, and were received with kindness by the inhabitants, as well as some traders from Canada, who were going to traffic with the Osages and Ottoes. They were all equally surprised and pleased at our arrival, for they had long since abandoned all hopes of ever seeing us return.

These Canadians have boats prepared for the navigation of the

Missouri, which seem better calculated for the purpose than those in any other form. They are in the shape of batteaux, about thirty feet long, and eight wide; the bow and stern pointed, the bottom flat, and carrying six oars only, and their chief advantage is their width and flatness, which saves them from the danger of rolling sands.

Having come sixty-eight miles, and the weather threatening to be bad, we remained at La Charette till the next morning,

Sunday, 21, when we proceeded, and as several settlements have been made during our absence, were refreshed with the sight of men and cattle along the banks. We also passed twelve canoes of Kickapoo Indians, going on a hunting excursion. At length, after coming forty-eight miles, we saluted, with heartfelt satisfaction, the village of St. Charles, and on landing were treated with the greatest hospitality and kindness by all the inhabitants of that place. Their civility detained us till ten o'clock the next morning,

Monday, 22, when the rain having ceased, we set out for Coldwater creek, about three miles from the mouth of the Missouri, where we found a cantonment of troops of the United States, with whom we passed the day, and then,

Tuesday, 23, descended to the Mississippi, and round to St. Louis, where we arrived at twelve o'clock, and having fired a salute went on shore and received the heartiest and most hospitable welcome from the whole village.

APPENDIX

APPENDIX.

Observations and reflections on the present and future state of Upper Louisiana, in relation to the government of the Indian nations inhabiting that country, and the trade and intercourse with the same. By captain Lewis.

WITH a view to a more complete development of this subject, I have deemed it expedient in the outset, to state the leading measures pursued by the provincial government of Spain, in relation to this subject; the evils which flowed from those measures, as well to the Indians as to the whites, in order that we may profit by their errors, and be ourselves the better enabled to apply the necessary correctives to the remnant of evils which their practice introduced.

From the commencement of the Spanish provincial government in Louisiana, whether by the permission of the crown, or originating in the pecuniary rapacity of their governors general, this officer assumed to himself exclusively the right of trading with all the Indian nations in Louisiana; and therefore proceeded to dispose of this privilege to individuals, for certain specific sums: his example was imitated by the governors of Upper Louisiana, who made a further exaction. Those exclusive permissions to individuals varied as to the extent of country or nations they embraced, and the period for which granted; but in all cases the exclusive licenses were offered to the highest bidder, and, consequently, the sums paid by the individuals purchasing, were quite as much as the profits of the trade would bear, and in many instances, from a spirit of opposition between coutending applicants, much more was given than ever the profits of the traffic would justify. The individual, of course, became bankrupt. This, however, was among the least of the evils flowing from this system to the Indian; it produced the evil of compelling him to pay such enormous sums for the articles he purchased, that his greatest exertions would not enable him to obtain as much as he had previously been in the habit of consuming, and which he therefore conceived necessary to him; for as this system progressed the demands of the governors became more exorbitant, and the trader, to meet his engagements, exacted higher prices from the Indians, though the game became scarcer in their country. The morals of the Indian were corrupted by placing before him the articles which he viewed as of the first necessity to him, at such prices, that he had it not in his power to purchase; he was therefore induced, in many instances, to take by force that which he had not the means of paying for; consoling himself with the idea, that the trader was compelled of necessity to possess himself of the peltries and furs, in order to meet his engagements with those from whom he had purchased his merchandise, as well as those who had assisted him in their transportation. He consequently could not withdraw himself from their trade, without inevitable ruin. The prevalence of this sentiment among the Indians, was strongly impressed on my mind by an anecdote related to me by a gentleman, who had for several years enjoyed, under the Spanish government, the exclusive privilege of trading with the Little Osages. It happened, that after he had bartered with them for all their peltries and furs which they had on hand, that they seized forcibly on a number of guns and a quantity of ammunition which he had still remaining; he remonstrated with them against this act of violence, and finally concluded by declaring that he would never return among them again, nor would he suffer any person to bring them merchandise thereafter. They heard him out very patiently, when one of their leaders pertly asked him; if he did not return the next season to obtain their peltries and furs, how he intended to pay the persons from whom he had purchased the merchandise they had then taken from him?

The Indians believed that these traders were the most powerful persons in the nation; nor did they doubt their ability to withhold merchandise from them; but the great thirst displayed by the traders for the possession of their peltries and furs, added to the belief that they were compelled to continue their traffic, was considered by the Indians a sufficient guarantee for the continuance of their intercourse, and therefore felt themselves at liberty to practise aggressions on the traders with impunity: thus they governed the trader by what they conceived his necessities to possess their furs and peltries, rather than governing themselves by their own anxiety to obtain merchandise, as they may most effectually be by a well regulated system. It is immaterial to the Indians how they obtain merchandise; in possession of a supply they feel independent. The Indians found by a few experiments of aggression on the traders, that as it respected themselves, it had a salutary effect; and although they had mistaken the legitimate cause of action on the part of the trader, the result being favourable to themselves, they continued their practice. The fact is, that the trader was compelled to continue his trade under every disadvantage, in order to make good his engagements to the governors; for having secured their protection, they were safe, both in person and property from their other creditors, who were, for the most part, the merchants of Montreal.

The first effect of these depredations of the Indians, was the introduction of a ruinous custom among the traders, of extending to them a credit. The traders, who visited the Indians on the Missouri, arrived at their wintering stations from the latter end of September to the middle of October: here they carried on their traffic until the latter end of March or beginning of April. In the course of the season they had possessed themselves of every skin the Indians had procured, of course there was an end of trade; but previous to their return, the Indians insist upon a credit being given on the faith of payment when he returned the next season. The trader understands his situation, and knowing this credit was nothing less than the price of his passport, or the privilege of departing in safety to his home, of course narrowed down the amount of this credit, by concealing, as far as he could, to avoid the suspicions of the Indians, the remnant of his merchandise. But the amount to be offered must always be such as they had been accustomed to receive; and which, in every case, bore a considerable proportion to their whole trade; say the full amount of their summer or redskin hunt. The Indians well knew that the traders were in their power, and the servile motives which induced them to extend their liberality to them, and were therefore the less solicitous to meet their engagements on the day of payment; to this indifference they were further urged by the traders distributing among them, on those occasions, many articles of the last necessity to them. The consequence was, that when the traders returned the ensuing fall, if they obtained only one half of their credits they were well satisfied, as this covered their real expenditure.

Again: if it so happen, in the course of the winter's traffic, that the losses of the trader, growing out of the indolence of the Indians, and their exorbitant exactions under the appellation of credit, should so reduce his stock in trade that he could not pay the governor the price stipulated for his license, and procure a further supply of goods in order to prosecute his trade, the license was immediately granted to some other individual, who, with an ample assortment of merchandise, visits the place of rendezvous of his predecessor, without the interpolation of a single season. It did not unfrequently happen, that the individuals engaged in this commerce, finding one of their number failing from the rapacity of the Indian nation, with which he had been permitted to trade, were not so anxious to possess themselves of the privilege of trading with that nation; the governor, of course, rather than lose all advantages, would abate of his demands considerably. The new trader thus relieved of a considerable proportion of the tax borne by his predecessor, and being disposed to make a favourable impression on the minds of the Indians, to whom he was about to introduce himself, would, for the first season at least, dispose of his goods to those Indians on more moderate terms than his predecessor had done. The Indians now find that the aggressions they have practised on their former trader, so far from proving detrimental to them, had procured not only their exoneration from the payment of the last credit given them by their former trader, but that the present trader furnished them goods on better terms than they had been accustomed to receive them. Thus encouraged by the effects of this rapacious policy, it was not to be expected that they would alter their plan of operation as it respected their new trader; or that they should appreciate the character of the whites in general in any other manner, than as expressed in a prevailing sentiment on this subject, now common among several nations on the Missouri, to wit: "*that the white men are like dogs, the more you beat them and plunder them, the more goods they will bring you, and the cheaper they will sell them.*" This sentiment constitutes, at present, the rule of action among the Kanzas, Sioux, and others; and if it be not broken down by the adoption of some efficient measures, it needs not the aid of any deep calculation to determine the sum of advantages which will result to the American people from the trade of the Missouri. These aggressions on the part of the Indians, were encouraged by the pusillanimity of the engagees, who declared that they were not engaged to fight.

The evils which flowed from this system of exclusive trade, were sensibly felt by the inhabitants of Louisiana. The governor, regardless of the safety of the community, sold to an individual the right of vending among the Indians every species of merchandise; thus bartering, in effect, his only efficient check on the Indians. The trader, allured by the hope of gain, neither shackled with discretion, nor consulting the public good, proceeded to supply the Indians, on whom he was dependent, with arms, ammunition, and all other articles they might require. The Indian, thus independent, acknowledging no authority but his own, will proceed without compunction of conscience or fear of punishment, to wage war on the defenceless inhabitants of the frontier, whose lives and property, in many instances, were thus sacrificed at the shrine of an *inordinate thirst for wealth* in their governors, which in reality occasioned all those evils. Although the governors could not have been ignorant that the misfortunes of the people were caused by the independence of the Indians, to which they were accessary, still they were the more unwilling to apply the corrective; because the very system which gave them wealth in the outset, in the course of its progress, afforded them many plausible pretexts to put their hands into the treasury of the king their master. For example; the Indians attack the frontier, kill some of the inhabitants, plunder many others, and agreeably to their custom of warfare, retire instantly to their villages with their booty. The governor informed of this transaction, promptly calls on the inhabitants to aid and assist in repelling the invasion. Accordingly a party assemble under their officers, some three or four days after the mischief had been done, and the Indians, one hundred, or one hundred and fifty miles from them, they pursue them, as they usually did, at no rapid pace, three or four days, and returned without overtaking the enemy, as they might have well known before they set out. On their return the men were dismissed, but ordered to hold themselves in readiness at a moment's warning. When at the end of some two or three months, the governor chose to consider the danger blown over, he causes receipts to be made out for the full pay of two or three months service, to which the signatures of the individuals are affixed; but as those persons were only absent from their homes ten or twelve days, all that was really paid them, did not amount to more than one fourth or one fifth of what they receipted for, and the balance of course was taken by the governor, as the reward for his faithful guardianship of the lives and property of his majesty's subjects.

The Spaniards holding the entrance of the Missouri, could regulate as they thought proper the intercourse with the Indians through that channel; but from what has been said, it will be readily perceived, that their traders, shackled with the pecuniary impositions of their governors, could never become the successful rivals of the British merchants on the west side of the Mississippi, which, from its proximity to the United States, the latter could enter without the necessity of a Spanish passport, or the fear of being detected by them. The consequence was that the trade of the rivers Demoin, St. Peter's, and all the country west of the Mississippi nearly to the Missouri, was exclusively enjoyed by the British merchants. The Spanish governors, stimulated by their own sordid views, declared that the honour of his majesty was grossly compromitted by the liberty that those adventurers took in trading with the natives within his territory, without their permission, and therefore took the liberty of expending his majesty's money by equipping and manning several galleys to cruise in the channels of the Mississippi in order to intercept those traders of the St. Peter's and Demoin rivers, in their passage to and from the entrance of the Oisconsing river; but after several unsuccessful cruises, and finding the Indians so hostile to them in this quarter, that they dare not land nor remain long in the channel without being attacked, they therefore retired and gave over the project. The Indians were friendly to the British merchants, and unfriendly to the Spanish, for the plain reason that the former sold them goods at a lower rate. The Ayaways, Sacks, Foxes and Yanktons of the river Demoin, who occasionally visited the Missouri, had it in their power to compare the rates at which the Spanish merchant in that quarter, and the British merchant on the Mississippi sold their goods; this was always much in favour of the latter; it therefore availed the Spaniards but little, when they inculcated the doctrine of their being their only legitimate fathers and friends, and that the British merchants were mere intruders, and had no other object in view but their own aggrandizement. The Indians, deaf to this doctrine, estimated the friendship of both by the rates at which they respectively sold their merchandise; and of course remained the firm friends of the British. In this situation it is not difficult for those to conceive who have felt the force of their machinations, that the British merchants would, in order to extend their own trade, endeavour to break down that of their neighbours on the Missouri. The attachments of the Indians to them, afforded a formidable weapon with which to effect their purposes, nor did they suffer it to remain unemployed.

The merchants of the Dog prairie, rivers Demoin and Ayaway, stimulated the nations just mentioned to the commission of acts of rapacity on the merchants of the Missouri, nor was Mr. Cameron and others, merchants of the river St. Peter's, less active with respect to the Cissitons, Yanktons of the plains, Tetons, &c. who resort the Missouri occasionally still higher up. War parties of those nations were consequently found lying in wait on the Missouri, to intercept the boats of the merchants of that river at the seasons they were expected to pass, and depredations were frequently committed, particularly by the Ayaways, who have been known in several instances to capture boats on the Missouri, in their descent to St. Louis, and compelled the crews to load themselves with heavy burdens of their best furs across the country to their towns, where they disposed of them to the British merchants. In those cases they always destroyed the periogues, and such of the peltries and furs as they could not carry off. It may be urged, that the British merchants knowing that the United States, at present, through mere courtesy, permit them to extend their trade to the west side of the Mississippi; or rather that they are mere tenants at will, and that the United States possess the means of ejecting them at pleasure; that they will, under these circumstances, be induced to act differently towards us than they did in relation to the Spanish government; but what assurance have we that this will be the effect of the mere change of governments without change of measures in relation to them. Suffer me to ask what solid grounds there are to hope that their gratitude for our tolerance and liberality on this subject, will induce them to hold a different policy towards us. None, in my opinion, unless we stimulate their gratitude by placing before their eyes the instruments of our power in the form of one or two garrisons on the upper part of the Mississippi. Even admit that the people were actuated by the most friendly regard towards the interests of the United States, and at this moment made a common cause with us to induce the Indians to demean themselves in an orderly manner towards our government, and to treat our traders of the Missouri with respect and friendship, yet, without some efficient check on the Indians, I should not think our citizens nor our traders secure; because the Indians, who have for ten years and upwards, derived advantages from practice on lessons of rapacity taught them by those traders, cannot at a moment be brought back to a state of primitive innocence, by the united persuasions of all the British traders. I hold it an axiom, incontrovertible, *that it is more easy to introduce vice into all states of society than it is to eradicate it;* and that this is still more strictly true, when applied to man in savage than in his civilized state. If, therefore, we wish, within some short period, to devest ourselves of the evils which flowed from the inculcation of those doctrines of vice, we must employ some more active agent than the influence of the same teachers who first introduced them. Such an agent, in my opinion, is the power of withholding their merchandise from them at pleasure; and to accomplish this, we must first provide the means of controlling the merchants. If we permit the British merchants to supply the Indians in Louisiana as formerly, the influence of our government over those Indians is lost. For the Indian in possession of his merchandise, feels himself independent of every government, and will proceed to commit the same depredations which they did when rendered independent by the Spanish system.

The traders give themselves but little trouble at any time to inculcate among the Indians a respect for governments; but are usually content with proclaiming their own importance. When the British merchants give themselves trouble to speak of governments, it is but fair to presume that they will teach the natives to respect the power of their own. And at all events, we know from experience that no regard for the blood of our frontier inhabitants will influence them at any time to withhold arms and ammunition from the Indians, provided they are to profit by furnishing them.

Having now stated, as they have occurred to my mind, the several evils which flowed from that system of intercourse with the Indians, pursued by the Spanish government, I shall next endeavour to point out the defects of our own, and show its incompetency to produce the wished for reform; then, with some remarks on the Indian character, conclude by submitting for the consideration of our government, the outlines of a plan which has been dictated as well by a sentiment of philanthropy towards the aborigines of America, as a just regard to the protection of the lives and property of our citizens; and with the further view also of securing to the people of the United States, exclusively, the advantages which ought of right to accrue to them from the possession of Louisiana.

We now permit the British merchants of Canada, indiscriminately with our own, to enter the Missouri, and trade with the nations in that quarter. Although the government of the U. States has not yielded the point that, as a matter of right, the British merchants have the privilege of trading in this quarter; yet from what has been said to them, they are now acting under a belief, that it will be some time before any prohibitory measures will be taken with respect to them; and are therefore making rapid strides to secure themselves in the affection of the Indians, and to break down, as soon as possible, the American adventurers, by underselling them, and thus monopolize that trade: this they will effect to an absolute certainty in the course of a few years. The old Northwest company of Canada have, within the last two years, formed a union with the Newyork company, who had previously been the only important rivals in the fur trade; this company, with the great accession of capital brought them by the Newyork company, have, with a view to the particular monopoly of the Missouri, formed a connexion with a British house in Newyork, another at New Orleans, and have sent their particular agent, by the name of Jacob Mires, to take his station at St. Louis. It may be readily conceived that the union of the Northwest and Newyork companies, who had previously extended their trade in opposition to each other, and to the exclusion of all unassociated merchants on the upper portion of the Mississippi, the waters of lake Winnipec and the Athebaskey country, would, after their late union, have a surplus of capital and a surplus of men, which they could readily employ in some other quarter: such was the Missouri, which, from the lenity of our government, they saw was opened to them; and I do believe, could the fact be ascertained, that the hope of future gain from the fur trade of that river, was one of the principal causes of the union between those two great rivals in the fur trade of North America. That this trade will be nurtured and protected by the British government, I have no doubt, for many reasons, which it strikes me could be offered, but which, not falling immediately within the purview of these observations on the fur trade of Louisiana, I shall forbear to mention.

As the Missouri forms only one of four large branches of the commerce of this united, or as it is still called, the Northwest company, they will have it in their power, not only to break down all single adventurers on the Missouri, but in the course of a few years to effect the same thing with a company of merchants of the United States, who might enter into a competition with them in this single branch of their trade. Nor is it probable that our merchants, knowing this fact, will form a company for the purpose of carrying on this trade, while they see the Northwest company permitted by our government to trade on the Missouri, and on the west side of the Mississippi: therefore, the Northwest company, on the present plan, having driven the adventurers of small capitals from these portions of our territory, will most probably never afterwards have a rival in any company of our own merchants. By their continuance they will acquire strength, and having secured the wished-for monopoly, they will then trade with the Indians on their own terms; and being possessed of the trade, both on the Mississippi and Missouri, they can make the price of their goods in both quarters similar, and though they may be excessively high, yet being the same they will run no risk of disaffecting the Indians by a comparison of the prices at which they receive their goods at those places. If then it appears, that the longer we extend the privilege to the Northwest company of continuing their trade within our territory, the difficulty of excluding them will increase: can we begin the work of exclusion too soon? For my own part I see not the necessity to admit, that our own merchants are not at this moment competent to supply the Indians of the Missouri with such quantities of goods as will, at least in the acceptation of the Indians themselves, be deemed satisfactory and sufficient for their necessities. All their ideas relative to their necessities are only comparative, and may be tested by a scale of the quantities they have been in the habit of receiving. Such a scale I transmitted to the government from fort Mandan. From a regard to the happiness of the Indians, it would give me much pleasure to see this scale liberally increased; yet I am clearly of opinion, that this effect should be caused by the regular progression of the trade of our own merchants, under the patronage and protection of our own government. This will afford additional security to the tranquillity of our much extended frontier, while it will give wealth to our merchants. We know that the change of government in Louisiana, from Spain to that of the United States, has withdrawn no part of that capital formerly employed in the trade of the Missouri; the same persons still remain, and continue to prosecute their trade. To these there has been an accession of several enterprising American merchants, and several others since my return have signified their intention to embark in that trade, within the present year; and the whole of those merchants are now unembarrassed by the exactions of Spanish governors. Under those circumstances is it fair for us to presume that the Indians are not now supplied by our own merchants, with quite as large an amount in merchandise as they had been formerly accustomed to receive? Should the quantity thus supplied not fully meet our wishes on liberal views, towards the Indians, is it not sounder policy to wait the certain progress of our own trade, than in order to supply this momentary deficiency, to admit the aid of the Northwest company, at the expense of the total loss of that trade; thereby giving them a carte blanch on which to write in future their own terms of traffic with the Indians, and thus throwing them into their hands, permit them to be formed into a rod of iron, with which, for Great Britain, to scourge our frontier at pleasure.

If the British merchants were prohibited from trading in upper Louisiana, the American merchants, with the aid of the profits arising from the trade of the lower portion of the Missouri and the western branches of the Mississippi, would be enabled most probably to become the successful rivals of the Northwest company in the more distant parts of the continent; to which we might look, in such case, with a well-founded hope of enjoying great advantages from the fur trade; but if this prohibition does not shortly take place, I will venture to predict that no such attempts will ever be made, and, consequently, that we shall for several generations be taxed with the defence of a country, which to us would be no more than a barren waste.

About the beginning of August last, two of the wintering partners of the Northwest company, visited the Mandan and Minnetaree villages on the Missouri, and fixed on a scite for a fortified establishment. This project once carried into effect, we have no right to hope for the trade of the upper portion of the Missouri, until our government shall think proper to dislodge them.

This season there has been sent up the Missouri, for the Indian trade, more than treble the quantity of merchandise that has ever been previously embarked in that trade at any one period. Of this quantity, as far as I could judge from the best information I could collect, two-thirds was the property of British merchants, and directly or indirectly that of the Northwest company. Not any of this merchandise was destined for a higher point on the Missouri than the mouth of the Vermillion river, or the neighbourhood of the Yanktons of the river Demoin; of course, there will be a greater excess of goods beyond what the Indians can purchase, unless they sell at one-third their customary price, which the American merchant certainly cannot do without sacrificing his capital.

On my return this fall, I met on the Missouri an American merchant by the name of Robert M'Clellan, formerly a distinguished partisan in the army under general Wayne: in a conversation with this gentleman, I learned that during the last winter, in his trade with the Mahas, he had a competitor by the name of Joseph La Croix (believed to be employed by the Northwest company, but now is an avowed British merchant)—that the prices at which La Croix sold his goods, compelled him to reduce the rates of his own goods so much as to cause him to sink upwards of two thousand dollars of his capital, in the course of his trade, that season; but that as he had embarked in this trade for two years past, and had formed a favourable acquaintance with the Mahas and others, he should still continue it a few seasons more, even at a loss of his time and capital, in the hope that government seeing the error would correct it, and that he might then regain his losses, from the circumstance of his general acquaintance with the Indians.

I also met in my way to St. Louis, another merchant, by the same name, a captain M'Clellan, formerly of the United States' corps of artillerists. This gentleman informed me that he was connected with one of the principal houses in Baltimore, which I do not now recollect, but can readily ascertain the name and standing of the firm, if it is considered of any importance; he said he had brought with him a small but well assorted adventure, calculated for the Indian trade, by way of experiment; that the majority of his goods were of the fine high-priced kind, calculated for the trade with the Spanish province of New Mexico, which he intended to carry on within the territory of the United States, near the border of that province; that connected with this object, the house with which he was concerned was ready to embark largely in the fur trade of the Missouri, provided it should appear to him to offer advantages to them. That since he had arrived in Louisiana, which was last autumn, he had endeavoured to inform himself of the state of this trade, and that from his inquiries, he had been so fully impressed with the disadvantages it laboured under from the free admission of the British merchants, he had written to his house in Baltimore, advising that they should not embark in this trade, unless these merchants were prohibited from entering the river.

I have mentioned these two as cases in point, and which have fallen immediately under my own observation: the first shows the disadvantages under which the trade of our own merchants is now actually labouring; and the second, that no other merchants will probably engage in this trade, while the British fur traders are permitted by our government to continue their traffic in Upper Louisiana. With this view of the subject, it is submitted to the government, with whom it alone rests to decide whether the admission or non-admission of those merchants is at this moment most expedient.

The custom of giving credits to the Indians, which grew out of the Spanish system, still exists, and agreeably to our present plan of intercourse with these people, is likely to produce more pernicious consequences than it did formerly. The Indians of the Missouri, who have been in the habit of considering these credits rather as a present, or the price of their permission for the trader to depart in peace, still continue to view it in the same light, and will therefore give up their expectations on that point with some reluctance; nor can the merchants well refuse to acquiesce, while they are compelled to be absent from the nations with which they trade five or six months in the year. The Indians are yet too vicious to permit them in safety to leave goods at their trading houses, during their absence, in the care of one or two persons; the merchant, therefore, would rather suffer the loss by giving the credit, than incur the expense of a competent guard, or doubling the quantity of his engagees, for it requires as many men to take the peltries and furs to market as it does to bring the goods to the trading establishment, and the number usually employed are not found at any time, more than sufficient to give a tolerable security against the Indians.

I presume that it will not be denied, that it is our best policy, and will be our practice to admit, under the restrictions of our laws on this subject, a fair competition among all our merchants in the Indian trade. This being the case then, it will happen, as it has already happened, that one merchant having trade with any nation, at the usual season gives them a credit and departs: a second knowing that such advance had been made, hurries his outfit and arrives at that nation, perhaps a month earlier in the fall than the merchant who had made this advance to the Indians: he immediately assembles the nation and offers his goods in exchange for their redskin hunt; the good faith of the Indians, with respect to the absent merchant, will not bind them to refuse; an exchange, of course, takes place; and when the merchant to whom they are indebted arrives, they have no peltry, either to barter or to pay him for the goods which they have already received: the consequences are, that the merchant who has sustained the loss becomes frantic; he abuses the Indians, bestows on them the epithets of liars and dogs, and says a thousand things only calculated to sour their minds, and disaffect them to the whites: the rival trader he accuses of having *robbed* him of his credits (for they never give this species of artifice among themselves a milder term) and calls him many opprobrious names; a combat frequently ensues, in which the principals are not the only actors, for their men will, of course, sympathise with their respective employers. The Indians are the spectators of those riotous transactions, which are well calculated to give them a contempt for the character of the whites, and to inspire them with a belief of the importance of their peltries and furs. The British traders have even gone further in the northwest, and even offered bribes to induce the Indians to destroy each other; nor have I any reason to doubt but what the same thing will happen on the Missouri, unless some disinterested person, armed with authority by government, be placed in such a situation as will enable him to prevent such controversies. I look to this custom of extending credits to the Indians, as one of the great causes of all those individual contentions, which will most probably arise in the course of this trade, as well between the Indians and whites, as between the whites themselves; and that our agents and officers will be always harrassed with settling these disputes, which they never can do in such a manner as to restore a perfect good understanding between the parties. I think it would be best in the outset, for the government to let it be understood by the merchants, that if they think proper to extend credits to the Indians, it shall be at their own risk, dependent on the good faith of the Indians for voluntary payment; that the failure of the Indians to comply with their contracts, shall not be considered any justification for their maltreatment or holding abusive language to them, and that no assistance shall be given them in any shape by the public functionaries to aid them in collecting their credits. If the government interfere in behalf of the traders by any regulation, then it will be the interest of every trader individually to get the Indians indebted to him, and to keep them so in order to secure in future their peltries and furs exclusively to himself. Thus, the Indians would be compelled to exchange without choice of either goods or their prices, and the government would have pledged itself to make the Indians pay for goods, of which they cannot regulate the prices. I presume the government will not undertake to regulate the merchant in this respect by law.

The difficulties which have arisen, and which must arise under existing circumstances, may be readily corrected by establishing a few posts, where there shall be a sufficient guard to protect the property of the merchants in their absence, though it may be left with only a single clerk: to those common marts, all traders and Indians should be compelled to resort for the purposes of traffic.

The plan proposed guards against all difficulties, and provides for a fair exchange, without the necessity of credit: when the Indian appears with his peltry and fur, the competition between the merchants will always insure him his goods on the lowest possible terms, and the exchange taking place at once, there can be no cause of controversy between the Indian and the merchant, and no fear of loss on the part of the latter, unless he is disposed to make a voluntary sacrifice, through a spirit of competition with others, by selling his goods at an under value.

Some of the stipulations contained in the licenses usually granted our Indian traders, are totally incompatible with the local situations, and existing customs and habits of almost all the Indian nations in Upper Louisiana. I allude more particularly to that clause in the license, which compels them to trade at Indian towns only. It will be seen by referrence to my statistical view of the Indian nations of Upper Louisiana, that the great body of those people are roving bands, who have no villages, or stationary residence. The next principal division of them, embracing the Panias, Ottoes, Kanzas, &c. have not their villages on the Missouri, and they even pass the greater portion of the year at a distance from their villages, in the same roving manner. The third, and only portion of those Indians, who can with propriety be considered as possessed of such stationary villages as seems to have been contemplated by this clause of the license, is confined to the Ayaways, Sioux, and Foxes of the Mississippi, and the Ricaras, Mandans, Minnetarees, and Ahwahaways of the Missouri. The consequence is, that until some further provision be made, that all the traders who have intercourse with any nations except those of the last class, will form their establishments at the several points on the Missouri, where it will be most convenient to meet the several nations with whom they wish to carry on commerce. This is their practice at the present moment, and their houses are scattered on various parts of the Missouri. In this detached situation, it cannot be expected that they will comply with any of the stipulations of their licenses. The superintendant of St. Louis, distant eight hundred or a thousand miles, cannot learn whether they have forfeited the penalty of their licenses or not: they may, therefore, vend ardent spirits, compromit the government, or the character of the whites, in the estimation of the Indians, or practice any other crimes in relation to those people, without the fear of detection or punishment. The government cannot with propriety, say to those traders, that they shall trade at villages, when in reality they do not exist; nor can they for a moment, I presume, think of incurring the expense of sending an Indian agent with each trader, to see that he commit no breach of the stipulations of his license. These traders must of course be brought together, at some general points, where it will be convenient for several nations to trade with them, and where they can be placed under the eye of an Indian agent whose duty it should be to see that they comply with the regulations laid down for their government. There are crimes which may be committed without a breach of our present laws, and which make it necessary that some further restrictions than those contained in the present licenses of our traders, should either be added under penalties in those licenses, or punished by way of a discretionary power, lodged in the superintendent, extending to the exclusion of such individuals from the Indian trade. Of this description I shall here enumerate three:

First, That of holding conversations with the Indians, tending to bring our government into disrepute among them, and to alienate their affections from the same.

Second, That of practising any means to induce the Indians to maltreat or plunder other merchants.

Third, That of stimulating or exciting by bribes or otherwise, any nations or bands of Indians, to wage war against other nations or bands; or against the citizens of the United States, or against citizens or subjects of any power at peace with the same.

These appear to me to be crimes fraught with more real evil to the community, and to the Indians themselves, than vending ardent spirits, or visiting their hunting camps for the purpose of trade; yet there are no powers vested in the superintendents, or agents of the United States, to prevent their repeated commission; nor restrictions or fines imposed by our laws, to punish such offences.

It is well known to me that we have several persons engaged in the trade of the Missouri, who have, within the last three years, been adopted as citizens of the United States, and who are now hostile to our government. It is not reasonable to expect, that such persons will act with good faith towards us. Hence, the necessity of assigning metes and bounds to their transactions among the Indians. On my way to St. Louis, last fall, I received satisfactory evidence that a Mr. Robideau, an inhabitant of St. Louis, had, the preceding winter, during his intercourse with the Ottoes and Missouris, been guilty of the most flagrant breaches of the first of those misdemeanors above mentioned. On my arrival at St. Louis, I reported the case to Mr. Broom, the acting superintendent, and recommended his prohibiting that person from the trade of the Missouri, unless he would give satisfactory assurances of a disposition to hold a different language to the Indians. Mr. Broom informed me, that the laws and regulations of the United States on this subject, gave him no such powers; and Mr. Robideau and sons still prosecute their trade.

The uncontrolled liberty which our citizens take of hunting on Indian lands, has always been a source of serious difficulty, on every part of our frontier, and is evidently destined to become quite as much so in Upper Louisiana, unless it be restrained and limited within consistent bounds. When the Indians have been taught, by commerce, duly to appreciate the furs and peltries of their country, they feel excessive chagrin at seeing the whites, by their superior skill in hunting, fast diminishing those productions, to which they have been accustomed to look as the only means of acquiring merchandise; and nine-tenths of the causes of war are attributable to this practice. The Indians, although well disposed to maintain a peace on any other terms, I am convinced will never yield this point; nor do I consider it as of any importance to us that they should; for with what consistency of precept and practice can we say to the Indians, whom we wish to civilize, that agriculture and the arts are more productive of ease, wealth, and comfort, than the occupation of hunting, while they see distributed over their forests a number of white men, engaged in the very occupation which our doctrine would teach them to abandon. Under such circumstances, it cannot be considered irrational in the Indians, to conclude, that our recommendations to agriculture are interested, and flow from a wish on our part to derive the whole emolument arising from the peltries and furs of their country, by taking them to ourselves.

These observations, however, are intended to apply only to such Indian nations as have had, and still maintain a commercial intercourse with the whites: such we may say are those inhabiting the western branches of the Mississippi, the eastern branches of the Missouri, and near the main body of the latter, as far up as the Mandans and Minnetarees. Here it is, therefore, that it appears to me expedient we should draw a line; and temporarily change our policy. I presume it is not less the wish of our government, that the Indians on the extreme branches of the Missouri to the west, and within the Rocky mountains, should obtain supplies of merchandise equally with those more immediately in their vicinity. To effect this, the government must either become the merchant themselves, or present no obstacles to their citizens, which may prevent their becoming so with those distant nations; but as the former cannot be adopted (though I really think it would be best for a time) then it becomes the more necessary to encourage the latter. Policy further dictates such encouragement being given, in order to contravene the machinations preparing by the Northwest company for practice in that quarter.

If the hunters are not permitted in those distant regions, the merchants will not be at the expense of transporting their merchandise thither, when they know that the natives do not possess the art of taking the furs of their country. The use of the trap, by which those furs are taken, is an art which must be learned before it can be practised to advantage. If the American merchant does not adventure, the field is at once abandoned to the Northwest company, who will permit the hunter to go, and the merchant will most probably be with him in the outset; the abundance of rich furs in that country, hold out sufficient inducement for them to lose no time in pressing forward their adventures. Thus those distant Indians will soon be supplied with merchandise; and while they are taught the art of taking the furs of their country, they will learn the value, and until they have learnt its value, we shall run no risk of displeasing them by taking it. When the period shall arrive that the distant nations shall have learned the art of taking their furs, and know how to appreciate its value, then the hunter becomes no longer absolutely necessary to the merchant, and may be withdrawn; but in the outset, he seems to form a very necessary link in that chain which is to unite these nations and ourselves in a state of commercial intercourse.

The liberty to our merchants of hunting, for the purpose of procuring food, in ascending and descending the navigable water-courses, as well as while stationary at their commercial posts, is a privilege which should not be denied them; but as the unlimited extent of such a privilege would produce much evil, it should certainly be looked on as a subject of primary importance: it should, therefore, enter into all those compacts which we may think proper to form with the Indians in that country, and be so shaped as to leave them no solid grounds of discontent.

The time to which licenses shall extend.

A view of the Indian character, so far as it is necessary it should be known, for the purposes of governing them, or maintaining a friendly commercial intercourse with them, may be comprised within the limits of a few general remarks.

The *love of gain* is the Indians' ruling passion, and the fear of punishment must form the corrective; to this passion we are to ascribe their inordinate thirst for the possession of merchandise, their unwillingness to accede to any terms, or enter into any stipulations, except such as appear to promise them commercial advantages, and the want of good faith, which they always evince by not complying with any regulations, which in practice do not produce to them those expected or promised advantages. The native justice of the Indian mind, will always give way to his impatience for the possession of the goods of the defenceless merchant, and he will plunder him, unless prevented by the fear of punishment; nor can punishment assume a more terrific shape to them, than that of *withholding every description of merchandise from them.* This species of punishment, while it is one of the most efficient in governing the Indians, is certainly the most humane, as it enforces a compliance with our will, without the necessity of bloodshed. But in order to compass the exercise of this weapon, our government must first provide the means of controlling their traders. No government will be respected by the Indians, until they are made to feel the effects of its power, or see it practised on others: and the surest guarantee of savage fidelity to any government, is a thorough conviction in their minds, that they do possess the power of punishing promptly, every act of aggression, which they may commit on the persons or property of their citizens. If both traders and Indians throughout Upper Louisiana, were compelled to resort to regulated commercial posts, then the trader would be less liable to be pillaged, and the Indians deterred from practising aggression; for when the Indians once become convinced, that in consequence of their having practised violence upon the persons or property of the traders, that they have been cut off from all intercourse with those posts, and that they cannot resort to any other places to obtain merchandise, then they will make any sacrifice to regain the privilege they had previously enjoyed; and I am confident, that in order to regain our favour in such cases, they would sacrifice any individual who may be the object of our displeasure, even should he be their favourite chief; for their thirst of merchandise is paramount to every other consideration; and the leading individuals among them, well knowing this trait in the character of their own people, will not venture to encourage or excite aggressions on the whites, when they know they are themselves to become the victims of its consequences.

But if, on the other hand, these commercial establishments are not general, and we suffer detached and insulated merchants, either British or American, to exercise their own discretion, in setting down where they may think proper, on the western branches of the Mississippi, for the purposes of trading with the Indians; then, although these commercial establishments may be so extended as to embrace the Missouri, quite to the Mandans, still they will lose a great part of their effects; because the roving bands of Tetons, and the most dissolute of the Siouxs being denied the permission to trade on the Missouri at any rate, would resort to those establishments on the Mississippi, and thus become independent of the trade of the Missouri, as they have hitherto been. To correct this, we have three alternatives: First, to establish two commercial posts in this quarter. Secondly, to prohibit all intercourse with the Sisitons, and other bands of Siouxs, on the river St. Peter's and the Raven's-wing river, informing those Indians that such prohibition has been the consequence of the malconduct of the Tetons, and thus leave it to them to correct them; or, Thirdly, to make an appeal to arms in order to correct the Tetons ourselves.

Impressed with a belief unalloyed with doubts, that the ardent wish of our government has ever been to conciliate the esteem, and secure the friendship of all the savage nations within their territory, by the exercise of every consistent and pacific measure in their power, applying those of coertion only in the last resort, I here proceed with a due deference to their better judgment, to develop a scheme which has suggested itself to my mind, as the most expedient that I can devise for the successful consummation of their philanthropic views towards those wretched people of America, as well as to secure to the citizens of the United States, all those advantages, which ought of right exclusively to accrue to them, from the possession of Upper Louisiana.

The situation of the Indian trade on the Missouri and its waters, while under the Spanish government.

The exclusive permission to trade with nations.

The giving by those exclusions, the right to individuals to furnish supplies, which rendered the Indians independent of the government.

The times of sending goods to the Indians, and of returning to St. Louis—the necessity of giving credits; therefore the disadvantages of.

The evils which grew out of the method pursued by the Spaniards, as well to themselves as to the Indians.

The independence of individuals of their own government.

The dependence of the Indians on those individuals, and their consequent contempt for the government, and for all other citizens whom they plundered and murdered at pleasure.

The present rapacity of the Indians, owing to this cause, aided also by the system of giving credits to the Indians, which caused contentions among the traders, which terminated by giving the Indians a contempt for the character of the whites.

The permission to persons to hunt on Indian lands, productive of many evils, the most frequent causes of war, hostile to the views of civilizing, and of governing the Indians.

The first principle of governing the Indians is to govern the whites—the impossibility of doing this without establishments, and some guards at those posts.

The Sisitons may be made a check on the Tetons by withholding their trade on the Mississippi.

Having stated the several evils which flowed from the Spanish system, I now state the Indian character, the evils which still exist, and what they will probably terminate in, if not redressed—the plan recommended to be pursued and the benefits which may be expected to result therefrom, conclude thus, it may be pretty confidently believed that it is not competent to produce the wished for reform among the Indians.

Hunters permitted in the Indian country pernicious—frequent cause of war between us.

Some of the stipulations of the licenses granted the traders, in application to the state of the Indians on the Missouri, of course not attended to. The incompetency of the Indian agents to see that any of the stipulations are complied with. Whiskey, or ardent spirits may, therefore, be introduced, and other corruptions practised without our knowledge. There is not at present allowed by law to the superintendant of Indian affairs, any discretionary powers, by which he can prohibit our newly acquired citizens of Louisiana, who may be disaffected to our government, from trading with the Indians: the law says, that any citizen of the United States, who can give sufficient security for the sum of five hundred dollars, for the faithful compliance with the stipulation of his license, shall be permitted to trade. An instance has happened in Mr. Robideau, &c.

The preceding observations of captain Lewis, although left in an unfinished state, are too important to be omitted. The premature death of the author has prevented his filling up the able outlinc that hc has drawn.

A summary statement of the rivers, creeks, and most remarkable places, their distances from each other, &c. their distances from the Mississippi, ascending the Missouri, across the Rocky mountains, and down the Columbia to the Pacific ocean, as was explored in the years 1804, 5, and 6, by captains Lewis and Clarke.

Names of remarkable places	The width of rivers and creeks in yards	Side on which they are situated	Distances from one place to another	Distances up the Missouri from the Mississippi
	Yards		Miles	Miles
To the village of St. Charles		N.E.	21	21
Osagew-oman's river	30	N.E.	20	41
Charrette's village and creek	20	N.E.	27	68
Shepherd's creek		S.W.	15	83
Gasconade river	157	S.W.	17	100
Muddy river	50	N.E.	15	115
Grand Osage river	397	S.W.	18	133
Murrow creek	20	S.W.	5	133
Cedar island and creek	20	N.E.	7	145
Leadmine hill		S.W.	9	154
Manitou creek	20	S.E.	8	162
Splitrock creek	20	N.E.	8	170
Saline, or Salt river	30	S.E.	3	173
Manitou river	30	N.E.	9	182
Goodwoman's river	35	N.E.	9	191
Mine river	70	S.W.	9	200
Arrow prairie		S.W.	6	206
Two Charleton rivers	30/70	N.E.	14	220
Ancient village of the Missouri nation, near which place Fort Orleans stood,		N.E.	16	236
Grand river	90	N.E.	4	240
Snake creek	18	N.E.	6	246
Ancient village of the Little Osages		S.W.	10	256
Tigers' island and creek	25	N.E.	20	276
Hubert's island and creek		S.W.	12	388
Fire-prairie creek		S.W.	12	300
Fort Point		S.W.	6	306
Haycabin creek	20	S.W.	6	312
Coalbank		S.W.	9	321
Bluewater river	30	S.W.	10	331
Kanzas river	230	S.W.	9	340
Little river Platte	60	N.E.	9	349

	Yards	Side	Miles	Miles
To the First old Kanzas village		S.W.	28	377
Independence creek, a mile below the second old Kanzas village		S.W.	28	405
St. Michael's prairie		N.E.	25	430
Nodawa river	70	N.E.	20	450
Wolf, or Loup river	60	S.W.	14	464
Big Nemaha river	80	S.W.	16	480
Tarkio creek	23	N.E.	3	483
Neeshnabatona river	50	N.E.	2	508
Little Nemaha river	48	S.W.	8	516
Baldpated prairie, the Neeshnabatona within 150 yards of the Missouri		N.E.	23	539
Weepingwater creek	25	S.W.	29	568
River Platt, or Shoal river	600	S.W.	32	600
Butterfly, or Papillon creek	18	S.W.	3	
Musquetoe creek	22	N.E.	7	610
Ancient village of the Ottoes		S.W.	11	
Ancient Ayaways village, below a bluff, on the northeast side		N.E.	6	
Bowyer's river	25	N.E.	11	
Council bluffs (establishment)		S.W.	12	650
Soldier's river	40	N.E.	39	689
Eaneahwaudepon, (Little Sioux river)	80	N.E.	44	733
Waucarde, or Badspirit creek		S.W.	55	788
Around a bend of the river to the northeast, the gorge of which is only 974 yards			21	809
To an island, 3 miles northeast of the Maha village			27	836
Floyd's bluff and river	35	N.E.	14	850
To the Big Sioux river	110	N.E.	3	853
Commencement of the copperas, cobalt, pirites, and alum bluffs		S.W.	27	880
Hot, or Burning bluffs		S.W.	30	910
Whitestone river	30	N.E.	8	918
Petit-arc, an old Maha village, at the mouth of Littlebow creek	15	S.W.	20	938
River Jacques, or James' river	90	N.E.	12	950
Calumet bluff (mineral)		S.W.	10	960
Ancient fortification, Goodman's island		S.W.	16	976
To Plum creek	12	N.E.	10	986
Whitepoint creek	28	S.W.	8	994
Quicourre	152	S.W.	6	1000
To the Poncar river and village	30	S.W.	10	1010
To the dome and village of the burrowing squirrels		S.W.	20	1030
Island of cedars			45	1075

	Yards	Side	Miles	Miles
To White river	300	S.W.	55	1130
To the Three rivers of the Sioux pass	35	N.E.	22	1152
An island in the commencement of the Big bend		N.E.	20	1172
the upper part of the Big bend, the gorge of which is 1¼ miles		S.W.	30	1202
To Tylor's river	35	S.W.	6	1208
Loisel's fort on Cedar island		S.W.	18	1226
Teton river	70	S.W.	37	1263
the upper of five old Ricara villages, reduced by the Sioux, and abandoned		S.W.	42	1305
To Chayenne river	400	S.W.	5	1310
an old Ricara village on Lahoocat's island			47	1357
Sarwarkarna river	90	S.W.	40	1397
Wetarhood river	120	S.W.	25	1422
the first Ricaras villages on an island		S.W.	4	
second Ricaras three villages		S.W.	4	1430
Stone-idol creek	18	N.E.	18	
Warreconne river	35	N.E.	40	1488
Cannonball river	140	S.W.	12	1500
Chesschetar river, near six old Mandan villages	38	S.W.	40	1540
Old Ricara and Mandan villages		S.W.	40	1580
To Fort Mandan (wintering post of 1804),		N.E.	20	1600
the Mandan villages on each side			4	1604
To Knife river, on which the two Minnetaree and Maha villages are situated near the mouth	80	S.W.	2	1606
the Island			11	
Miry river	10	N.E.	16	1633
Island in the Little basin			28	
Little Missouri river	134	S.W.	29	1690
Wild-onion creek	16	N.E.	12	
Goose-egg lake	300	N.E.	9	
Chaboneau's creek	20	S.W.	16	1727
Goatpen creek, Mouse river, waters of lake Winnipec near the Missouri	20	N.E.	16	1743
To Hall's strand, lake, and creek		N.E.	47	1790
White-earth river	60	N.E.	40	1840
Rochejaune, or Yellowstone river	858	S.W.	40	1880
To Martha's river	50	N.E.	60	1940
Porcupine river	112	N.E.	50	1990
To the Littledry creek	25	S.W.	40	2030
Bigdry creek	100	S.W.	9	
Littledry river	200	S.W.	6	2045
Gulf in the Island bend			32	

	Yards	Side	Miles	Miles
To Milk river	150	N.E.	13	2090
Bigdry river	400	S.W.	25	
Werner's run	10	N.E.	9	
Pine creek	20	N.E.	36	2160
Gibson's river	35	N.E.	17	2177
Brownbear-defeated creek	40	S.W.	12	
Bratton's river	100	N.E.	24	2213
Burntlodge creek	50	S.W.	6	
Wiser's creek	40	N.E.	14	2233
Muscleshell river	110	S.W.	37	2270
Grouse creek	20	N.E.	30	
North-mountain creek	30	N.E.	36	2336
South-mountain creek	30	S.W.	18	2354
Ibex island			15	
Goodrich's island			9	2378
Windsor's creek	30	N.E.	7	2385
Elk rapid (swift water)			15	2400
Thomson's creek	28	N.E.	27½	2427
Judith's river	100	S.W.	11½	2439½
Ash rapid (swift water)			4	
Slaughter river	40	S.W.	11	2454
Stonewall creek, above the natural walls	30	N.E.	26	2480
Maria's river	186	N.E.	41	2521
Snow river	50	S.W.	19	
Shields's river	35	S.W.	28	2568
The foot of the entrance of Portage river, five miles below the Great falls	45	S.W.	7	2575

Leaving the Missouri below the falls, and passing by land to the navigable waters of the Columbia river.

Names of remarkable places	Width of the rivers and creeks	Distance from one place to another	Distance from the falls of the Missouri	Distance from the Mississippi
	Yards	Miles	Miles	Miles
To the entrance of Medicine river	137	18	18	2593
Fort Mountain, passing through the plain between Medicine river and the Missouri, near the Missouri		15	33	2608

	Yards	Miles	Miles	Miles
Rocky mountains, to a gap on the ridge, which divides the waters of the Missouri from those of the Columbia, passing the north part of a mountain and crossing Dearborn's river		35	68	2643
Fork of Cohahlarishkit river from the north, passed four creeks from the north	45	40	108	2683
To Seaman's creek from the north	20	7	115	
Werner's creek from the north	35	10	125	2700
the east fork of Clarke's river, at the entrance of Cohahlarishkit	120	30	155	3730
To Clarke's river, below the forks	150	12	167	2742
Traveller's-rest creek, on the west side of Clarke's river, about the forks	25	5	172	2747
the Fork's of Traveller's-rest creek, at a right-hand road		18	190	
Hot springs on the creek		13	203	2778
Quamash glades, passing the head of the creek to a branch of Kooskooskee river		7	210	
North branch of Kooskooskee river, a left-hand road leads off at five miles		7	217	
Junction of the roads on the top of a snowy mountain, the left-hand road, passing by a fishery		10	227	2802
Hungry creek from the right, passing on a dividing mountain, covered with deep snow, except on two places, which are open, with a southern exposure at 8 and 36 miles		54	281	2856
To a Glade upon Hungry creek		6	287	
Glade upon a small branch of do		8	295	
Glade on Fish creek	10	9	304	
To Collins's creek	25	13	317	
Quamash flats		11	328	2903
Kooskooskee, or Flathead's river, in a pine country	120	12	340	2915

NOTE. In passing from the falls of the Missouri, across the Rocky mountains to the navigable waters of the Columbia, you have two hundred miles of good road, one hundred and forty miles of high, steep, rugged mountains, sixty miles of which is covered from two to eight feet deep with snow in the last of June.

Remarkable places descending the Columbia	Width of the rivers and creeks	The wide on which they are situated	Distance from one place to another	Distance descending the Columbia	Distance from the Mississippi
	Yards	Side	Miles	Miles	Miles
To the entrance of Rockdam creek	20	N.	8	8	2923
Chopunnish river	120	N.	5	13	2928
Colter's creek	35	N.	37	50	2978
Lewis's river, at the entrance of the Kooskooskee river	200	S.	23	73	2988
the Sweathouse village and run		S.	7	80	
Pilot's village		N.	11	91	3006
Kemooenim creek	20	S.	48	139	
Drewyer's river, below the narrows of Lewis's river	30	N.	5	144	3059
Cave rapid			28	172	
Basin rapid (bad)			34	206	3121
Discharge rapid (bad)			14	220	3135
the Columbia at the mouth of Lewis's river, from the east		S.E.	7	227	2142
Wollawollah river, passed eleven large mat lodges of that nation	40	S.E.	16	243	3158
Muscleshell rapid (bad) passed thirty-three mat lodges of the Wollawollahs			25	268	3183
Pelican rapid, passed forty-eight lodges of the Pishquitpahs nation		N.	22	290	3205
twenty-one lodges of the Wahowpum nation, residing on three islands, at the commencement of the high country		N.	18	308	3223
To eight lodges of the Wahowpums at Short rapid		N.	27	335	3250
the Rocky rapid, nine lodges of the same nation		N.	13	348	3263
the river La Page (bad rapid)	40	S.	9	357	3272
twenty-seven lodges of the Eneshure nation, at Fishstack rapid		N.	10	367	3282
Towahnahiooks river	180	S.	8	375	3290
the Great falls of the Columbia river of 57 feet 8 inches, near which there are forty mat lodges of the Eneshure nation		N.	4	379	3294
the Short narrows, 45 yards wide			2	381	3296

	Yards	Side	Miles	Miles	Miles
Skilloot village of twenty-one large wood houses, at the long narrows, from 50 to 100 yards wide........		N.	4	385	3300
Chilluckittequaw village of eight large wood houses.....................		N.	14	390	3314
Cataract river, a few miles below a village of seven houses, and immediately above one of eleven houses of the Chilluckittequaw nation....	60	N.	10	409	3324
Sepulchre rock, opposite to a village of houses of Chilluckittequaws.....		N.	4	413	3328
River Labiche, opposite to twenty-six houses of the Smackshop nation, houses scattered on the north side	46	S.	9	422	3337
Little Lake creek, three houses of the Smackshop nation..............	28	N.	10	432	3347
Cruzatte's river..................	60	N.	12	444	3359
The Grand rapid, just below the village of the Yehuh tribe of the Shahala nation of fourteen wood houses		N.	6	450	3365
Clahclellah village of the Shahala nation, near the foot of the rapids; seven houses..................		N.	6	456	3371
Wahclellah village of the Shahala nation, twenty-three houses, just below the entrance of the Beacon-rock creek.....................		N.	6	462	3377
Tide water					
Phoca rock in the river, sixty-feet above water.................			11	473	3383
To Quicksand river..................	120	S.	9	482	3397
Seal river..................	80	N.	3	485	
Neechaokee village, opposite to the Diamond island..................		S.	4	489	
Shahala village of twenty-five temporary houses..................		S.	12	501	3416
Multnomah river..................	500	S.	14	515	3430
Multnomah village..................		S.	6	521	
Quathlahpotle village..............		N.	8	529	
Tahwahnahiooks river..............	200	N.	1	530	3445
Cathlahaws creek and village........	18	N.	10	540	3455
Lower extremity of Elallah or Deer island.........................		S.	6	546	

	Yards	Side	Miles	Miles	Miles
Coweliskee river, about the entrance, and up this river the Skilloot nation reside	150	N.	13	559	3474
Fanny's island		S.	16	577	3490
the Sea-otter island			12	587	3502
the upper village of the Wahkiacum nation		N.	6	593	3508
the Cathlamahs village of nine large wood houses, S. of Seal islands		S.	14	607	3522
Point William, opposite Shallow bay		S.	10	617	3532
Point Meriwether, above Meriwether's bay		S.	9	626	3541
Clatsop village, below Meriwether's bay, and seven miles northwest of Fort Clatsop		S.	8	634	3549
Point Adams, at the entrance of the Columbia into the Pacific ocean, or Great South Sea, in latitude 46° 15′ north, and longitude 124° 57′ west from Greenwich		S.	6	640	3555

NOTE. Fort Clatsop is situated on the west side of, and three miles up the Netul river from Meriwether bay, and seven miles east from the nearest part of the seacoast;—at this fort captain M. Lewis, and captain W. Clarke, passed the winter of 1805 and 1806.

The road by which we went out by the way of the Missouri to its head is 3096 miles, thence by land, by way of Lewis's river over to Clarke's river, and down that to the entrance of Traveller's-rest creek, where all the roads from different routes meet, then across the rugged part of the Rocky mountains to the navigable waters of the Columbia, 398 miles; thence down the river 640 miles, to the Pacific ocean; making a total distance of 4134 miles. On our return in 1806, we came from Traveller's-rest creek directly to the falls of the Missouri river, which shortens the distance about 579 miles, and is a much better route, reducing the distance from the Mississippi to the Pacific ocean to 3555 miles. 2575 miles of this distance is up the Missouri to the falls of that river; thence passing through the plains, and across the Rocky mountains to the navigable waters of the Kooskooskee river, a branch of the Columbia, 340 miles; 200 miles of which is a good road, 140 miles over a tremendous mountain, steep and broken, 60 miles of which is covered several feet deep with snow, on which we passed the last of June: from the navigable part of the Kooskooskee we descended that rapid river 73 miles to its entrance into Lewis's river, and down that river 154 miles to the Columbia, and thence 413 miles to its entrance into the Pacific ocean. About 180 miles of this distance is tide-water. We passed several bad rapids and narrows, and one considerable fall, 268 miles above the entrance of this river, of 37 feet 3 inches.—The total distance descending the Columbian waters 640 miles, making a total of 3555 miles, on the most direct route from the Mississippi, at the mouth of the Missouri, to the Pacific ocean.

ESTIMATE OF THE WESTERN INDIANS

Names of Indian nations and their places of general residence	Number of houses or lodges	Probable number of souls
1. Shoshonee nation resides in spring and summer on the west fork of Lewis's river, a branch of the Columbia, and in winter and fall on the Missouri....................	60	300
2. Ootlashoot tribe of the Tushshepah nation reside in spring and summer in the Rocky mountains on Clarke's river, and winter and fall on the Missouri and its waters......	33	400
3. Chopunnish nation, residing on the Kooskooskee river, below the forks, and on Colter's creek, and who sometimes pass over to the Missouri........................	33	2000
4. Pelloatpallah band of Chopunnish reside on the Kooskooskee, above the forks, and on the small streams which fall into that river, west of the Rocky mountains and Chopunnish river, and sometimes pass over to the Missouri..	33	1600
4. Kimooenim band of Chopunnish nation reside on Lewis's river, above the entrance of the Kooskooskee, as high up that river as the forks..............................	33	800
6. Yeletpo band of Chopunnish reside under the southwest mountains, on a small river which falls into Lewis's river, above the entrance of the Kooskooskee, which they call Weaucum..	33	250
7. Willewah band of Chopunnish reside on a river of the same name, which discharges itself into Lewis's river on the southwest side, below the forks of that river........	33	500
8. Soyennom band of Chopunnish on the north side of the east fork of Lewis's river, from its junction to the Rocky mountains, and on Lamaltar creek..................	33	400
9. Chopunnish of Lewis's river, below the entrance of the Kooskooskee, on either side of that river to its junction with the Columbia..................................	40	2300
10. Sokulk nation reside on the Columbia, above the entrance of Lewis's river, as high up as the entrance of Clarke's river..	120	2400
11. Chimnahpum reside on the northwest side of the Columbia, both above and below the entrance of Lewis's river, and on the Tapteel river, which falls into the Columbia 15 miles above Lewis's river........................	42	1860

	Houses	Souls
12. Wollawollah nation on both sides of the Columbia from the entrance of Lewis's river, as low as the Muscleshell rapid, and in winter pass over to the Tapteel river......	46	1600
13. Pishquitpahs nation resides on the Muscleshell rapid, and on the north side of the Columbia to the commencement of the high country; this nation winter on the waters of the Tapteel river........	71	2600
14. Wahowpum nation resides on the north branch of the Columbia, in different bands from the Pishquitpahs, as low as the river Lapage; the different bands of this nation winter on the waters of Tapteel and Cataract rivers.....	33	700
15. Eneshure nation resides at the upper part of the Great narrows of the Columbia on either side—are stationary..	41	1200
16. Eskeloot nation resides at the upper part of the Great narrows of the Columbia; on the north side is the great mart for all the country........	21	1000
17. Chilluckittequaw nation residing next below the narrows, and extending down on the north side of the Columbia to the river Labiche........	32	1400
18. Smockshop band of Chilluckittequaws resides on the Columbia, on each side of the entrance of the river Labiche to the neighbourhood of the great rapids of that river...	24	800
19. Shahala nation resides at the grand rapids of the Columbia, and extends down in different villages as low as the Multnomah river, consisting of the following tribes: viz. Yehuh, above the rapids, Clahclellah, below the rapid, the Wahclellah, below all the rapids, and the Neerchokioon (1 house 100 lodges) on the south side, a few miles above the Multnomah river........	62	2800
20. *Wappatoo Indians*		
Nechacokee tribe resides on the south side of the Columbia, a few miles below Quicksand river, and opposite the Diamond island........	1	100
Shoto tribe reside on the north side of the Columbia, back of a pond, and nearly opposite the entrance of the Multnomah river........	8	460
Multnomah tribe resides on Wappatoo island, in the mouth of the Multnomah, the remains of a large nation	6	800
Clannahqueh tribe of Multnomah resides on Wappatoo island, below the Multnomahs........	4	130
Nemalquinner tribe of Multnomahs reside on the northeast side of the Multnomah river, three miles above its mouth........	4	200
Cathlacommatups, a tribe of Multnomahs, reside on the south side of the Wappatoo island on a slur of the Multnomah........	3	170

	Houses	Souls
Cathlanaquiahs, a tribe of Multnomahs, reside on the southwest side of Wappatoo island....................	6	400
Clackstar nation reside on a small river, which discharges itself on the southwest side of Wappatoo island.........	28	1200
Claninnatas resides on the southwest side of Wappatoo island..	5	200
Cathlacumups reside on the main shore, southwest of Wappatoo island....................................	6	450
Clannarminnamuns reside on the southwest side of the Wappatoo island....................................	12	280
Quathlahpohtle nation reside on the southwest side of the Columbia, above the entrance of Tahwahnahiooks river, opposite the lower point of Wappatoo island...........	14	900
Cathlamahs reside on a creek which falls into the Columbia on the north side, at the lower part of the Columbian valley, north side...................................	10	200
21. Skilloot nation resides on the Columbia, on each side in different villages, from the lower part of the Columbian valley as low as Sturgeon island, and on either side of the Coweliskee river...	50	2500
Hullooellell reside on the Coweliskee		
22. Wahkiacums reside on the north side of the Columbia, opposite the Marshy islands..........................	11	200
23. Cathlamahs reside on the south side of the Columbia, opposite to the Seal islands..........................	9	300
24. Chinnooks reside on the north side of the Columbia at the entrance of, and on Chinnook river..................	28	400
25. Clatsop nation resides on the south side of the Columbia, and a few miles along the southeast coast, on both sides of point Adams..	14	200
26. Killamucks nation resides from the Clatsops of the coast along the southeast coast for many miles.............	50	1000
Indian information. The following nations speak the Killamuck language:		
27. Lucktons reside on the seacoast to the southwest of the Killamucks..		20
Kahuncles reside on the seacoast southwest of the Lucktons..		400
Lukawis do. do. to the S.S.E. large town.......		800
Youikcones do. do. do. large houses......		700
Neeketoos do. do. do. large town.......		700
Ulseahs do. do. do. small town.......		150
Youitts do. do. do. do.		150
Sheastuckles reside on the seacoast to the southeast of the Lucktons......................large town.......		900
Killawats do. do. do. do.		500

	Houses	Souls
28. Cookkoo-oose nation reside on the seacoast, to the south of the Killawats		1500
Shallalah nation reside on the same course to the south		1200
Luckkarso nation do. do. do.		1200
Hannakallal nation do. do. do.		600
Indians along the N.W. coast		
29. Killaxthocles tribe reside on the seacoast, from the Chinnooks to the N.N.W.	8	100
Chiltz nation reside from the Killaxthokles along the N.N.W. coast	38	700
Clamoctomichs reside from the Chiltz along the N.N.W. coast	12	260
Potoashs reside on the same coast northwestwardly of the Clamoctomichs	10	200
Pailsh tribe reside from the Potoash on the northwest coast	10	200
Quiniilts reside from the Pailsh along the northwest coast	60	1000
Quieetsos reside from the Quiniilts along the northwest coast	18	250
Chillates reside from the Quieetos along the northwest coast	8	150
Calasthocle reside from the Chillate northwest along the same coast	10	200
Quinnechart nation reside on the seacoast and creek, north and northwest of the Calasthocles		2000
30. Clarkamus nation reside on a large river of the same name, which heads in Mount Jefferson, and discharges itself into the Multnomah, forty miles up that river on its northeast side; this nation has several villages on either side		1800
31. Cushhooks nation reside on the northeast bank of the Multnomah, immediately below the falls of that river, about sixty miles above its entrance into the Columbia		650
32. Charcowah nation reside on the southwest bank of the Multnomah, immediately above the falls; they take the salmon in that river		200
33. Callahpoewah nation inhabit the country on both sides of the Multnomah, above the Charcowahs for a great extent		2000
34. Shoshonee (or Snake Indians) residing in winter and fall on the Multnomah river, southwardly of the southwest mountains, and in spring and summer on the heads of the Towanahiooks, La Page, Yaumalolam, and Wollawollah rivers, and more abundantly at the falls of the Towanahiooks, for the purpose of fishing		3000
35. Shoshonees on the Multnomah and its waters; the resi-		

	Houses	Souls
dence of them is not well known to us, or the Indians of the Columbia		6000
36. Shobarboobeer band of Shoshonees reside on the south-west side of the Multnomah river, high up the said river		1600
37. Shoshonees residing on the south fork of Lewis's river, and on the Nemo, Walshlemo, Shallette, Shushpella-nimmo, Shecomshink, Timmoonumlarwas, and the Cop-coppakark rivers, branches of the south fork of Lewis's river		3000
We saw parts of the following tribes at the Long narrows:		
38. Skaddals nation reside on Cataract river, twenty-five miles north of the Big narrows		200
Squannaroos reside on Cataract river, below the Skaddals		120
Shallattoos reside on Cataract river, above them		100
Shanwappoms reside on the heads of Cataract and Tap-teel rivers		400
39. Cutsahnim nation reside on both sides of the Columbia, above the Sokulks, and on the northern branches of the Tapteel river, and also on the Wahnaachee river	60	1200
Lahanna nation reside on both sides of the Columbia, above the entrance of Clarke's river	120	2000
Coospellar nation reside on a river which falls into the Columbia, to the north of Clarke's river	30	1600
Wheelpo nation reside on both sides of Clarke's river, from the entrance of Lastaw to the great falls of Clarke's river	130	2500
Hihighenimmo nation reside from the entrance of the Lastaw into Clarke's river, on both sides of the Lastaw, as high as the forks	45	1300
Lartielo nation reside at the falls of the Lastaw river, below the great Wayton lake, on both sides of the river	30	600
Skeetsomish nation resides on a small river of the same name, which discharges itself into the Lastaw, below the falls, around the Wayton lake, and on two islands within the said lake	12	2000
Micksucksealton tribe of the Tushshepah reside on Clarke's river, above the great falls of that river, in the Rocky mountains	25	300
Hohilpos, a tribe of the Tushshepah reside on Clarke's river, above the Micksucksealtons, in the Rocky moun-tains	25	300
Tushshepahs nation reside on a north fork of Clarke's river in spring and summer, and the fall and winter on the Missouri. The Ootlashoots is a band of this nation	35	430
Whole number of Indians W. of Rocky Mountains		80,000

Thermometrical observations, showing also the rise and fall of the Mississippi (Missouri); appearances of weather, winds, &c. commencing at the mouth of the river.

Duboes in latitude 38° 55′ 19″ $\frac{6}{10}$ north, and longitude 89° 57′ 45″ west, January 1, 1804.

Thermometer on the north side of a tree in the woods.

Explanations of the notations of the weather

f means fair weather.
r means rain.
h means hail.
l means lightning.
c a s means cloudy after snow intervening.
c a r s means cloudy after rain and snow.
c means cloudy.
s means snow.
t means thunder.
a after, as *f a r* means fair after rain, which has intervened since the last observation.

Notations of the river

r means risen in the last 24 hours, ending at sunrise.
f means fallen in the last 24 hours, ending at sunrise.

Notations of thermometer

a means above naught.
b means below naught.

Day of the month	Therm. at sun-rise	Weather	Wind	Therm. at four o'clock	Weather	Wind	River: r and f.	River: Feet	River: Inches
1804	Deg.			Deg.					
Jan. 1		c.			c.				
2		c. a. s.			c.				
3				2½ a.	f.	N.W. by W.			
4	11 a.	f.	W.			W.			
5		f.	W.		f.	W.			
6		f.	N.W.W.	30 a.	f.	N.W.W.			
7		h.	S.W.		c.a.r.h.	S.W.			
8		f.	S.W.		f.	S.W.			
9		f.	S.W.W.	1 b.	c.	N.W. by W.			
10		f.			f.				6
11									
12									
13		c. s.	S.W.		r. s.	S.W.			
14		f. a. s.			f.				
15									
16									
17	8 b.	f.	N.W.	1½ b.	f.	N.W.	f.		
18	1 b.	c.	N.W.W.	1 a.	f. a. s.	N.W.W.	f.		
19	13 a.	c.	N.W.	11 a.	c.	N.W.	f.		
20	5 b.	f.	N.W.	8 a.	c.	N.W.	f.		
21	7 a.	c. s.	N.E.	17 a.	s. h.	N.E.	f.		
22	11 a.	s.	Shifting	13 a.	s.	N.W.	f.		
23	11 a.	c.	N.E.	17 a.	c.	N.	f.		
24	4 a.	c.	N.W.	11 a.	c.	W.	f.		
25	2 b.	f.	W.N.W.	16 a.	f.	W.	f.		
26		c.	S.W.		c.	S.W.	f.		
27		f.			f.				
28	5 a.	c. s.	N.W.	18 a.	c. s.	N.W.	r.		
29	16 a.	f.	W.	23 a.	f.		r.		
30	22 a.	c. s.	N.	16 a.	f. a. s.	f. a. s.	r.		
31	10 a.	f.	S.W. by W.	15 a.	f.	W.	r.		
Feb. 1	10 a.	f.	S.W.	20 a.	f.	S.W.S.	r.		1½
2	12 a.	f.	N.W.	10 a.	f.	N.W.	r.		1½
3	12 a.	f.	S.W.	19 a.	f.	W.			
4	17 a.	f.	S.W.	28 a.	f.	S.	r.		½
5	18 a.	f.	S.E.	31 a.	c. a. f.	S.E.S.	r.	2	6½
6	19 a.	f.	N.W.	15 a.	c.	S.			

Day of the month		Therm. at sun-rise	Weather	Wind	Therm. at four o'clock	Weather	Wind	River		
								r. and f.	Feet	Inches
1804		Deg.			Deg.					
Feb.	7	29 a.	r. a. c.	S.E.	30 a.	r. c.	S.E.	f.		8
	8	22 a.	c. a. r.	N.W.	20 a.	c. a. s.	N.	r.	1	
	9	10 a.	f. a. s.	N.N.E.	12 a.	c.	N.E.	r.	2	
	10	3 a.	f.	N.E.	17 a.	f.	S.W.	r.	1	4
	11	18 a.	c. a. h.	S.E.	31 a.	s. a. h.	S.E.	r.	1	
	12	15 a.	f.	S.S.E.	25 a.	f.	S.W.	f.		2
	13	12 a.	f.	N.W.	20 a.	f.	W.	r.		1
	14	15 a.	f.	S.W.	32 a.	f.	S.W.			
	15	18 a.	f.	S.W.	32 a.	f.	W.			
	16	28 a.	c.	S.E.	30 a.	c. a. r.	S.E.	r.		2½
	17	15 a.	c. a. r.	S.W.	32 a.	f.	W.	r.		2
	18	10 a.	f.	N.W.				r.		7½
	19	10 a.	f.	N.W.						
	20	10 a.	f.	N.W.	28 a.		S.W.	f.		2½
	21	20 a.	f.	N.W.	34 a.		N.W.	f.		1½
	22	14 a.	f.	N.E.	26 a.		N.E.	r.		1½
	23	6 a.	f.	N.W.	24 a.		N.W.	r.		1
	24	6 a.	f.	N.E.	26 a.		N.E.	f.		2
	25	20 a.	f.	N.E.	28 a.		S.S.W.			
	26	16 a.	f.	N.E.	30 a.		N.E.	f.		½
	27	4 a.	c.	N.E.	24 a.	r. s.	N.W.	f.		1
	28	4 a.	c. s.	N.W.	6 a.	c. a. s.	N.W.	f.		2
	29	8 a.	h. s.	N.W.	12 a.	c. a. s.	N.W.	f.		2½
Mar	1	20 b.	f.	N.W.	4 b.		N.W.	f.		9
	2	19 b.	f.	N.W.	14 a.		E.	f.		8
	3	18 b.	f.	E.	10 a.		S.W.	f.		6½
	4	4 b.	f.	N.E.	12 a.		E.	f.		5
	5	2 a.	f.	N.W.	12 a.		N.W.	f.		3
	6	4 b.	f.	N.W.	2 a.		N.W.	f.		3
	7	16 b.	c. & s.	N.W.	10 a.	c.	N.W.			
	8	2 b.	c. s.	N.W.	12 a.	s.	N.W.	f.		1½
	9	10 a.	c.	N.W.	10 a.	c.	N.W.	r.		2
	10	6 a.	c.	N.W.	12 a.	f.	N.W.	r.		2½
	11	12 a.	f.	E.	20 a.	f.	S.W.	f.		2½
	12	14 a.	f.	N.E.	16 a.	f.	N.E.	r.		1½
	13	8 a.	f.	N.W.	12 a.	f.	N.W.	f.		1½
	14	4 a.	f.	N.E.	10 a.	f.	N.E.	f.		4½
	15	6 b.	c. s.	N.W.	40 a.	r. a. s.	N.E.	r.		5
	16	2 b.	f.	E.	40 a.	f.	S.S.W.	r.		11
	17	12 a.	f.	N.E.	38 a.	f.	N.E.	r.		7

Day of the month	Therm. at sun-rise	Weather	Wind	Therm. at four o'clock	Weather	Wind	River		
							r. and f.	Feet	Inches
1804	Deg.			Deg.					
Mar. 18	2 a.	f.	E.	44 a.	f.	N.E.	f.		3
19	2 a.	f.	N.E.	52 a.	f.	S.S.W.	f.		2½
20	4 a.	f.	E.	60 a.	f.	S.S.W.	f.		1½
21	26 a.	f.	S.S.W.	36 a.	f.	N.W.	f.		2
22	22 a.	f.	N.W.	40 a.	f.	N.W.	f.		2
23	14 a.	f.	N.E.	44 a.	f.	N.E.	r.		4
24	6 a.	f.	E.	52 a.	f.	S.S.W.	r.	1	5½
25	16 a.	f.	S.S.W.	46 a.	f.	E.	r.	2	
26	28 a.	f.	E.	44 a.	f.	E.	r.		10
27	34 a.	r. & t.	E.	42 a.	f. a. r.	N.E.	r.		7
28	34 a.	c.	N.E.	44 a.	c.	E.	r.		5½
29	20 a.	r. a. t.	N.E.	30 a.	h. r.	N.E.	r.		1
30		c. a. r.	N.W.		f.	N.W.	r.		2
31		f.	N.W.		f.	N.W.	r.		2
April 1		f.	N.E.		f.	N.E.	r.		2½
2	8 a.	f.			f.	N.E.	r.		3½
3	42 a.	f.	N.E.		r.	N.E.	r.		3½
4	44 a.	c. a. r.	N.W.				r.		11
5	24 a.	c. a. r.	N.E.		t. a. r.		r.		2
6	18 a.	c. a. r.	N.W.		s. a. r.		f.		4½
7	10 a.	f. a. c.	N.W.		c.		f.		2
8	10 a.	c.	N.E.		c. r.		f.		2½
9	18 a.	f. a. c.	N.E.		c.		f.		2
10	10 a.	f.	N.W.		f.		f.		6½
11	10 a.	f.	N.E.		f.		f.		7½
12	16 a.	c.	N.W.		f. a. c.		f.		7
13	36 a.	c.	N.E.		c.		f.		6½
14	22 a.	f.	S.W.		f.		f.		5
15	22 a.	f.	N.W.				f.		6½
16	36 a.	c.	N.W.		f. a. c.		f.		5½
17	26 a.	f. a. c.	N.W.		f.		f.		5
18	16 a.	f. a. c.	N.N.W.		c.		f.		3
19	34 a.	r.	S.S.E.				f.		4
20	34 a.	c. r.	S.E.	37 a.	r.	S.E.	f.		3½
21	31 a.	r.	S.W.	42 a.	f. a. r.	W.	r.	1	2
22	28 a.	c.	N.W.	34 a.	c.	N.W.	r.	1	6
23	22 a.	f.	N.W.	64 a.	f.	W.	f.		1
24	36 a.	f.	N.W.	44 a.	f.	N.W.	r.		8
25	26 a.	f.	N.W.	38 a.	c.	N.W.	r.		2½
26	16 a.	f.	N.W.	58 a.	f.	N.W.	f.		6

Day of the month		Therm. at sun-rise	Weather	Wind	Therm. at four	Weather	Wind	River		
								r. and f.	Feet	Inches
1804		Deg.			Deg.					
April	27	28 a.	c. & r.	W.	62 a.	f.	S.W.	f.		8
	28	30 a.	f.	N.W.	64 a.	f.	N.W.	f.		7
	29	32 a.	f.	N.W.	52 a.	f.	S.E.	f.		7
	30	18 a.	f.	S.E.	56 a.	f.	N.E.	f.		6
May	1	20 a.	f.	S.E.	54 a.	f.	N.E.	f.		4½
	2	19 a.	f.	S.E.	68 a.	f.	S.S.E.	f.		6
	3	24 a.	f.	S.S.E.	72 a.	f.	S.S.W.	f.		4½
	4	40 a.	t. c. r.	S.	56 a.	c. a. r.	S.	r.		2
	5	42 a.	t. c. r.	W.	58 a.	c. a. r.	W.	r.		2½
	6	34 a.	f.	S.W.	70 a.	f.	S.W.	f.		2½
	7	38 a.	f.	S.E.	52 a.	f.	S.S.E.	f.		4½
	8	44 a.	f.	N.E.	62 a.	f.	S.W.	f.		4
	9	42 a.	f.	E.	76 a.	f.	S.W.	f.		2
	10	46 a.	c.	N.E.	67 a.	f.	N.W.	f.		3½
	11	46 a.	f.	E.	70 a.	f.	S.W.	f.		2½
	12	36 a.	f.	E.	72 a.	f.	W.	f.		3
	13	42 a.	c. a. r.	W.	40 a.	c. a. r.	N.W.	f.		2
	14	34 a.	c.	S.E.	56 a.	f.	N.			
	*									
Sept.	19	46 a.	f.	S.E.	71 a.	f.	S.E.			
	20	51 a.	f.	S.E.	70 a.	f.	S.E.			
	21	58 a.	f.	S.W.	88 a.	f.	S.W.			
	22	52 a.	f.	E.	82 a.	f.	S.E.			
	23	50 a.	f.	S.E.	86 a.	f.	S.E.			
	24	54 a.	f.	E.	82 a.	f.	W.			
	25	56 a.	f.	S.W.	79 a.	f.	W.			
	26	54 a.	f.	W.	78 a.	f.	S.W.			
	27	52 a.	f.	W.	86 a.	f.	S.W.			
	28	45 a.	f.	S.E.	80 a.	f.	S.E.			
	29	45 a.	f.	S.E.	67 a.	f.	S.E.			
	30	42 a.	c. a. r.	S.E.	52 a.	c. a. r.	S.E.			
Oct.	1	40 a.	c.	S.E.	46 a.	c.	S.E.			
	2	39 a.	f.	S.E.	75 a.	c.	N.			
	3	40 a.	c.	N.W.	45 a.	c. a. r.	N.			
	4	38 a.	c. a. r.	N.W.	50 a.	c.	N.W.			

* Here is an hiatus in the manuscript, which it is not in our power to fill up, viz. from the 14th of May to September. The party were then just beginning the ascent of the Missouri, and it is probable that amongst the many other important things which engrossed their attention this was omitted.

Day of the month	Therm. at sun-rise	Weather	Wind	Therm. at four o'clock	Weather	Wind	River		
							r. and f.	Feet	Inches
1804	Deg.			Deg.					
Oct. 5	36 a.	f.	N.W.	54 a.	f.	N.W.			
6	43 a.	f.	N.W.	60 a.	f.	N.W.			
7	45 a.	c.	S.E.	58 a.	f.	S.E.			
8	48 a.	f.	N.W.	62 a.	f.	N.W.			
9	45 a.	c.	N.E.	50 a.	c. a. r.	N.			
10	42 a.	f. a. r.	N.W.	67 a.	f.	N. W.			
11	43 a.	f.	N.W.	59 a.	f.	N.W.			
12	42 a.	f.	S.	65 a.	f.	S.E.			
13	43 a.	f.	S.W.	49 a.	c. a. r.	S.E.			
14	42 a.	r.	S.E.	40 a.	r.	S.E.			
15	46 a.	r.	N.	57 a.	f. a. r.	N.W.			
16	45 a.	c.	N.E.	50 a.	f.	N.E.			
17	47 a.	f.	N.W.	54 a.	f.	N.W.			
18	30 a.	f.	N.W.	68 a.	f.	N.W.			
19	43 a.	f.	S.E.	62 a.	f.	S.			
20	44 a.	f.	N.W.	48 a.	f.	N.			
21	31 a.	s.	N.W.	34 a.	s.	N.W.			
22	35 a.	c. a. s.	N.E.	42 a.	c.	N.E.			
23	32 a.	s.	N.W.	45 a.	c.	N.E.			
24	33 a.	s. a. f.	N.W.	51 a.	c. a. s.	N.W.			
25	31 a.	c.	S.E.	50 a.	c.	S.E.			
26	42 a.	f.	S.E.	57 a.	f.	S.E.			
27	39 a.	f.	S.W.	58 a.	f.	S.W.			
28	34 a.	f.	S.W.	54 a.	f.	S.W.			
29	32 a.	f.	S.W.	59 a.	f.	S.W.			
30	32 a.	f.	S.W.	52 a.	f.	S.W.			
31	33 a.	f.	W.	48 a.	f.	W.			
Nov. 1	31 a.	f.	N.W.	47 a.	f.	N.W.			
2	32 a.	f.	S.E.	63 a.	f.	S.E.			
3	32 a.	f.	N.W.	53 a.	f.	N.W.			
4	31 a.	f.	N.W.	43 a.	c.	W.			
5	30 a.	c.	N.W.	58 a.	c.	N.W.			
6	31 a.	c.	S.W.	43 a.	c.	W.			
7	43 a.	c.	S.	62 a.	c.	S.			
8	38 a.	c.	S.	39 a.	c.	W.			
9	27 a.	f.	N.W.	43 a.	f.	N.W.			
10	34 a.	f.	N.W.	36 a.	c.	N.W.			
11	28 a.	f.	N.W.	60 a.	f.	N.W.			
12	18 a.	f.	N.	31 a.	f.	N.E.			
13	18 a.	s.	S.E.	28 a.	c. a. s.	S.E.	f.		$1\frac{1}{2}$

Day of the month	Therm. at sun-rise	Weather	Wind	Therm. at four o'clock	Weather	Wind	River		
							r. and f.	Feet	Inches
1804	Deg.			Deg.					
Nov. 14	24 a.	s.	S.E.	32 a.	c. a. s.	S.E.	r.		1
15	22 a.	c.	N.W.	31 a.	c. a. s.	N.W.	r.		½
16	25 a.	c.	N.W.	30 a.	f.	S.E.	r.		¼
17	28 a.	f.	S.E.	34 a.	f.	S.E.	r.		¼
18	30 a.	f.	S.E.	38 a.	f.	W.	r.		¼
19	32 a.	f.	N.W.	48 a.	f.	N.W.	r.		1
20	35 a.	f.	N.W.	50 a.	f.	W.	r.		1¼
21	33 a.	c.	S.	49 a.	f.	S.E.	r.		
22	37 a.	f.	W.	45 a.	f.	N.W.	r.		½
23	38 a.	f.	W.	48 a.	f.	N.W.			
24	36 a.	f.	N.W.	34 a.	f.	N.W.			
25	34 a.	f.	W.	32 a.	f.	S.W.			
26	15 a.	f.	S.W.	21 a.	f.	W.			
27	10 a.	f.	S.E.	19 a.	c.	S.E.	f.		3
28	12 a.	s.	S.E.	15 a.	s.	E.	f.		4
29	14 a.	c. a. s.	N.E.	18 a.	f.	W.	f.		2½
30	17 a.	f.	W.	23 a.	f.	W.	f.	2	
Dec. 1	1 b.	f.	E.	6 a.	f.	S.E.	r.	1	
2	38 a.	f.	N.W.	36 a.	f.	N.W.	r.		1
3	26 a.	f.	N.W.	30 a.	f.	N.W.	r.		1
4	18 a.	f.	N.	29 a.	f.	N.	r.		1
5	14 a.	c.	N.E.	27 a.	s.	N.E.			
6	10 a.	s.	N.W.	11 a.	c. a. s.	N.W.			
7	0 a.	f.	N.W.	1 b.	c.	N.W.	r.	2	½
8	12 b.	s.	N.W.	5 b.	f. a. s.	N.W.			
9	7 a.	f.	E.	10 b.	f.	N.W.			
10	10 b.	c.	N.	11 b.	c.	N.	r.		½
11	21 b.	f.	N.	18 b.	f.	N.	f.		½
12	38 b.	f.	N.	16 b.	f.	N.			
13	20 b.	f.	S.E.	4 b.	c.	S.E.			
14	2 b.	c.	S.E.	2 a.	s.	S.E.	f.		1
15	8 b.	c. a. s.	W.	4 b.	c. a. s.	W.			
16	22 b.	f.	N.W.	4 b.	f.	N.W.	f.		1
17	45 b.	f.	N.	28 b.	f.	N.	r.		3
18	32 b.	f.	W.	16 b.	f.	S.W.	r.		1
19	2 b.	c.	S.W.	16 a.	f.	S.	r.		1
20	24 a.	f.	N.W.	22 a.	c.	W.	r.		2
21	22 a.	f.	N.W.	22 a.	c.	N.W.	r.		2
22	10 a.	f.	N.W.	23 a.	f.	N.W.	r.		2½
23	18 a.	c.	S.W.	27 a.	c.	W.	f.		1

Day of the month	Therm. at sun-rise	Weather	Wind at sun-rise	Therm. at four o'clock	Weather	Wind at four o'clock	River		
							r. and f.	Feet	Inches
1804	Deg.			Deg.					
Dec. 24	22 a.	s.	S.W.	31 a.	c. a. s.	W.	f.		2½
25	15 a.	s.	N.W.	20 a.	c. a. s.	N.W.	f.		1
26	18 a.	c.	N.W.	21 a.	f.	N.W.			
27	4 b.	c.	N.W.	14 a.	c.	N.W.			
28	12 a.	f.	N.	13 a.	f.	N.W.	r.		2½
29	9 b.	f.	N.	3 a.	f.	N.	r.		1
30	20 b.	f.	N.	11 b.	f.	N.	r.		½
31	10 b.	f.	S.E.	12 a.	c.	S.W.	r.		1½
1805									
Jan. 1	18 a.	s.	S.E.	34 a.	f.	N.W.	r.		1
2	4 b.	s.	N.W.	8 b.	f. a. s.	N.			
3	14 b.	c.	N.	4 b.	s.	S.E.			
4	28 a.	c. a. s.	W.	4 b.	c.	N.W.	r.		2½
5	20 b.	c.	N.W.	18 b.	s.	N.E.	r.		2
6	11 b.	c. a. s.	N.W.	16 b.	f.	N.W.	r.		3
7	22 b.	f.	N.W.	14 b.	f.	W.	f.		1
8	20 b.	f.	N.W.	10 b.	f.	N.W.	r.		1
9	21 b.	f.	W.	18 b.	f. a. c.	N.W.			
10	40 b.	f.	N.W.	28 b.	f.	N.W.			
11	38 b.	f.	N.W.	14 b.	f.	N.W.	f.		½
12	20 b.	f.	N.W.	16 b.	f.	N.W.	r.		1
13	34 b.	f.	N.W.	20 b.	f.	N.W.			
14	16 b.	s.	S.E.	8 b.	c. a. s.	S.E.			
15	10 b.	f.	E.	3 a.	c.	S.W.	r.		1
16	36 a.	c.	W.	16 a.	f.	S.W.	r.		2½
17	2 b.	c.	W.	12 b.	f.	N.W.			
18	1 b.	f.	N.W.	7 a.	f. a. c.	N.W.	f.		1
19	12 a.	c.	N.E.	6 b.	f.	N.W.	r.		1
20	28 a.	f.	N.E.	9 b.	c.	S.E.	r.		½
21	2 b.	c.	N.E.	8 a.	f.	S.E.			
22	10 a.	f. a. h.	N.W.	19 a.	c.	N.W.	r.		1¾
23	20 b.	s.	E.	2 b.	c. a. s.	N.	f.		2½
24	12 b.	c.	N.W.	2 b.	f.	N.W.	r.		¼
25	26 b.	f.	N.W.	4 b.	f. a. c.	W.			
26	12 a.	c.	N.E.	20 a.	f. a. c.	S.E.			
27	20 a.	c.	S.E.	16 a.	c.	N.W.	r.		2
28	2 b.	f.	N.W.	15 a.	f.	S.W.			
29	4 a.	f.	S.W.	16 a.	f.	W.	r.		½
30	6 a.	c.	N.W.	14 a.	c.	N.W.	r.		1
31	2 b.	c. a. s.	N.W.	8 a.	f. a. c.	N.W.	f.		1

Day of the month		Therm. at sun-rise	Weather	Wind at sun-rise	Therm. at four o'clock	Weather	Wind at four o'clock	River		
								r. and f.	Feet	Inches
1805		Deg.			Deg.					
Feb.	1	6 a.	c.	N.W.	16 a.	f.	N.W.	r.		2½
	2	12 b.	f.	N.W.	3 a.	f.	S.	f.		1
	3	8 b.	f.	S.W.	2 a.	f.	W.			
	4	18 b.	f.	N.W.	9 b.	f.	W.			
	5	10 a.	f.	N.W.	20 a.	f.	N.W.	r.		1
	6	4 b.	f.	N.W.	12 a.	f.	W.	r.		½
	7	18 a.	f.	S.E.	29 a.	c.	S.	r.		½
	8	18 a.	f.	N.W.	28 a.	c.	N.E.	f.		1
	9	10 a.	f.	S.E.	33 a.	c.	S.E.			
	10	18 a.	c. a. s.	N.W.	12 a.	c.	N.W.			
	11	8 b.	f.	N.W.	2 b.	f.	N.W.			
	12	14 b.	f.	S.E.	2 a.	f.	W.			
	13	2 b.	c.	S.E.	10 a.	c.	N.W.	f.		1
	14	2 a.	c. a. s.	N.W.	2 b.	f.	N.W.			
	15	16 b.	f.	S.W.	6 b.	f.	W.			
	16	2 a.	f.	S.E.	8 a.	f.	W.	f.		1
	17	4 a.	c.	S.E.	12 a.	f.	N.W.			
	18	4 a.	s.	N.E.	10 a.	f.	S.			
	19	4 a.	f.	S.E.	20 a.	f.	S.			
	20	2 a.	f.	S.	22 a.	f.	S.			
	21	6 a.	f.	S.	30 a.	f.	S.			
	22	8 a.	c.	N.	32 a.	c. a. r.				
	23	18 a.	f.	N.W.	32 a.	f.	W.	r.		½
	24	8 a.	f.	N.W.	32 a.	f.	W.			
	25	16 a.	f.	W.	38 a.	f.	N.W.			
	26	20 a.	f.	N.E.	31 a.	f.	N.			
	27	26 a.	f.	S.E.	36 a.	f.	E.	f.		½
	28	24 a.	f.	E.	38 a.	c.	S.E.			
Mar.	1	28 a.	c.	W.	38 a.	f.	N.W.			
	2	28 a.	f.	N.E.	36 a.	f.	N.E.	r.		1½
	3	28 a.	c.	E.	39 a.	f.	N.W.			
	4	26 a.	f.	N.W.	36 a.	f.	N.W.			
	5	22 a.	f.	E.	40 a.	f.	N.W.			
	6	26 a.	c.	E.	36 a.	f.	E.	r.		2
	7	12 a.	f.	E.	26 a.	c.	E.	r.		2
	8	7 a.	c.	E.	12 a.	f.	E.	r.		2½
	9	2 a.	c.	N.	18 a.	f.	N.W.	r.		2
	10	2 b.	f.	N.W.	12 a.	f.	N.W.	r.		3½
	11	12 a.	c.	S.E.	26 a.	f. a. c.	N.W.	r.		4½
	12	2 b.	f. a. s.	N.	10 a.	f.	N.W.	r.		5

Day of the month		Therm. at sun-rise	Weather	Wind at sun-rise	Therm. at four o'clock	Weather	Wind at four o'clock	River		
								r. and f.	Feet	Inches
1805		Deg.			Deg.					
Mar.	13	1 b.	f.	S.E.	28 a.	f.	S.W.	r.		3½
	14	18 a.	f.	S.E.	40 a.	f.	W.			
	15	24 a.	f.	S.E.	38 a.	f.	W.	f.		1
	16	32 a.	c.	E.	42 a.	c.	W.	f.		3
	17	30 a.	f.	S.E.	46 a.	f.	S.W.	r.		2
	18	24 a.	c.	N.	34 a.	c.	N.	f.		1
	19	20 a.	c. a. s.	N.	31 a.	f.	N.W.	r.		1
	20	28 a.	c.	N.W.	28 a.	f.	N.W.	r.		3
	21	16 a.	c.	E.	26 a.	s. & h.	S.			
	22	22 a.	f. a. s.	S.	36 a.	f.	S.W.	f.		4
	23	34 a.	f.	W.	38 a.	c. a. r.	N.W.	f.		4
	24	28 a.	c. a. s.	N.E.	30 a.	c. a. s.	N.	r.		1
	25	16 a.	f.	E.	32 a.	f.	S.	r.		5
	26	20 a.	f.	S.E.	46 a.	f.	W.	r.		4½
	27	28 a.	f.	S.E.	60 a.	f.	S.W.	r.		9
	28	40 a.	f.	S.E.	64 a.	f.	S.W.	r.		1
	29	42 a.	f.	N.W.	52 a.	f.	N.W.	f.		11
	30	28 a.	f.	N.W.	49 a.	f.	N.W.	r.	1	1
	31	35 a.	c. a. r.	S.E.	45 a.	c.	S.E.	r.		9
April	1	33 a.	c.	N.W.	43 a.	c. a. t.	W.	f.		11
	2	28 a.	c. a. r.	N.W.	38 a.	f. a. c.	W.	f.		5
	3	24 a.	f.	N.	44 a.	f.	N.	f.		4
	4	36 a.	f.	S.	55 a.	f.	N.W.	f.		4
	5	30 a.	f.	N.W.	39 a.	f.	N.	f.		2
	6	19 a.	f.	N.	48 a.	c.	N.W.	f.		1
	7	28 a.	f.	N.	64 a.	f.	S.W.	r.		2
	8	19 a.	f.	N.W.	56 a.	f.	N.W.	f.		2
	9	38 a.	f.	S.E.	70 a.	f.	S.W.	f.		½
	10	42 a.	f.	E.	74 a.	f.	S.W.	r.		⅓
	11	42 a.	f.	N.W.	76 a.	f.	W.	f.		½
	12	56 a.	f.	N.W.	74 a.	c. r. t. l.	W.	r.		½
	13	58 a.	f.	S.E.	80 a.	f.	S.E.	f.		1
	14	52 a.	c.	S.E.	82 a.	f.	S.W.	f.		¾
	15	51 a.	f.	E.	78 a.	f.	S.W.	f.		½
	16	54 a.	f.	S.E.	78 a.	f.	S.	f.		½
	17	56 a.	f.	N.E.	74 a.	c.	N.W.	f.		½
	18	52 a.	f.	N.E.	64 a.	c.	N.			
	19	54 a.	c.	N.W.	56 a.	c.	N.W.			
	20	40 a.	c.	N.W.	42 a.	c. a. s.	N.W.			
	21	28 a.	f.	N.W.	40 a.	c.	N.W.	f.		½

Day of the month	Therm. at sun-rise	Weather	Wind	Therm. at four o'clock	Weather	Wind	River		
							r. and f.	Feet	Inches
1805	Deg.			Deg.					
April 22	34 a.	f. a. c.	W.	40 a.	f.	N.W.	r.		2
23	34 a.	f.	W.	52 a.	c.	N.W.	r.		2
24	40 a.	f.	N.	56 a.	f.	N.	r.		1
25	36 a.	f.	N.	52 a.	f.	N.W.	r.		2
26	32 a.	f.	S.	63 a.	f.	S.E.	r.		3
27	36 a.	f.	S.W.	64 a.	f.	N.W.	f.		2
28	44 a.	f.	S.E.	63 a.	f.	S.E.	f.		1½
29	42 a.	f.	N.E.	64 a.	f.	E.	f.		1½
30	50 a.	f.	N.W.	58 a.	f.	S.E.	f.		½
May 1	36 a.	c.	E.	46 a.	c. a. f.	N.E.	f.		1½
2	28 a.	s.	N.E.	34 a.	c. a. s.	N.W.	f.		1
3	26 a.	f.	W.	46 a.	c.	W.	f.		¼
4	38 a.	c.	W.	48 a.	f. a. c.	W.			
5	38 a.	f.	N.W.	62 a.	f. a. r.	S.E.	r.		1
6	48 a.	f.	E.	61 a.	c. a. r.	S.E.	r.		2
7	42 a.	c.	S.	60 a.	f.	N.E.	r.		1½
8	41 a.	c.	E.	52 a.	c. a. r.	E.	f.		¼
9	38 a.	f.	E.	58 a.	f.	W.	r.		¾
10	38 a.	f. a. c.	W.N.W.	62 a.	c. a. r.	N.W.	f.		¾
11	44 a.	f.	N.E.	60 a.	c.	S.W.			
12	52 a.	f.	S.E.	54 a.	c. a. r.	N.W.	r.		2
13	52 a.	c. a. r.	N.W.	54 a.	f. a. c.	N.W.	f.		2¼
14	32 a.	f.	S.W.	52 a.	c.	S.W.	f.		1¾
15	48 a.	c. a. r.	S.W.	54 a.	c.	N.W.	f.		¾
16	48 a.	c.	S.W.	67 a.	f.	S.W.			
17	60 a.	f.	N.E.	68 a.	f.	S.W.			
18	58 a.	f.	W.	46 a.	c. a. r.	N.W.	f.		1
19	38 a.	f.	E.	68 a.	f. a. c.	S.W.			
20	52 a.	f.	N.E.	76 a.	f.	E.	f.		1
21	50 a.	f.	S.W.	76 a.	f.	N.W.			
22	46 a.	c.	N.W.	48 a.	c.	N.W.	f.		½
23	32 a.	f.	S.W.	54 a.	f.	S.W.	f.		½
24	32 a.	f.	N.W.	68 a.	f.	S.E.	r.		3½
25	46 a.	f.	S.W.	82 a.	f.	S.W.	r.		2
26	58 a.	f.	S.W.	80 a.	f.	S.W.	r.		½
27	62 a.	f.	S.W.	82 a.	f.	S.W.			
28	62 a.	c.	S.W.	72 a.	c. & r.	S.W.	r.		½
29	62 a.	c. a. r.	S.W.	67 a.	r.	S. W.	r.		1
30	56 a.	c. a. r.	S.W.	50 a.	r.	S.W.	r.		5
31	48 a.	c. a. r.	W.	53 a.	c. a. r.	S.W.	r.		1½

Day of the month	Therm. at sun-rise	Weather	Wind at sun-rise	Therm. at four o'clock	Weather	Wind at four o'clock	River		
							r. and f.	Feet	Inches
1805	Deg.			Deg.					
June 1	50 a.	c.	S.W.	62 a.	c.	S.E.	r.		1½
2	56 a.	c. a. r.	S.W.	68 a.	f.	S.W.			
3	46 a.	f.	S.W.	60 a.	f.	S.W.			
4	48 a.	f. a. c.	N.E.	61 a.	f.	S.W.	f.		¾
5	40 a.	r.	S.W.	42 a.	c. a. r.	N.E.	f.		¾
6	35 a.	c. a. r.	N.E.	42 a.	r. a. r.	N.E.	f.		1½
7	40 a.	c. a. r.	S.W.	43 a.	r. a. r.	S.W.	f.		1½
8	41 a.	r. a. r.	S.W.	48 a.	f. a.	S.W.	f.		1¼
9	50 a.	f.	S.W.	52 a.	f.	S.W.	f.		1
10	52 a.	f.	S.W.	68 a.	f. a. r.	S.W.	r.		2
11	54 a.	f.	S.W.	66 a.	f.	S.W.			
12	54 a.	f.	S.W.	64 a.	f. a. r.	S.W.			
13	52 a.	f.	S.W.	72 a.	f.	S.W.	r.		¾
14	60 a.	f.	S.W.	74 a.	f.	S.W.	f.		¾
15	60 a.	f.	S.W.	76 a.	f.	S.W.	f.		½
16	64 a.	c. r.	S.W.	58 a.	f.	S.W.	r.		½
17	50 a.	c.	S.W.	57 a.	c.	S.W.	f.		½
18	48 a.	c.	S.W.	64 a.	f. a. c.	S.W.	f.		½
19	52 a.	f.	S.W.	70 a.	f.	S.W.	f.		½
20	49 a.	c.	S.W.	74 a.	f. a. r.	S.W.	f.		¼
21	49 a.	f.	S.W.	70 a.	c.	S.W.	f.		¼
22	45 a.	c.	S.W.	54 a.	f.	S.W.	f.		½
23	48 a.	f.	S.E.	65 a.	c.	S.E.	f.		¼
24	49 a.	c. a. r.	S.E.	74 a.	f. a. c.	S.W.	f.		
25	47 a.	c. a. r.	S.W.	72 a.	f.	S.W.			
26	49 a.	f.	S.W.	78 a.	f.	S.W.	r.		½
27	49 a.	f.	S.W.	77 a.	f. a. r. h.	S.W.	r.		1¼
28	46 a.	f.	S.W.	75 a.	c. a. f.	S.W.	r.		2
29	47 a.	r. t. l.	S.W.	77 a.	f. a. r.	S.W.	r.		4½
30	49 a.	f.	S.W.	76 a.	f.	S.W.	r.		2¼
July 1	59 a.	f.	S.W.	74 a.	f.	S.W.	r.		½
2	60 a.	f. a. r.	S.W.	78 a.	f.	S.W.			
3	56 a.	f.	S.W.	74 a.	c.a.f.a.r.	S.W.			
4	52 a.	f.	S.W.	76 a.	f. a. r.	S.W.	f.		¾
5	49 a.	t. & r.	S.W.	72 a.	f.	S.W.	f.		½
6	47 a.	c. a. h.	S.W.	74 a.	f. a. c.	S.W.	f.		¼
7	54 a.	c. a. f.	S.W.	77 a.	f. a. c.	S.W.	f.		¼
8	60 a.	f.	S.W.	78 a.	f. a. r.	S.W.	f.		¼
9	56 a.	f.	S.W.	76 a.	c. a. r.	N.W.			¼
10	52 a.	f. a. r.	S.W.	66 a.	f.	S.W.			

Day of the month	Therm. at sun-rise	Weather	Wind at sun-rise	Therm. at four o'clock	Weather	Wind at four o'clock	River		
							r. and f.	Feet	Inches
1805	Deg.			Deg.					
July 11	46 a.	f.	S.W.	70 a.	f.	S.W.			
12	50 a.	f.	S.W.	74 a.	f.	S.W.	f.		1/4
13	42 a.	f.	S.W.	76 a.	f.	S.W.	f.		1/4
14	45 a.	f.	S.W.	78 a.	c. a. r.	S.W.			
15	60 a.	f. a. r.	S.W.	76 a.	f.	S.W.	f.		1 1/2
16	53 a.	f.	S.W.	80 a.	f.	S.W.	f.		3/4
17	58 a.	f.	S.W.	81 a.	f.	S.W.	f.		1 1/2
18	60 a.	f.	S.W.	84 a.	f.	S.W.	f.		1/2
19	62 a.	f.	S.W.	68 a.	c. a. h. r.	S.W.	f.		1/2
20	59 a.	f. a. r.	S.W.	60 a.	f.	N.W.			
21	60 a.	f.	N.W.	67 a.	f.	N.W.	f.		1/2
22	52 a.	f.	N.W.	80 a.	f.	N.E.			
23	54 a.	f.	S.W.	80 a.	c.	S.W.	f.		1/2
24	60 a.	f.	S.W.	90 a.	f.	S.W.	f.		3/4
25	60 a.	f.	S.W.	86 a.	f.	S.W.	f.		1/2
26	60 a.	f.	S.W.	82 a.	c. a. r.	S.W.	f.		3/4
27	52 a.	c.	S.W.	80 a.	c. a. r.	S.W.	f.		3/4
28	49 a.	f. a. r.	S.W.	90 a.	f.	S.W.	f.		1/2
29	54 a.	f. a. r.	N.	82 a.	f.	N.E.	r.		1/2
30	50 a.	f.	S.E.	80 a.	f.	S.E.			
31	48 a.	f.	S.W.	92 a.	f.	S.W.			
Aug. 1	54 a.	f.	S.W.	91 a.	f.	S.W.	f.		1/2
2	48 a.	f.	N.W.	81 a.	f.	N.W.	f.		1/2
3	50 a.	f.	N.E.	86 a.	f.	N.E.	f.		1/2
4	48 a.	f.	S.	92 a.	f.	S.	f.		1/2
5	49 a.	f.	S.E.	79 a.	f.	S.E.	f.		1/4
6	52 a.	f.	S.W.	71 a.	c.	S.W.			
7	54 a.	c. a. r.	S.W.	80 a.	c.	S.W.			
8	54 a.	f. a. r.	S.W.	82 a.	c. a. f.	S.W.			
9	58 a.	f.	N.E.	78 a.	c.	S.W.			
10	60 a.	c. a. r.	S.W.	68 a.	t. l. r.	S.W.			
11	58 a.	c. a. r. h.	N.E.	70 a.	f.	S.W.			
12	58 a.	f. a. r. h.	W.	72 a.	f.a.r.a.h.	N.W.			
13	52 a.	c. a. f.	N.W.	70 a.	f. a. r.	N.W.			
14	51 a.	f. a. r.	N.W.	76 a.	f.	N.W.			
15	52 a.	f.	S.E.	74 a.	f.	S.W.			
16	48 a.	f.	S.W.	70 a.	f.	S.W.			
17	42 a.	f.	N.E.	76 a.	f.	S.W.			
18	45 a.	c.	S.W.	78 a.	r.	S.W.			
19	30 a.	f. a. r.	S.W.	71 a.	f. a. r.	S.W.			
20	32 a.	f.	S.W.	74 a.	f.	S.W.			

Day of the month	Therm. at sun-rise	Weather	Wind at sun-rise	Therm. at four o'clock	Weather	Wind at four o'clock	River		
							r. and f.	Feet	Inches
1805	Deg.			Deg.					
Aug. 21	19 a.	f.	S.E.	78 a.	f.	E.			
22	22 a.	f.	E.	70 a.	f.	E.			
23	35 a.	f.	E.	72 a.	f.	S.E.			
24	40 a.	f.	S.E.	76 a.	f. a. r.	S.E.			
25	32 a.	f. a. r.	S.E.	65 a.	c.	S.E.			
26	31 a.	f.	S.E.	45 a.	f.	S.E.			
27	32 a.	f.	S.E.	56 a.	f.	S.E.			
28	35 a.	f.	S.W.	66 a.	f.	S.W.			
29	32 a.	f.	S.W.	68 a.	f.	S.W.			
30	34 a.	c.	N.E.	59 a.	c.	N.E.			
31	38 a.	c. a. r.	N.E.	58 a.	c. a. r. h.	N.E.			
Sept. 1	38 a.	c.	N.W.	67 a.	c.	N.W.			
2	36 a.	c. a. r.	N.E.	60 a.	c. a. r. h.	N.E.			
3	34 a.	c. a. r.	N.E.	52 a.	c. a. r.	N.E.			
4	19 a.	r. a. s.	N.E.	34 a.	c. a. r.	N.E.			
5	17 a.	c. a. s.	N.E.	29 a.	c. a. r. s.	N.E.			
6		c. a. r.	N.E.		r.	N.E.			
7		c. a. r.	N.E.		c. a. r.	N.E.			
8		c.	N.E.		c. a. r.	N.E.			
9		c. a. r.	N.E.		f. a. r.	N.E.			
10		f.	N.W.		f.	N.W.			
11		f.	N.W.		f.	N.W.			
12		f.	N.W.		f.	N.E.			
13		c.	N.E.		r.	N.E.			
14		c. a. r.	S.W.		c. a. r.	S.W.			
15		c. a. s.	S.W.		s.	S.W.			
16		c. a. s.	S.W.		f.	S.W.			
17		f.	S.W.		f.	S.W.			
18		f.	S.W.		f.	S.W.			
19		f.	S.W.		f.	S.W.			
20		f.	S.W.		f.	S.W.			
21		f.	S.E.		f.	S.W.			
22		f.	S.W.		f.	S.W.			
23		f.	S.W.		f.	S.W.			
24		f.	S.E.		f.	S.E.			
25		f.	E.		f.	S.W.			
26		f.	E.		f.	S.W.			
27		f.	E.		f.	S.W.			
28		f.	E.		f.	S.W.			
29			E.		f.	S.W.			
30			E.		f.	S.W.			

October			November			December		
Day of month	Wind	Weather	Day of month	Wind	Weather	Day of month	Wind	Weather
1	E.	f.	1	N.E.	f.	1	E.	c. a. r.
2	N.	f.	2	S.W.	f.	2	S.W.	c. a. r.
3	E.	f.	3	N.E.	f. a. fog.	3	E.	f. a. r.
4	E.	f.	4	W.	c. a. r.	4	S.E.	r.
5	E.	f.	5	S.W.	r. c. r.	5	S.W.	r.
6	E.	f.	6	S.W.	r. a. r.	6	S.W.	r.
7	E.	f.	7	S.W.	r. a. r. fog.	7	N.E.	f. a. r.
8	E.	f.	8	S.W.	f. a. r.	8	N.E.	c.
9	S.W.	c.	9	S.	r.	9	N.E.	c. r.
10	N.W.	f.	10	N.W.	r. a. r.	10	N.E.	r.
11	E.& S.W.	c.	11	S.W.	r.	11	S.W.	r.
12	E.& S.W.	f.	12	S.W.	h. r. t. & l.	12	S.W.	r.
13	S.W.	f. a. r.	13	S.W.	r.	13	S.W.	r.
14	S.W.	f.	14		r.	14	S.W.	r.
15	S.W.	f.	15	S.E.	f. a. r.	15	S.W.	c. a. r.
16	S.W.	f.	16	W.S.W.	f.	16	S.W.	r.
17	S.E.	f.	17	E.	c. a. f.	17	S.W.	f. a. r. & h.
18	S.E.	f.	18	S.E.	f. a. c.	18	S.E.	c. a. r. s. h.
19	S.E.	f.	19	S.E.	c. a. r.	19	S.W.	h. r. & c.
20	S.W.	f.	20	S.E.	f. a. r.	20	S.W.	f. a. r. & h.
21	S.W.	f.	21	S.E.	c. a. r.	21	S.W.	r.
22	S.W.	f.	22	S.S.E.	r.	22	S.W.	r.
23	S.W.	f.	23	S.W.	c. a. r.	23	S.W.	r. h. & t.
24	S.W.	f.	24	W.	f. a. r.	24	S.W.	r.
25	W.	f.	25	E.S.E.	c. a. r.	25	S.W.	c. r.
26	W.	f.	26	E.N.E.	r.	26	S.W.	r. a. t. & l.
27	W.	f.	27	S.W.	r.	27	S.W.	r.
28	N.W.	r. a. f.	28	S.W.W.	r.	28	S.E.	r.
29	W.	f. a. r.	29	S.W.	r.	29	S.E.	c. a. r.
30	S.E.	r. a. r.	30	S.W.	f. a. r. & h.	30	S.E.	f. a. r.
31	S.W.	f. a. r.				31	S.W.	r.

Day of the month		Weather	Wind at sun-rise	Weather	Wind at four o'clock
1806					
Jan.	1	c. a. r.	S.W.	r. a. c.	S.W.
	2	c. a. r.	S.W.	r.	S.W.
	3	c. a. r. h. t. & l.	S.W.	c. a. r. h. & f.	S.W.
	4	c. a. r. & h.	S.W.	r. a. f. & r.	S.E.
	5	r.	S.E.	r.	S.E.
	6	c. a. r.	S.E.	f.	E.
	7	f.	N.E.	c. a. f.	S.E.
	8	f.	N.E.	c. a. f.	S.E.
	9	f.	S.W.	c. a. f.	S.W.
	10	f. a. r.	S.W.	c. a. f.	S.W.
	11	c.	S.W.	c. a. r.	S.W.
	12	f. a. c.	N.W.	c.	N.W.
	13	r.	S.W.	r.	S.W.
	14	f. a. r.	N.W.	c. a. f.	S.
	15	r. a. c. & r.	S.E.	r. a. r.	S.
	16	r. a. r.	S.W.	r. a. r.	S.W.
	17	c. a. r.	S.W.	c.	S.W.
	18	r. a. r.	S.W.	c. a. r.	S.W.
	19	c. a. r.	S.	c. a. r.	S.W.
	20	r. a. r.	S.W.	r. a. r.	S.W.
	21	c. a. r.	S.W.	c. a. r.	S.W.
	22	r. a. r.	S.W.	c. a. r.	S.W.
	23	c. a. r. t. & l.	S.W.	c. a. f.	S.W.
	24	c. a. r. & s.	S.E.	c. a. r. h. & s.	E.
	25	h. a. r. h. s.	N.E.	c. a. r. h. & s.	N.E.
	26	c. a. h. & s.	N.E.	c. a. s.	N.E.
	27	f. a. s.	N.E.	f.	N.E.
	28	f.	N.E.	f.	N.E.
	29	f.	N.E.	f.	N.E.
	30	s. a. s.	N.	s. a. s.	W.
	31	f. a. c.	N.E.	f.	N.E.
Feb.	1	f.	N.E.	f.	N.E.
	2	f.	N.E.	c. a. s.	S.W.
	3	c. a. s. & r.	N.W.	c. a. f.	N.E.
	4	f.	N.E.	f.	N.E.
	5	f.	N.E.	f.	N.E.
	6	f.	N.E.	c.	S.W.
	7	c.	S.W.	c.	S.W.
	8	c. a. s. r. h.	S.W.	c. a. f. r. h. & s.	S.W.
	9	c. a. r. & h.	S.W.	c. a. r. & h.	S.W.
	10	c. a. r. h. s.	N.	c. a. f. & c.	S.W.
	11	c. a. f. & c.	S.W.	r. a. f. & r.	S.W.
	12	r. a. r. & c.	S.W.	r. a. c. & r.	S.W.
	13	c. a. r.	S.W.	c. a. r.	S.W.

Day of the month		Weather	Wind at sun-rise	Weather	Wind at four o'clock
1806					
Feb.	14	c. a. f. & s.	S.W.	r. a. r. f. & r.	S.W.
	15	c. a. r. & f.	S.	c. a. r. & f.	S.W.
	16	r. a. s. & r.	S.W.	r. a. f. & r.	S.W.
	17	c. a. r. h. & s.	S.W.	r. a. f. h. s. & r.	S.W.
	18	c. a. r. & h.	S.W.	r. a. r. & h.	S.W.
	19	r. a. r.	S.W.	r. a. r.	S.W.
	20	c. a. r.	S.W.	c. a. r.	S.W.
	21	r. a. c. & r.	S.W.	r. a. c. & r.	S.W.
	22	f. a. r.	N.E.	c. a. f.	N.E.
	23	f.	S.W.	c. a. f.	S.W.
	24	c. a. f. & c.	S.W.	r. a. c. & r.	S.
	25	r. a. r.	S.	r. a. r.	S.
	26	f. a. r.	N.E.	c. a. f. & r.	S.
	27	c. a. r.	S.W.	r. a. r.	S.W.
	28	r. a. r.	S.W.	c. a. c. & f.	S.W.
Mar.	1	f. a. r. & c.	S.W.	r. a. c. & r.	S.W.
	2	r. a. c. & r.	S.	r. a. c. & r.	S.
	3	c. a. r.	S.	c. a. r.	S.
	4	r. a. c. & r.	S.	r. a. r.	S.
	5	c. a. r.	N.E.	c. a. r.	S.
	6	f. a. r.	S.E.	c. a. f.	S.E.
	7	r. a. r. & h.	S.E.	r. a. f. r. h. c. & f.	S.E.
	8	h. & r. a. h. r. & s.	S.	r. a. r. & h.	S.E.
	9	s. & h. a. r. s. & h.	S.W.	r. a. h. & r.	S.W.
	10	s. & r. a. h. r. & s.	S.W.	f. a. r. h. & s.	S.W.
	11	f. a. r. h. & s.	S.E.	f. a. r. & h.	S.E.
	12	f. a. c.	N.E.	c. a. f.	N.E.
	13	f. a. r.	N.E.	f.	N.E.
	14	c. a. f.	N.E.	c.	N.E.
	15	c. a. c.	N.E.	f.	N.E.
	16	r. a. f. & c.	S.W.	c. a. f. c. r.	S.W.
	17	c. a. r.	S.W.	r. a. f. h. s. & r.	S.W.
	18	r. a. c. & r.	S.W.	r. a. f. r. & h.	S.W.
	19	r. & h. a. c. r. & h.	S.W.	r. a. f. r. & h.	S.W.
	20	r. a. r. & h.	S.W.	r.	S.W.
	21	r. a. r.	S.W.	c. a. r.	N.E.
	22	r. a. r.	S.W.	r. a. c. & r.	S.W.N.E.
	23	r. a. r.	S.W.	f. a. c. & r.	S.W.
	24	r. c. a. & r.	S.W.	f. a. c.	N.W.S.W.
	25	c. a. f.	S.E.	r. a. c. & r.	S.E.
	26	c. a. r.	N.W.	c. a. f. & c.	S.E.
	27	r. a. c.	S.E.	r. a. c. & r.	S.E.
	28	c. a. r.	N.	f. a. f. & r.	S.W.
	29	c. a. r. & f.	S.	c. a. r.	S.W.

Day of the month	Weather	Wind at sun-rise	Weather	Wind at four o'clock	Columbia River		
					r. and f.	Feet	Inches
1806							
Mar. 30	c.	E.	f. a. c.	S.W.			
31	f.	S.E.					
April 1	c. a. f.	S.E.	c. a. f.	S.E.	r.		1
2	c.	S.E.	c. a. f.	S.E.	f.		⅓
3	c. a. r.	S.W.	c. a. r.	W.	f.		3½
4	c. a. r.	S.W.	c. a. r.	S.W.	f.		4½
5	c. a. r.	S.W.	c. a. f. & c.	S.W.	f.		2½
6	f. a. c.	S.W.	f.	S.W.	f.		1
7	f.	S.W.	f.	S.W.	r.		½
8	f.	E.	f.	E.	r.		1½
9	f.	W.	f.	W.			
10	c. a. r.	W.	c. a. r.	S.W.	r.		1
11	r. a. r.	W.	c. a. r.	S.W.	r.		2
12	c. a. r.	W.	r. a. c. & r.	W.	r.		2
13	r. a. c. & r.	W.	c. a. r. & f.	W.	r.		2½
14	f.	W.	f.	W.	r.		1
15	f.	W.	f.	W.			
16	f. a. c.	S.W.	f.	S.W.	f.		2
17	f.	N.E.	c. a. f.	S.W.	f.		2
18	f. a. r.	S.W.	f.	S.W.	f.		1
19	c. a. r.	S.W.	c.	S.W.	f.		3
20	f. a. r.	S.W.	c. a. r.	S.W.	f.		2½
21	f.	N.E.	f.	E.	f.		2
22	f.	N.W.	f.	W.	f.		1
23	f. a. c.	E.	f.	N.E.	f.		4
24	f.	N.W.	f.	N.W.	f.		2
25	f.	N.E.	f.	N.E.	f.		2
26	f. a. c.	N.W.	f.	N.E.	f.		2½
27	f. a. r.	S.E.	f.	N.W.	f.		1½
28	f. a. t.	S.W.	f.	N.E.	f.		2
29	f. a. c.	N.W.	f.	N.W.	f.		1
30	c. a. r.	N.W.	f. a. c.	N.W.	f.		2
May 1	c. a. r.	S.W.	c.	S.W.			
2	f. a. c.	N.E.	f.	S.W.			
3	c. a. h. r. s.	S.W.	c. a. r. h. s.	S.W.			
4	f. a. h.	S.W.	c. a. r. & h.	S.W.			
5	f.	S.W.	f.	S.W.			
6	r. a. c. r.	N.E.	f. a. r.	N.E.			
7	f. a. c.	N.E.	f.	S.W.			

Day of the month		Weather	Wind at sun-rise	Weather	Wind at four o'clock	Kooskooskee River		
						r. and f.	Feet	Inches
1806								
May	8	f.	S.W.	f.	S.W.			
	9	f.	S.W.	f. a. c.	W.			
	10	c. a. r. & s.	S.W.	f. a. s.	S.W.			
	11	f. a. r.	S.W.	f. a. c.	S.W.			
	12	f.	E.	f.	S.W.			
	13	f.	S.W.	f.	S.W.			
	14	f.	S.W.	f.	S.W.			
	15	f.	N.	f. a. c.	N.W.			
	16	c.	S.E.	c. a. r.	S.E.	r.		6
	17	r. a. r.	S.E.	c. a. r.	S.E.	r.		10¾
	18	c. a. r.	S.E.	c.	S.E.	r.		2
	19	r. a. r.	S.E.	c. a. r.	S.E.	f.		4
	20	r. a. r.	N.W.	c. a. r.	S.E.	r.		2
	21	c. a. r.	S.E.	f. a. c.	S.E.	f.		1
	22	f.	S.E.	f.	S.E.	f.		2
	23	f.	N.W.	f.	N.W. S.E.	f.		1½
	24	f.	S.E.	f.	N.W.	f.		1
	25	c. a. r. & t.	N.W.	f.	N.W.	r.		9½
	26	f. a. r.	S.E.	f.	N.W.	r.		6
	27	c.	S.E.	r. a. f. r. t. l.	S.E.	r.		6½
	28	c. a. r. t. & l.	S.E.	c. a. f. r. t. l.	S.E.	r.		11
	29	c. a. r. & t.	S.E.	c. a. r.	N.W.	r.	1	5
	30	c. a. r.	S.E.	f.	S.E.	f.		6
	31	c. a. f.	S.E.	f.	S.E.	r.	1	1
June	1	f. a. r. t. & l.	S.E.	f. a. c.	N.W.			
	2	c. a. c.	N.W.	f. a. c.	S.E.			
	3	c. a. f. & c.	S.E.	c. a. f.	S.E.			
	4	c. a. r.	S.E.	f. a. c.	N.W.			
	5	f.	S.E.	f.	N.W.			
	6	f.	S.E.	f.	N.W.			
	7	c. a. r.	N.W.	c. a. f. r. h.	N.W.			
	8	c.	S.E.	c. a. f.	N.W.			
	9	c.	S.E.	f. a. c.	N.W.			
	10	f.	S.E.	f.	N.W.			
	11	f.	S.E.	f.	N.W.			
	12	f. a. r. l. & t.	S.E.	f.	N.W.			
	13	c.	S.E.	c. a. f.	N.W.			
	14	f.	S.E.	f.	N.W.			
	15	c.	N.W.	r. a. f. & r.	N.W.			

Day of the month		Weather	Wind at sun-rise	Weather	Wind at four o'clock	River r. and f.	River Feet	River Inches
1806								
June	16	f. a. c.	S.E.	c. a. f.	S.E.			
	17	c. a. r.	E.	c. a. f. & r.	S.E.			
	18	c. a. r.	E.	c. a. r. & h.	S.W.			
	19	f. a. c.	S.E.	f.	N.W.			
	20	f.	S.E.	f.	N.W.			
	21	f.	S.E.	f.	N.W.			
	22	f.	N.W.	f.	N.W.			
	23	f.	N.W.	f.	N.W.			
	24	f.	N.W.	f.	N.W.			
	25	c. a. r.	S.E.	c. a. r.	N.W.			
	26	c. a. r.	S.E.	f.	S.E.			
	27	f. a. r.	S.E.	f.	S.E.			
	28	f.	S.E.	f.	S.E.			
	29	f.	S.E.	f. a. h. r. t.	S.E.			
	30	f.	S.E.	f.	N.W.			
July	1	c. a. f.	N.W.	f.	N.W.			
	2	f.	S.E.	f.	N.W.			
	3	f.	S.E.	f.	S.W.			
	4	f.	S.W.	f.	S.W.			
	5	f.	N.E.	f.	S.W.			
	6	f.	S.W.	c. a. r. t. & l.	S.W.			
	7	c. a. r.	W.	f. a. r.	S.W. by W.			
	8	f. a. r.	W.	f.	S.W.			
	9	c.	S.W.	f.	S.W.			
	10	f.	S.E.	f.	S.W.			
	11	f.	S.E.	f.	N.N.E.			
	12	f.	S.E.	f.	N.W.			
	13	f.	S.S.E.	f.	N.E.			
	14	f.	N.W.	f.	N.W.			
	15	f.	S.E. by E.	f.	N.E.			
	16	c.	N.E.	c.	N.E.			
	17	f. a. r. h. t. l.	S.E.	f.	S.W.			
	18	f.	S.W.	f.	S.E.			
	19	f.	N.W.	f.	S.E.			
	20	f.	N.E.	f.	N.E.			
	21	f.	N.E.	c.	N.E.			
	22	f. a. t. l. & r.	N.E.	c.	N.E.			
	23	f.	N.E.	c.	S.E.			
	24	f.	S.W.	r.	S.W.			

Day of the month	Weather	Wind at sun-rise	Weather	Wind at four o'clock	River		
					r. and f.	Feet	Inches
1806							
July 25	c.	E.	c. a. r.	S.W.			
26	c.	S.S.W.	f. a. r.	N.W.			
27	f.	N.E.	f.	S.W.			
28	c. a. r.	N.E.	f.	N.W.			
29	c. a. r. t. & l.	N.E.	f.	N.			
30	f. a. r. t. & l.	N.W.	f. a. r.	S.E.			
31	f.	N.W.	c. a. r.	N.E.			
Aug. 1	c. a. r.	N.W.	r.	N.	r.	5	$\frac{1}{2}$
2	c. a. r.	N.	f. a. r.	N.	r.	3	
3	f.	S.W.	f.	S.W.	r.	2	$\frac{1}{4}$
4	f.	N.W.	f.	N.E.	f.	6	$\frac{1}{2}$
5	f.	N.E.	f.	N.E.	f.	7	
6	c. a. r. t. l.	S.W.	f.	N.E.	f.	2	$\frac{1}{4}$
7	r.	N.E.	c. a. r.	N.	f.	2	$\frac{1}{2}$
8	f.	N.	f.	N.W.	f.		
9	f.	N.E.	f.	N.E.	f.	1	$\frac{1}{4}$
10	f.	E.	c.	E.	f.		$\frac{3}{4}$
11	f.	N.W.	f.	N.W.	f.	2	
12	f.	S.W.	c.	S.W.	f.	2	$\frac{1}{4}$
13	f. a. r.	S.W.	f.	S.W.	f.	2	$\frac{1}{2}$
14	f.	N.E.	f.	S.W.	f.	3	$\frac{1}{2}$
15	f.	N.W.	f.	N.W.	f.	2	
16	f.	N.W.	f.	N.W.	f.	3	$\frac{1}{2}$
17	c.	S.E.	c.	S.E.			
18	c. a. r.	S.E.	f.	S.E.	f.	1	$\frac{1}{2}$
19	t. l. & r.	S.E.	c.	S.E.	f.		$\frac{3}{4}$
20	c. a. t. l. & r.	S.W.	f.	N.W.	f.	1	$\frac{1}{4}$
21	f.	S.E.	f.	N.W.	f.	2	$\frac{1}{2}$
22	c. a. r.	S.W.	f.	S.E.	f.	4	
23	c.	S.E.	r.	N.W.	f.	1	$\frac{1}{2}$
24	f.	N.E.	f.	N.W.	f.	2	
25	f.	S.W.	f.	N.W.	f.	1	$\frac{1}{4}$
26	f.	S.E.	f.	S.E.	f.		$\frac{3}{4}$
27	f.	S.E.	f.	S.E.	f.	1	$\frac{1}{4}$
28	f.	S.E.	f.	N.W.			
29	c.	N.W.	f. a. r.	S.E.	f.		$\frac{1}{2}$
30	c. a. r.	S.E.	f.	S.E.			
31	c. a. r. t. l. w.	S.E.	c. a. r.	S.E.			

Day of the month 1804.		REMARKS AND REFLECTIONS.
January	1	Snow one inch deep.
	2	Some snow last night.
	3	Hard wind.
	4	River covered with ice out of the Missouri.
	5	River Du Bois rise.
	6	do. do. do.
	7	do. do. do.
	8	do. do. do. and discharge ice.
	9	Some snow last night.
	10	The Missouri rise.
	13	Snowed last night.
	17	River covered with ice, some 5½ inches thick.
	19	do. do. do.
	20	No ice passing to-day.
	21	Ice running out of the Missouri 9 inches thick. Snow 2½ inches deep.
	22	Ice running out of the Missouri, snow 5¾ inches deep.
	23	Ice stopped.
	24	The trees covered with ice.
	28	Ice running, cold &c.
February	1	The wind blew hard, no frost, snow disappearing fast.
	2	Frost this morning, the snow has disappeared in spots.
	3	Frost this morning, the snow thaws considerably.
	4	Frost, number of swan and geese from N. and S.
	5	Immense quantity of ice running, some of which is 11 inches thick.
	6	A quantity of soft ice running, white frost, the snow disappeared, swans passing.
	7	A small qnantity of floating ice passing, swans passing.
	8	Many swan from N. W. Creek rose and took off the water mark.
	9	The river rose 2 feet: large quantity of drift ice from the Missouri.
	10	Ice still drifting in considerable quantities: some geese pass from the south.

February 11 The sugar maple runs freely: swans pass from the north.
12 Pigeons, geese and ducks of various kinds have returned.
13 The first appearance of the blue crains.
14 But little drift ice: the Mississippi is not broken up: sugar trees run.
15 Immense quantity of swans.
27 The river rose three inches and fell immediately.
28 Began to snow, and continued all day.
29 Snow all night, and until eleven o'clock A. M. and cleared away.

March 7 Saw the first brant return.
8 Rain succeeded by snow and hail.
9 Cloudy in the morning.
19 The weather has been generally fair but very cold, the ice run for several days in such quantities, that it was impossible to pass the river; visited St. Charles; saw the first snake, which was the kind usually termed the garter snake; saw also a beetle of a black colour, with two red stripes on his back, passing each other crosswise from the but of the wing to the extremity of the same.
20 Heard the first frogs on my return from St. Charles.
25 Saw the first white crane return.
26 The weather warm and fair.
27 The buds of the spicewood appeared, and the tassels of the mail cottonwood were larger than a large mulberry, and with the shape and colour of that fruit: some of them had fallen from the trees. The grass begins to spring; the weather has been warm, and no falling weather until this time, though the atmosphere has been very smoky and thick; a heavy fall of rain commenced, which continued until twelve at night, attended with thunder and lightning. Saw large insects which resembled musquitoes, but doubt whether they are really those insects or the fly which produces them, they attempted to bite my horse, but I could not observe that they made any impression with their beaks.
31 Windy.

April 1 The spicewood is in full bloom, the dog's-tooth violet, and May apple appeared above ground. A northern light appeared at 10 o'clock P. M. very red.

5 At St. Louis the buds of the peaches, apples and cherries appear.
6 A large flock of pellicans appear.
7 The leaves of some of the apple trees have burst their coverts and put forth, the leaves of the greenwood bushes have put forth.—Many of the wild plants have sprung up and appear above ground.
10 No appearance of the buds of the Osage apple; the Osage plum has put forth its leaves and flower buds, though it is not yet completely in blow.
13 The peach trees are partly in bloom; the brant, geese, duck, swan, crane and other aquatic birds have disappeared very much within a few days, and have gone further north I presume; the summer ducks raise their young in this neighbourhood, and are now here in great numbers.
17 Peach trees in full bloom; the weeping willow has put forth its leaves, and are one fifth of their size: the violet, the dove's-foot and cowslip are in blow, the dog's-tooth violet is not yet in bloom. The trees of the forest, particularly the cotton-wood, begin to obtain from the size of their buds, a greenish cast at a distance; the gooseberry, which is also in this country and black, have put forth their leaves—frost.
26 The white frost killed much fruit near Kahokia, while that at St. Louis escaped with little injury.
30 White frost; slight; did but little injury.

May 5 Thundered and lightened excessively this morning.
10 Distant thunder: sultry this evening.
12 The wind at four was uncommonly hard.
25 Strawberries in the prairies ripe, and abundant.
27 Service berries or wild currants ripe and abundant.
30 Mulberries begin to ripen; abundant in the bottom of the river.

June 10 Purple raspberries ripe and abundant.
11 Many small birds are now sitting; some have young: the whippoorwill sitting.
16 The wood duck now have its young; these ducks are abundant, and except one solitary pelican and a few geese, these ducks were the only aquatic fowl we have yet seen.

July 1 Saw some geese with their young; caught several; they are not yet feathered, nor can they fly; the old geese are in the same situation at this season.

4 A great number of young geese and swan in a lake opposite to the mouth of Fourth of July creek: in the lake there is also an abundance of fish of various species, the pike, perch, carp, cat, sunperch, &c. &c.

12 The deer and bear are becoming scarce, and the elk begin to appear.

23 Catfish is very common, and easy taken in any part of this river; some are nearly white, particularly above the Platte river.

Sept. 19 The leaves of the cotton-wood begin to fade: yesterday saw the first brant passing from the northwest to southeast.

20 The antelope is now rutting; the swallow has disappeared twelve days.

21 The elk is now rutting; the buffaloe is nearly ceased; the latter commence the latter end of July or the first of August.

22 A little foggy this morning; a great number of green-legged plover are passing down the river, also some geese and brant.

23 The air remarkably dry; plums and grapes fully ripe; in thirty-six hours two spoonfulls of water evaporated in a saucer.

27 Saw a large flock of white gulls, with wings tipped with black.

October 1 The leaf of the ash, poplar, and most of the shrubs begin to turn yellow, and decline.

3 The earth and sand which form the bars of this river are so fully impregnated with salt, that it shoots and adheres to the little sticks which appear on the surface; it is pleasant and seems nitrous.

5 Slight white frost last night: geese and brant passing south.

6 Frost last night: saw teel, mallards and gulls.

9 Wind blew hard this morning; saw some brant and geese passing to the south.

14 Cotton-wood all yellow, and the leaves begin to fall: abundance of grapes and red berries; the leaves of all

the trees as ash, elm, &c. except the cotton-wood, are now fallen

17 Saw a large flock of white brant with black wings: antelopes are passing to the Black mountains to winter, as is their custom.

18 Hard frost last night, the clay near the water edge was frozen, as was the water in the vessels exposed to the air.

19 No mule-deer seen above the Chayenne river.

20 Much more timber than usual: saw the first black haws that we have seen for a long time.

29 The wind was so hard, that it was extremely disagreeable: the sand was blown on us in clouds.

Nov. 3 Wind blew hard all day.

7 A few drops of rain this evening; saw the aurora-borealis at 10 P. M.; it was very brilliant in perpendicular columns, frequently changing position.

8 Since we have been at our present station, the river has fallen 9 inches.

9 Very hard frost this morning.

10 Many geese passing to the south; saw a flock of the crested cherry birds passing to the south.

13 Large quantity of drift ice running this morning, the river having appearances of closing for this winter.

16 Hard frost this morning attached to the timber and boughs of the trees.

17 The frost of yesterday remained on the trees until 2 P. M. when it descended like a shower of snow; swans passing from the north.

20 Little soft ice this morning; the boat in much danger from ice, &c.

29 The snow fell eight inches deep, it drifted in heaps in the open ground.

30 The Indians pass the river on the ice.

Decr. 5 Wind blew excessively hard this night from the north-west.

7 Last night the river blocked up opposite fort Mandan.

8 The ice one and a half inches thick on the part that had not previously frozen; the buffaloe appear.

14 Captain Clark set out with a hunting party on the ice with sleighs.

Decr. 15 Snow fell half inch.
24 Snow very inconsiderable.
27 The trees are all white with the frost which attached itself to their boughs.
28 It blew very hard last night; the frost fell like a shower of snow.

1805
January 3 The snow is nine inches deep.
6 At 12 o'clock to-day two luminous spots appeared on each side of the sun, extremely bright.
8 The snow is now ten inches deep, accumulating by frosts.
12 Singular appearance of three distinct *Halos* or luminous rings about the moon appeared this evening at half after nine, P. M. and continued one hour; the moon formed the centre of the middle ring, the other two which lay north and south of the moon, and had each of them a limb passing through the moon's centre, and projecting north and south, a semidiameter beyond the middle ring, to which last they were equal in dimensions, each ring appearing to extend an angle of fifteen degrees of a great circle.
15 A total eclipse of the moon last night visible here, but partially obscured by the clouds.
19 Ice now three feet thick on the most rapid part of the river.
23 The snow fell about four inches deep last night, and continues to snow.
It frequently happens that the sun rises fair and in about fifteen or twenty minutes it becomes suddenly turbid, as if the moon had some chemical effect on the atmosphere.
31 The snow fell two inches last night.
Feb. 8 The black and white speckled woodpecker has returned.
14 The snow fell three inches deep last night.
March 2 The snow has disappeared in many places, the river partially broken up.
3 A flock of ducks passed up the river this morning.
12 Snow but slight, disappeared to-day.
19 But little snow, not enough to cover the ground. Collected some roots, herbs and plants, in order to send

by the boat, particularly the root said to cure the bite of a mad dog and rattlesnake.

The Indians raise a kind of artichokes, which they say is common in the prairies; well tasted.

21 Some ducks in the river opposite the fort.

24 But little snow.

25 A flock of swan returned to-day: the ice in the river has given way in many places, and it is with difficulty it can be passed.

26 The ice gave way in the river about 3 P. M. and came down in immense sheets; very near destroying our new canoes; some geese pass to-day.

27 The first insect I have seen, was a large black gnat to-day; the ice drifting in great quantities.

28 Ice abates in quantity, wind hard, river rises thirteen inches, and falls twelve inches.

29 A variety of insects make their appearance, as flies bugs, &c. The ice ceases to run, supposed to have formed an obstruction above.

30. The ice comes down in great quantities; the Mandans take some floating buffaloe.

31 Ducks and geese passing: the ice abates in quantity.

April 1 A fine refreshing shower of rain fell about 2 P. M. this was the first shower of rain that we had witnessed since the 15th September, 1804, though it has several times fallen in small quantities, and was noticed in the diary of the weather; the cloud came from the west, and was attended by hard thunder and lightning. I have observed that all thunder-clouds in the western part of the continent, proceed from the westerly quarter, as they do in the Atlantic states. The air is remarkably dry and pure in this open country; very little rain or snow, either winter or summer. The atmosphere is more transparent than I ever observed it in any country through which I have passed.

4 Observed a flock of brant passing up the river to-day: the wind blew very hard, as it does frequently in this quarter. There is scarcely any timber to break the winds from the river, and the country on both sides being level plains, wholly destitute of timber, the

winds blow with astonishing violence, in this open country, and form a great obstruction to the navigation of the Missouri, particularly with small vessels, which can neither ascend nor descend should the wind be the least violent.

April 6 This day a flock of cherry or cedar birds were seen, one of the men killed several of them. They are common in the United States, usually associate in large flocks, and are frequently destructive to the cherry orchards, and in winter in the lower parts of the states of Maryland and Virginia feed on the berries of the cedar. They are a small bluish-brown bird, crested with a tuft of dark brown feathers, with a narrow black stripe passing on each side of the head underneath the eye, from the base of the upper beak to the back of the head; it is distinguished more particularly by some of the shorter feathers of the wing, which are tipped with red spots, which have much the appearance, at a little distance, of sealing-wax.

8 The killdeer and large hawk have returned; the only bird that I observed during the winter at fort Mandan, was the Missouri magpie, a bird of the corvus genus, the raven in immense numbers, the small woodpecker, or sapsucker as they are sometimes called, the beautiful eagle, or calumet-bird, so called from the circumstance of the natives decorating their pipe-stems with its plumage, and the prairie-hen or grouse.

9 The crows have also returned, saw the first to-day; the musquitoes revisit us, saw several of them.

10 The lark, bald-eagle, and the large plover have returned; the grass begins to spring up, and the leaf-buds of the willow to appear.

11 The lark-woodpecker, with yellow wings, and a black spot on the breat, common to the United States have appeared, with sundry small birds. Many plants begin to appear above the ground; saw a large white gull to-day; the eagle are now laying their eggs; and the geese have mated. The elm, large leafed willow, and the bush which bears a red berry is in bloom.

13 The leaves of the choke-cherry are about half grown, the cotton-wood is in bloom; the flower of this tree re-

sembles that of the aspin in form, and is of a deep purple colour.

15 Several flocks of white brant with black wings pass us to day, on their flight to the northwest; the trees now begin to assume a green appearance, though the earth at the depth of about three feet is not yet thawed, which we discover by the banks of the river falling in and disclosing a strata of frozen earth.

16 Saw the first leather-wing bat; it appeared about the size of those common to the United States.

18 A heavy dew this morning, which is the first and only one we have seen since we passed the Council bluffs last summer; there is but little dew in this open country. Saw a flock of pellican pass from southwest to northeast; they appeared to be on a long flight.

19 The trees have now put forth their leaves; the gooseberries, currant, service berries, and wild plums are in bloom.

21 White frost last night, the earth frozen along the water's edge.

23 Saw the first robbin, also the brown curlew.

28 Vegetation has progressed but little since the 18th; in short, the change is scarcely perceptible.

May 2 The wind continued so violent from 12 o'clock yesterday, until five o'clock this evening, that we were unable to proceed; the snow which fell last night and this morning, has not yet disappeared; it forms a singular contrast with the trees which are now in leaf.

3 At 4 P. M. the snow had not yet entirely disappeared; the new horns of the elk begin to appear.

4 The snow has disappeared; saw the first grasshoppers today; there are great quantities of a small blue beetle feeding on the willows.

8 The bald eagle, of which there are great numbers, now have their young; the turtle-dove appears.

9 The chokecherry is now in bloom.

17 The geese have their young; the elk begin to produce their young; the antelope and deer as yet have not; the small species of whip-poor-will begin to cry; the blackbird, both large and small have appeared. We

have had scarcely any thunder and lightning; the clouds are generally white, and accompanied with wind only.

May 18 Saw the wild rose in bloom. The brown thrush or mocking bird have appeared; had a good shower of rain to-day, it continued about two hours; this is the first shower that deserves the appellation of *rain*, which we have seen since we left fort Mandan; no thunder, &c.

22 Saw some particles of snow fall to-day, which did not lie in sufficient quantity on the ground to be perceptible.

23 Hard frost last night; ice in the eddy water along the shore, and the water froze on the oars this morning; strawberries in bloom; saw the first kingfisher.

25 Saw the king-bird or bee-martin; the grouse disappear; killed three of the bighorn animals.

26 The last night was much the warmest that we have experienced; found the covering of our blanket sufficient: the air is extremely dry and pure.

28 A slight thunder storm, the air was turbid in the forenoon, and appeared to be filled with smoke; we supposed it to proceed from the burning of the plains, which we are informed are frequently set on fire by the Snake Indians to compel the antelopes to resort to the woody and mountainous country which they inhabit; saw a small white and black woodpecker, with a red head, the same which is common to the Atlantic states.

30 The rain commenced about 4 o'clock in the evening, and continued moderately through the course of the night; more rain has now fallen than we have experienced since the 15th of September last.

31 The antelopes now bring forth their young; from the size of the young of the bighorn, I suppose they bring forth their young as early at least as the elk.

June 5 Great numbers of sparrows, larks, curlews and other smaller birds common to prairies, are now laying their eggs and sitting; their nests are in great abundance; the large bats, or nighthawks, and the common buzzards appear; first saw the mountain-cock near the entrance of Maria's river.

15 The deer now begin to bring forth their young; the young magpies begin to fly. The brown and grizly bear begin to copulate.

27 At 1 P. M. a black cloud which arose in the southwest came on, accompanied with a high wind and violent thunder and lightning; a great quantity of hail also fell during this storm, which lasted about two hours and a half. The hail which was generally about the size of pigeons' eggs, and not unlike them in form, covered the ground to one inch and a half. For about twenty minutes during this storm, hail fell of an enormous size with violence almost incredible. When the hail-stones struck the ground, they would rebound to the height of ten or twelve feet, and pass twenty or thirty before they touched again. During this immense storm, I was with the greater part of the men on the portage; the men saved themselves, some by getting under a canoe, others by putting sundry articles on their heads, two were knocked down, and seven had their legs and thighs much bruised. Captain Lewis weighed one of those hail stones which weighed three ounces, and measured seven inches in circumference; they were generally round and perfectly solid. I am convinced that if one of these had struck a man on his naked head, it would certainly have fractured his skull; young black-birds are abundant and beginning to fly.

July 6 A heavy wind from the southwest, attended with rain about the middle of the last night; about day had a violent thunderstorm, attended with hail and rain; the hail covered the ground, and was near the size of musquet balls; one black-bird was killed with the hail; I am astonished that more have not suffered in a similar manner, as they are abundant, and I should suppose the hail-stones sufficiently heavy to kill them.

August 7 The river which we are now ascending, is so inconsiderable, and the current so much of a stand, that I relinquished paying further attention to its state.

21 Most astonishing was the difference between the height of the mercury at sunrise and at 4 P. M. to-day. There was the difference of fifty-nine degrees, and this in the space of eight hours, yet we experience

this wonderful transition without feeling it near so sensibly as I should have expected.

Nov. 3 A thick fog continued until 12 o'clock, at which time it cleared off, and was fair the remainder of the day.

5 Commenced raining at 2 P. M. and continued at intervals all day; saw fourteen striped snakes to-day.

7 A thick fog this morning which continued until 11 A. M, at which time it cleared off, and continued fair about two hours, and began to rain; several showers during the evening.

12 Violent wind from the southwest, accompanied with hail thunder and lightning, the thunder excessively loud, which continued from 3 till 6 A. M. when it cleared off for a short time; afterwards a heavy rain succeeded, which lasted until twelve o'clock, when it cleared off for an hour, and again become cloudy: the rain has been pretty generally falling since the 7th instant.

15 The after part of this day is fair and calm, for the first time since the 12th instant, and no rain.

20 Rained moderately from 6 o'clock A. M. until 1 P. M. on the 21st, after which it became cloudy without rain.

22 The wind violent from the S. S. E. throwing the water of the river over our camp, and rain continued all day.

26 Rained all day; some hard showers; wind not so hard as it has been for a few days past; some rain on the morning of the 23d, and night of the 24th instant.

27 Rained moderately all day; a hard wind from the southwest, which compelled us to lie by on the isthmus of point William on the south side.

28 The wind which was from the southwest shifted in the after part of the day to the northwest, and blew a storm which was tremendous; rained all the last night and to-day without intermission.

29 Rained all last night hard, and to-day moderately.

30 Rained and hailed at intervals throughout the last night, some thunder and lightning.

Decr. 3 Fair from 12 to 2 P. M. rained all the last night and this morning; rained the night of the 1st and the morning of the 2nd, and cloudy the remainder of the day;

rained at intervals the night of the 2nd instant, with constant, hard, and sometimes violent winds.

5 Rained yesterday, last night, and moderately to-day, all day the wind violent.

6 Rained all last night and to-day until 6 o'clock, at which time it cleared away and became fair; the winds also ceased to blow violent.

7 Rained from ten to twelve last night; fair day; a hard wind from the northwest, and a shower of rain at 2 P. M.

10 Rained all day, and the air cool; I returned from the ocean; a violent wind last night from the southwest; rained the greater part of the night of the 8th, and all day the 9th instant.

15 Rained at short intervals from the 10th instant, until 8 A. M. to-day.

16 Rained all the last night; cold wind violent from the southwest, accompanied with rain.

17 Rained all the last night and this morning until 9 o'clock, when we had a shower of hail, which lasted about an hour, and then cleared off.

18 Rained, snowed, and hailed at intervals all the last night; several showers of hail and snow until meridian.

19 Rained last night, and several showers of hail and rain this evening; the air cool.

20 Some rain and hail last night, rain continued until 10 A. M.

23 Rained all last night, and moderately all day, with several showers of hail, accompanied with hard claps of thunder &c.; rained 21st and 22d all day and night.

25 Rained at intervals last night and to-day.

26 Rained and blew hard all last night and to-day; some hard claps of thunder and sharp lightning.

29 Rained moderately without much intermission from the 26th until 7 A. M. this morning, hard wind from southeast.

30 Hard wind and some rain last night; to-day tolerably fair.

31 Rained last night and all this day.

1806.

January 1 The changes of the weather are exceedingly sudden, sometimes though seldom the sun is visible for a few moments, the next it hails and rains, then ceases and remains cloudy; the wind blows and it again rains; the wind blows by squalls most generally, and is almost invariably from southwest; these vicissitudes of the weather happen two, three or more times in half a day; snake seen 25th December.

3 The thunder and lightning of the last evening was violent, a singular occurrence for the time of year; the loss of my thermometer I most sincerely regret. I am confident that the climate here, is much warmer than in the same parallel of latitude on the Atlantic ocean, though how many degrees it is now out of my power to determine. Since our arrival in this neighbourhood on the 7th of November, we have experionced one slight white frost only, which happened on the morn- of the 16th of that month; we have yet seen no ice, and the weather is so warm, that we are obliged to cure our meat with smoke and fire to save it; we lost two parcels by depending on the air to preserve it, though it was cut in very thin slices, and sufficiently exposed.

10 Various flies and insects now alive and in motion.

12 The wind from any quarter off the land or along the northwest coast, causes the air to become much cooler; every species of water fowl common to this country at any season of the year, still continue with us.

14 Weather perfectly temperate, I never experienced a winter so warm as the present has been.

23 When the sun is said to shine, or the weather fair, it is to be understood that it barely casts a shadow, and that the atmosphere is hazy, of a milky white colour.

25 It is now perceptibly colder than it has been this winter.

26 The snow this evening is four and three-quarter inches deep: the isicles continue suspended from the eaves of the houses during the day; it now appears something like winter, for the first time this season.

27 The sun shone more bright this morning than it has done since our arrival at this place; the snow since 4 P. M. yesterday, has increased to the depth of six inches, and this morning is perceptibly the coldest that we have had. I suspect the mercury would stand at twenty degrees above naught; the breath is perceptible in our room by the fire.

28 Last night exposed a vessel of water to the air, with a view to discover the depth to which it would frieze in the course of the night, but unfortunately the vessel was only two inches deep, and it friezed the whole thickness; how much more it might have frozen had the vessel been deeper, is therefore out of my power to decide; it is the coldest night that we have had, and I suppose the mercury this morning would have stood as low as fifteen degrees above naught.

31 Notwithstanding the cold weather, the swan, white brant, geese and ducks still continue with us; the sandhill crane also continues; the brown or speckled brant are mostly gone, some few are still to be seen; the cormorant, and a variety of other water fowls still remain. The winds from the land brings us cold and clear weather, while those obliquely along either coast or off the ocean brings us warm, damp, cloudy and rainy weather; the hardest winds are always from the southwest. The blue-crested corvus has already began to build its nest; the nest is formed of small sticks, usually in a pine tree.

February 3 The rain which fell in the latter part of the night froze, and made a slight incrustation on the snow which fell some days past, and also on the boughs of the trees &c.; yesterday it continued fair until 11 A. M. when the wind veered about to southwest, and the horizon was immediately overcast with clouds, which uniformly takes place when the wind is from that point.

4 All the water-fowls before enumerated still continue with us; the birds which resemble the robbin have now visited us in small numbers; saw two of them yesterday about the fort; they are gentle.

Febr 8 The rain of the last night has melted down the snow which has continued to cover the ground since the 24th of January; the feeling of the air and other appearances seem to indicate that the rigor of the winter has passed; it is so warm that we are apprehensive our meat will spoil, we therefore cut it in small pieces and hang it separately on sticks. Saw a number of insects flying about: the small brown flycatch continues with us; this is the smallest of all the American birds except the humming-bird.

15 The robbin has returned and is singing, which reminds us of spring; some other small birds passed on their flight from the south, but were so high that we could not distinguish of what kind they were; the robbin had left this place before our arrival in November.

16 At 11 A. M. it became fair, and the insects were flying about; at half past 12 o'clock it clouded up and began to rain.

24 Much warmer this morning than usual; aquatic and other birds, heretofore enumerated, continue with us still; the sturgeon and a small fish like the anchovy begin to run, they are taken in the Columbia about forty miles above us: the anchovey is exquisitely fine.

28 Saw a variety of insects in motion this morning, some small bugs as well as flies; a brown fly with long legs, about half the size of the common house fly was the most numerous; this is the first insect that has appeared; it is generally about the sinks or filth of any kind; the yellow and brown flycatch has returned, it is a very small bird with a tail as long proportionally as a sparrow.

March 1 A great part of this day was so warm, the fire was unnecessary, notwithstanding its being cloudy and raining.

6 Saw a spider this morning, though the air is perceptibly colder than it has been since the 1st instant. At 9 A. M. it clouded up and continued so the remainder of the day: even the easterly winds which have heretofore given us the only fair weather which we have enjoyed, seem now to have lost their influence in this respect.

7 The elk now begin to shed their horns. A bird of a scarlet colour as large as a common pheasant with a long tail has returned, one of them was seen to-day near the fort by captain Clark's black man; I could not obtain a view of it.

11 It became cloudy at 10 A. M. and rained attended with some hail; at six P. M. it become fair, and the wind changing to northeast it continued fair during the night: the snow had all disappeared by 4 P. M. this evening.

12 It was fair in the morning, but became cloudy at 3 P. M. and continued so during the day.

13 Saw a number of insects in motion; among others saw for the first time this spring and winter, a downy black fly about the size of the common house fly. The plants begin to appear above the ground, among others the rush, of which the natives eat the root, which resembles in flavor the sweet potatoe.

15 The sorrel with an oval, obtuse, and ternate leaf has now put forth its leaves, some of them have already nearly obtained their growth; the birds were singing very agreeably this morning, particularly the common robbin.

16 The anchovy has ceased to run; the white salmon trout have succeeded them; the weather is so warm that insects of various species are every day in motion.

22 The leaves and petals of the flower of the green huckleberry have appeared, some of the leaves have already obtained one fourth of their size.

24 The brown briery shrub with a broad pinnate leaf has began to put forth its leaves; the polecat calwort is in bloom; saw the blue-crested fisher; birds are singing this morning: the black alder is in bloom.

25 The elder, gooseberry and honeysuckle are now putting forth their leaves; the nettle and a variety of other plants are springing up; the flowers of the broadleafed thorn are nearly blown; several small plants in bloom.

26 The humming-bird has appeared; killed one of them and found it the same with those common to the United States.

March 27 The small or bank martin appeared to-day; saw one large flock of them; water-fowl very scarce; a few cormorant, geese, and the red-headed fishing duck are all that are to be seen; the red flowering currant are in bloom; this I take to be the same species I first saw on the Rocky mountains; the fruit is a deep purple berry, covered with a gummy substance, and not agreeably flavoured: there is another species not covered with gum which I first found on the waters of the Columbia, about the 12th of August last.

28 This evening we saw many swan passing to the north as if on a long flight; vegetation is not by several days as forward here as at fort Clatsop when we left that place; the river rising fast; the water is turbid; the tide only swells the water a little, it does not stop the current; it is now within two feet of its greatest height.

30 The grass is about sixteen inches high in the river bottoms; the frogs are now abundant.

April 1 From the best opinion I could form of the state of the Columbia on the first of April, it was about nine feet higher than when we descended it in the beginning of November last.

6 The cottonwood has put forth its leaves and begins to assume a green appearance at a distance; the sweet willow has not yet burst its bud, while the leaves of the red and broad-leafed willow are of some size; it appears to me to be the most backward in vegetating of all the willows; the narrow-leafed willow is not found below tide-water on this river.

8 The male flowers of the cottonwood are falling; the gooseberry has cast the petals of its flowers, and its leaves have obtained their full size; the elder which is remarkably large, has began to bloom, some of its flowrets have expanded their corollas; the service-berries, choke-cherries, the growth which resembles the beach, the small birch and gray willow have put forth their leaves.

9 The vining honeysuckle has put forth shoots of several inches; the dog-toothed violet is in bloom, as is also both the species of the mountain-holly, the straw-

berry, the bear's-claw, the cowslip, the violet, common striped, and the wild cress or tongue grass.

11 The geese are yet in large flocks and do not yet appear to have mated; what I have heretofore termed the broad-leafed ash, is now in bloom; the fringe tree has cast the corolla and its leaves have nearly obtained their full size; the saccacommis is in bloom.

12 The duckinmallard, which breed in the neighbourhood, is now laying its eggs; vegetation is rapidly progressing in the bottoms, though the snow of yesterday and to-day reaches within a mile of the base of the mountains at the rapids of the Columbia.

16 At the Rock-fort camp saw the prairie lark, a species of the peaweet, the blue-crested fisher, the party-coloured corvus, and the black pheasant; a species of hyacinth, native of this place, bloomed to-day; it was not in bloom yesterday.

26 The last evening was cloudy; it continued to threaten rain all night, but without raining; the wind blew hard all night, the air cold, as it is invariably when it sets from the westerly quarter.

May 1 Having left the river we could no longer observe its state, it is now declining, though it has not been as high this season by five feet as it appears to have been the last spring; the Indians inform us that it will rise higher in this month, which I presume is caused by the snows of the mountains.

3 The mountains on our right seem to have had an increase of snow last evening.

10 It began to rain and hail about sunset this evening, which was shortly after succeeded by snow; it continued to fall without intermission until 7 A. M. and lay 8 inches deep on the plain where we were; the air was very keen; a sudden transition this day; yesterday the face of the country had every appearance of summer; after nine A. M. the sun shone, but was frequently obscured by clouds which gave us light showers of snow; in the after part of the day the snow melted considerably, but there was too great a portion to be dissipated by the influence of one day's sun.

May 11 The crimson haw is not more forward now at this place than it was when we lay at Rock-fort camp in April.

20 A nest of the large blue or sandhill crane was found by one of our hunters; the young were in the act of leaving the shell; the young of the party coloured corvus begin to fly.

22 The air is remarkably dry and pure, it has much the feeling and appearance of the air in the plains of the Missouri: since our arrival in this neighbourhood on the 7th instant all the rains noted in the diary of the weather were snows on the plain, and in some instances it snowed on the plains when only a small mist was perceptible in the bottoms at our camp.

27 The dove is cooing, which is the signal, as the Indians inform us of the approach of the salmon. The snow has disappeared on the high plains, and seems to be diminishing fast on the spurs and lower regions of the Rocky mountains.

28 The river from sunrise yesterday to sunrise this morning rose one foot ten inches; drift-wood running in considerable quantities, and the current incredibly swift though smooth.

29 The river rose six inches in the course of yesterday, and one foot five inches in the course of the last night; it is now as high as there are any marks of its having been in the spring 1805; at ten A. M. it arrived at its greatest height, having rose one and a half inches from sunrise to that time; in the balance of the day it fell seven inches; the natives inform us that it will take one more rise before it begins to subside for the season, and then the passage of the mountains will be practicable.

30 The river continued to fall until 4 A. M. having fallen three inches by that time since sunrise; it was now at a stand until dark, after which it began again to rise.

June 2 The river from sunrise until 10 A. M. yesterday rose one and a half inches, from that time until dark fell four and a half inches, and in the course of last night rose again eight inches—the Indians inform us that the present rise is the greatest which it annually takes; that when the water subsides to about the height it was at the time we arrived here, the mountains will be passable. I have no doubt but the melting of the mountain snows in the beginning of June is what causes the annual inundation of the lower portion of the Missouri from the first to the middle of July.

4 Yesterday the water was at its greatest height at noon, between that time and dark it fell fifteen inches, and in the course of the night rose one and a half inches; from the Indian information the water will now subside, and may therefore be said to be at its greatest annual height on the 3rd instant at noon.

5 The river fell three and a half inches in the course of the day; this fluctuating state of the river is no doubt caused by the influence of the sun in the course of the day on the snows on the mountains; the accession of water thus caused in the day does not reach us until night, when it produces a rise in the river. The wild rose is in bloom. The river fell ten inches in the course of this day.

6 In the course of last night the river rose a little, but fell an inch by morning lower than it was last evening; the seven bark and the yellow vining honeysuckle are just in bloom; a few of the does have produced their young.

7 The river fell three inches last night and seven yesterday; the gooseberry is fully grown; also, the service-berry.

10 The river fell one inch last night and five and a half yesterday; it appears to be falling fast, and in the course of a few days will be as low as it was when we first arrived here: it is now about six feet lower than it has been.

16 On the top of the hills the dog-tooth violet is just in bloom, grass about two inches high; small huckleberry just putting forth its leaves.

22 Strawberries ripe at the Quamash flats; they are but small and not abundant.

29 The quamash and strawberries are just beginning to bloom at the flats on the head of the Kooskooskee river. The sunflower is also just beginning to bloom,

which is two months later than those on the sides of the western mountains near the falls of the Columbia.

July 5 A dew this morning; the nights are cool; the musquetoes are troublesome until a little after dark when the air becomes cool, and the musquetoes disappear.

6 I arrived in an open plain in the middle of which a violent wind from the northwest accompanied with hard rain lasted from four until half past five P. M. Quamash in those plains at the head of Wisdom river is just beginning to bloom, and the grass is about six inches high.

7 A small shower of rain at 4 this morning was companied with wind from the S. S. W.

8 A heavy shower of rain was accompanied with wind from the southwest from four to five P. M.

9 Last night it was very cold and wind hard from the northwest; the river is twelve inches higher than it was last summer; there is more snow on the adjacent mountains than was at that time.

10 A large white frost last night; the air extremely cold; ice three quarters of an inch thick on standing water.

11 A slight frost last night; the air cool; the musquetoes retired a little after dark, and did not return until about an hour after sunrise.

17 A heavy shower of rain accompanied with hail, thunder and lightning at 2 A. M. with hard wind from the southwest; after the shower was over it cleared away and became fair.

20 The river Rochejhone falls about half an inch in twenty-four hours, and becomes much clearer than above. The grasshoppers are extremely numerous, and have destroyed every species of grass from one to ten miles above on the river, and a great distance back.

22 A few drops of rain last night at dark, the cloud appeared to hang to the southwest: wind blew hard from different points from five to eight P. M. at which time it thundered an lightened. The river by eleven A. M. to-day had risen fifteen inches, and the water was of a milky white colour.

23 The river has fallen within the last twenty-four hours seven inches. The wind was violent from the southwest for about three hours last night, from one to three A. M.

24 River falling a little; it is six feet lower than the highest appearance of its rise; rained from three to four P. M. but slightly; the wind violent from the southwest.

25 Several showers of rain with hard wind from the south and southwest the fore part of the day. The brooks on each side are high and the water muddy.

26 A slight shower this morning with hard wind from the southwest. The river falling but very slowly, one inch in twenty-four hours.

28 A few drops of rain a little before daylight. River still falling a little.

29 A few drops of rain accompanied with hard peals of thunder and sharp lightning last night: wind hard from the northeast.

30 A slight shower of rain accompanied with thunder and lightning: several showers in the course of this day; it cleared away in the evening and became fair. River falling a little. Great quantities of coal in the bluffs on either side.

31 The wind blew hard and it was showery all day, though there was not much rain: the clouds came up from the west and northwest frequently in the course of the day.

August 22 The rains which have fallen in this month are most commonly from flying clouds which pass in different directions; those clouds are always accompanied with hard winds, and sometimes with thunder and lightning. The river has been falling moderately since the third of the month; the rains have made no other impression on the river than causing it to be more muddy, and probably preventing its falling fast.

END OF VOLUME III